MASTERING

BASIC ENGLISH LAW

MACMILLAN MASTER SERIES

Banking
Basic English Law
Basic Management
Biology
British Politics
Business Communication
Chemistry
COBOL Programming
Commerce
Computer Programming
Computers
Data Processing
Economics
Electrical Engineering
Electronics
English Grammar
English Language
English Literature
French
French 2

German
Hairdressing
Italian
Keyboarding
Marketing
Mathematics
Modern British History
Modern World History
Nutrition
Office Practice
Pascal Programming
Physics
Principles of Accounts
Social Welfare
Sociology
Spanish
Statistics
Study Skills
Typewriting Skills
Word Processing

MASTERING
BASIC ENGLISH LAW

W.T. MAJOR

M.A. LL.B. Barrister
formerly Principal Lecturer in Law at the
City of London Polytechnic

LAW SERIES EDITOR
M. C. OLIVER

M.A. Barrister
formerly Dean of the Faculty of Law at the
City of London Polytechnic

MACMILLAN

First published 1985

Published by
MACMILLAN EDUCATION LTD
Houndmills, Basingstoke, Hampshire RG21 2XS
and London
Companies and representatives
throughout the world

Typeset by TECSET Ltd, Sutton, Surrey

Printed in Great Britain by
Anchor Brendon Ltd,
Tiptree, Essex

British Library Cataloguing in Publication Data
Major, W.T.
Mastering basic English law.—(Macmillan
master series)
1. Law—England
I. Title
344.2   KD662
ISBN 0-333-38289-7
ISBN 0-333-37402-9 Pbk
ISBN 0-333-37403-7 Pbk export

CONTENTS

CONTENTS

III CONTRACTS

CONTENTS

CONTENTS

PREFACE

AND

ACKNOWLEDGEMENTS

The main purpose of this book is to meet the needs of readers preparing for professional or business examinations with a paper on the general principles of law, such as are encountered by students of accountancy, banking and business studies. Parts I and II have been designed to cover most syllabuses of this kind, while Part III goes on to deal with those commercial law subjects which are sometimes required for such examinations.

The book may be used as a complete self-study course comprising explanatory text, chapter summaries, exercises and workshop problems. Alternatively, it may be found useful as an auxiliary text for readers attending college courses.

The author gratefully acknowledges the work done by Lady Oliver, the law series editor. She was always most generous with advice and assistance during the writing of the text and at proof stage, causing many substantial improvements to be made. Nevertheless, the author remains responsible for the accuracy and completeness of all parts of the book.

August 1985   W. T. MAJOR

ACKNOWLEDGEMENTS

The author and publishers wish to thank The Controller of Her Majesty's Stationery Office for Nos 1–14 of *Appendix: Unfair Contract Terms Act 1977.*

Every effort has been made to trace all the copyright-holders but if any have been inadvertently overlooked the publishers will be pleased to make the necessary arrangement at the first opportunity.

TO
Tom

TABLE OF CASES

Y

TABLE OF STATUTES

PART I
PRELIMINARY MATTERS

HISTORICAL

BACKGROUND

The expression 'English law' means the law governing England and Wales. One of the most remarkable characteristics of English law is its long period of gradual development – a period which is virtually unbroken since 1066.

The study of English law must include a minimum of history. Indeed, some of the vital legal concepts can be understood only against their historical background. In this chapter we are concerned with the historical approach to the following concepts: custom, common law, equity and legislation.

1.1 HOW LAW DEVELOPED FROM CUSTOM

Before the Norman Conquest (1066) there was no body of law which could properly be called English law. Life was governed by customary rules which varied from one locality to another. Each local community had its own court by which local custom was enforced. However, important changes occurred over the three centuries following the Norman Conquest. During this period, the courts of the Kings of England gradually gained control over the local courts. Through this exercise of central authority, a unified system of law slowly came into existence and became known as *the common law*. It was said that the common law was common to all men within the King's jurisdiction.

Since local custom preceded both legislation and judicial precedent, it must be regarded as the original source of law.

1.2 THE COMMON LAW

The replacement of local custom by the common law was part of the process of extension of the power of the Crown during the mediaeval period. The Crown's achievement was the result of a combination of factors as follows.

(a) The King's writ

In mediaeval jurisprudence the King was the Fountain of Justice. It was, accordingly, the King's responsibility to deal with any case in which one of his subjects contended that justice had been denied him in a local court. Claimants were granted writs by the King as a means of starting the legal process and these writs defined rights and obligations which were enforceable only in the King's courts. In the course of time, the writs became formalised so that disputes in civil matters became determinable by the common law rather than by local custom. It was of particular importance that disputes concerning the title to land were removed from the local jurisdiction.

The Norman kings had introduced a special kind of feudalism by which all land was owned by the King. The King's subjects could not own land. This rule applied to high and low alike. Even the mightiest subjects could own no more than an interest in land known as an *estate* in land. It followed that any dispute over an estate was necessarily one which affected the King's interest and should, therefore, be dealt with by the King's judges in the courts of common law. By the time of Henry II (1154-1189), any suitor was entitled to make an entirely fictitious allegation that there was a defect in the proceedings before a feudal court so as to have the matter transferred out of the local jurisdiction. This was permitted by the so-called writ of *Pone*.

(b) Serious crime

The criminal jurisdiction exercised by the Sheriffs after the Conquest was gradually taken over by the King's judges as they went on circuit to various parts of the country.

(c) The Grand Assize

Henry II introduced the Grand Assize to enable a defendant to claim trial of a right concerning land held by freehold tenure (8.1(a)) in the King's courts.

(d) The Petty Assize

Henry II introduced the Petty Assize also. Its purpose was to enable a person summarily to regain land from which he had been wrongfully ousted.

(e) The King's Peace

Breach of the King's Peace was redressable only by a plea of the Crown which, if successful, gave rise to forfeiture of property or a fine. This was a valuable source of Crown revenue. As the power of the Crown increased, so was the scope of this plea widened. Indeed, until 1851, it was necessary to allege in every indictment that the offence was committed *contra pacem domini regis*. This means against the peace of our lord the King.

1.3 EQUITY

When the writ system was first evolved, it was flexible enough to bring about a remarkable development of the common law at the expense of local custom and local courts. However, the system was eventually formalised and embodied in the register of writs. The point was reached where no writ could be issued which was not in the same terms as one of those contained in the register. There resulted a rigidity which prevented any substantial development of the principles of common law.

As time went on, the common law became less and less able to provide a just rule or remedy for all cases. A suitor unable to find a registered writ drawn to suit his claim would have no remedy at common law, but he might petition the King himself - the Fountain of Justice. When such petitions were first made, they were heard by the King in Council. Perhaps the most important matter here is that the petitions were determined according to conscience - the King's conscience. By the end of the fifteenth century, the Chancellor would deal with petitions in his own name, thus giving rise to the Court of Chancery. Notions of conscience continued to govern the approach of this court because the Chancellor was not only a high official of state but also a cardinal and the King's confessor. As a judge he had to act as keeper of the King's conscience.

Where the application of a rule of common law produced an unfair result or where a common law remedy was not appropriate, the Court of Chancery might give relief to its petitioners according to equity and good conscience. At first, the early Chancellors varied one from another in their approach. In those days it was said that equity was as long as the Chancellor's foot. However, in the course of time, the Chancery judges followed their own precedents. As a result, equity became a body of law based on precedent and came to have its own procedures, its own substantive rules and its own remedies.

1.4 LEGISLATION

Law was promulgated by the early mediaeval kings in the form of charters, statutes and ordinances. This early legislation did not carry the same force as a modern Act of Parliament. There were two reasons for this. First, the superiority of legislation over case law was not then established. Secondly, before the introduction of printing, there was often a serious uncertainty as to the wording of the original instrument. Nevertheless, some of these early statutes had an abiding influence over the development of the common law. Consider the following three examples.

(a) The Statute of Marlborough (1267)

The effect of this statute was to widen the effect of the writ of entry so that it could be used to cover any dispute over title to land.

(b) The Statute of Gloucester (1278)

This statute was originally intended to restrict the jurisdiction of the common law judges over personal actions. It provided that no action involving less than forty shillings could be commenced in the King's courts. The judges defeated this intention by the unexpected way in which they interpreted this provision. By their interpretation, the judges took an eventual monopoly of the jurisdiction over personal actions.

(c) The Statute of Westminster II (1285)

This statute was really a compilation of several statutes, each known by its Latin name which was no more than the first two or three words of its text. *In consimili casu* allowed new writs to be granted where it was not possible exactly to fit the case into the formula of one of the existing writs in the register. It led to what were called 'actions on the case' or 'case'. It brought a welcome new flexibility to the common law. *Nisi prius* extended the jurisdiction of the travelling assize judges to include civil proceedings. Before the statute, their jurisdiction was criminal only and personal actions were tried in London regardless of the inconvenience involved.

Later, during the fifteenth century, the legislative power of the king was transferred to Parliament. At the same time, the superiority of legislation over the common law was firmly established and, also, the certainty of the statute was assisted by the invention of printing. The stage was set for the development of legislative techniques by Parliament.

It should be understood that legislation had the potential to achieve great reforms; precedent could merely bring about changes of a piecemeal and random nature. By the second half of the nineteenth century, legislation was a source of law of far greater importance than either the common law or equity.

1.5 LOCAL CUSTOM

In the main the customs existing at the time of the Norman Conquest were eventually absorbed into the common law or replaced by a Norman rule as part of the common law. In some cases they were discarded. Exceptionally, some local customs survived the process of unification. A local custom could survive only where it existed within the jurisdiction of a local court which continued to enforce it. Here are three examples of local custom which continued as local exceptions to the common law:

(a) Gavelkind

Before the Conquest the most widespread custom governing the tenure of land was *gavelkind*. After the Conquest, the Norman rule of primogeniture displaced *gavelkind* in most parts of the country. It is said that the men of Kent were allowed to retain this Saxon custom of *gavelkind* as a reward for services rendered to William at the battle of Hastings. By this custom, the land yielded husbandry service or rent, as opposed to the more general military service. Land held by *gavelkind* descended to all sons equally – the youngest son being entitled to inherit the homestead. In the common law courts it was presumed that land in Kent was held by *gavelkind* until the contrary was proved. *Gavelkind* was abolished by the Administration of Estates Act 1925.

(b) Borough English

The custom of postremo-geniture obtained in certain boroughs and manors whose jurisdictions were able to resist the introduction of the Norman rule of primogeniture with regard to the succession of land. By this custom, the youngest son inherited his father's land to the exclusion of all his brothers and sisters. This custom originated in pastoral tribal communities in which young men, on reaching full age, would depart from their father's house with an allotment of animals to seek new pastures. The end result was that the youngest son remained at home to inherit all. The name 'Borough English' derives from a case tried in Nottingham in 1327. At that time Nottingham consisted of two boroughs, one of which was French and the other English. They were called *Burgh Frauncoyes* and *Burgh Engloys*. In the case of 1327 the court took notice that land in Burgh Engloys was held by the custom which involved the succession of the youngest son.

(c) Ancient demesne

The manors of ancient demesne were, according to Coke (2.11), 'the ancient demesnes of the Crown of England'. They were the manors in the actual possession of the Crown during the reigns of Edward the Confessor (1042–1066) and of William I (1066–1087). These manors are described as such in the Domesday Book. The *socage tenants* of these manors were known as *tenants in ancient demesne* and, in consequence, they enjoyed certain customary immunities. Questions concerning their land could be decided only by the court of ancient demesne of the manor or, later, by the Court of Common Pleas. Land held by this tenure could pass by common law conveyance independently of the will of the lord of the manor. It should be understood that a socage tenant was one whose tenure was by agricultural service rather than military service.

1.6 THE LAW MERCHANT

Until the seventeenth century any dispute between one merchant and another would not have been dealt with by a court of common law. Such mercantile disputes were within the jurisdiction of the courts of the fairs (the so-called *piepowder* courts, from *pieds poudrés*) and the staple courts. The great advantage of the piepowder courts was the speedy procedure, speed being of obvious importance to travelling merchants. The staple courts were set up in towns where merchants dealt in some basic commodity such as wool or cloth, the purpose being to ensure that customs dues were paid. By the fifteenth century, appeal lay from these courts to the Court of Common Pleas. By the end of the seventeenth century the staple courts had virtually ceased to exist. The law merchant – never originally part of the common law – was derived from the international practices and customs of merchants. After being absorbed into the common law, the law merchant became the basis of great developments of contract law which could never have occurred under the old common law. The law merchant enriched the common law sufficiently to cover bills of exchange, agency, partnership, insurance and sale of goods. Much of this law was codified during the nineteenth century in statutes such as the Bills of Exchange Act 1882, the Partnership Act 1890 and the Sale of Goods Act 1893.

SUMMARY

1 The common law is the law which is common to the whole of England and Wales.

2 The common law replaced the various local customs which were in force at the time of the Norman Conquest.

3 This process resulted from the exercise of central power by the courts of the kings over the local courts in all parts of the country.

4 The eventual formalisation of the writ system destroyed the original flexibility of the common law. This led to the development of equity in the Court of Chancery. Equity is a body of case law based on good conscience.

5 Certain early mediaeval legislation had an abiding influence on the common law.

6 Some local customs survived the unification process of the common law. These local customs continued to be enforced in their local jurisdictions as exceptions to the common law. Examples of local custom are:
gavelkind, Borough English and ancient demesne.

7 The law merchant was derived from the customs internationally followed by merchants. The law merchant was first applied in England by the courts of piepowder and the courts of staple.

8 The law merchant was ultimately absorbed into the common law and was very largely codified by Parliament in the nineteenth century.

EXERCISES

1 What is the common law? Comment on the early development of the common law.

2 Examine the several factors which enabled the Crown to extend its power over the whole country during the mediaeval period.

3 What is equity? How did equity originate?

4 Give three examples of early legislation and comment on each.

5 Give some examples of local customs which survived to become exceptions to the common law, in particular in local jurisdictions.

CHAPTER 2

SOURCES OF LAW

In this chapter we shall be concerned with the way in which rules of law are created and altered.

Almost all rules of law owe their existence either to Acts of Parliament or to decisions of the courts. In other words, the main sources of law are legislation and judicial precedent. These sources of law give authority to the rules, making them part of the law.

There are two subsidiary sources of law, namely, local custom and books of authority. These sources once enjoyed a considerable significance, but nowadays they are seldom encountered. The main sources support almost all rules of law.

In the study of law, the rules should be known. This is obvious. Also, the source of each rule should be known. This is, perhaps, not so obvious but it is the case. A lawyer can construct a legal argument only by citing the authority (statute or decision) for each rule or principle which he uses.

As the reader progresses through the chapters of this book it will be seen that all the most important rules of law are explained with their respective sources. Rules and sources have been explained together and should be learned together.

2.1 LEGISLATION

Modern legislation may be expressed in the form of an Act of Parliament or as delegated legislation.

Parliament is sovereign. There is, in theory, no limit to the legislative power of Parliament. An Act of Parliament may make any new law. Parliament may amend or repeal any existing law. The courts are bound to apply the rules contained in an Act of Parliament. In *British Railways Board* v. *Pickin* (1973) the House of Lords restated the principle that the courts have no power to disregard an Act of Parliament. Nor have the courts any power to examine parliamentary proceedings to determine whether an Act has been passed as a result of any irregularity or fraud.

The legislative process starts with the drafting of a Bill by parliamentary draftsmen, usually under the supervision of a government minister. The Bill must then be introduced into either the House of Commons or the House of Lords. The Bill must pass through the several parliamentary stages as set out below in one single session. The Bill is then qualified for the Royal Assent and thus becomes an Act of Parliament.

Normally the concurrence of both Houses is required but, by the Parliament Act 1911, the Royal Assent may, in some circumstances, be given to a Bill which has not been passed by the Lords.

Acts of Parliament may be public or private. A public Act applies generally to the United Kingdom. A private Act applies only to a particular local authority mentioned in the Act.

Where a public Bill is introduced in the House of Commons it will pass through the following stages.

(a) First reading

The Clerk of the House of Commons reads the short title of the Bill. This is an important formality which registers the introduction of the Bill. There is, obviously, no debate at this stage.

(b) Second reading

After the first reading, the Bill is printed so that it can be debated and voted on. The following stages occur only if the Bill passes the vote at this stage.

(c) Committee stage

At this stage the Bill is dealt with in detail, clause by clause, in committee. The committee will usually be a Standing Committee. In important cases, the Committee may be of the whole House. Again, a vote is taken and, if the Bill is passed, the following stages occur.

(d) Report stage

The Bill, as amended in Committee, comes again before the whole House of Commons. Here it will be decided whether the Bill needs further consideration in Committee, or whether it can proceed to the next stage.

(e) Third reading

The House of Commons now votes on the Bill to accept or reject it. If it is passed, it is sent to the House of Lords where it passes through the same stages as in the Commons. The Bill is eventually returned to the House of Commons with amendments by the Lords.

(f) Discussion of the Lords' amendments

If the Commons do not object to the Lords' amendments, the Bill will pass to the next and final stage. Where the Commons object to the amendments, discussion usually takes place with a view to reaching an agreement with the Lords.

(g) The Royal Assent

Once the Royal Assent has been given, the Bill becomes an Act of Parliament.

2.2 KINDS OF STATUTE

Statutes may be classified according to purpose, i.e., reform, codification, consolidation or taxation, as follows.

(a) Law reform

Reform of the law will be carried out by statute whenever Parliament intends to alter existing rules. This may occur when the rule of common law resulting from a House of Lords decision is considered to be unsatisfactory. An important example is the Law Reform (Frustrated Contracts) Act 1943, which reversed a rule fundamental to the law of frustration of contracts arising from the *Fibrosa* case (1943).

Massive reforms were achieved by the Judicature Acts of 1873 and 1875. These Acts swept away the existing system of separate courts of common law and equity. The system was entirely replaced by the Supreme Court with jurisdiction to apply both common law and equity.

Another example of reform in depth through legislation is to be found in the Law of Property Act 1925 and its accompanying statutes.
These statutes completely modernised the system of land law which had endured in what was virtually its mediaeval form until 1925.

Law reform by statute has been rationalised by the work of the Law Commission since 1965. It is the duty of the Law Commission to keep the law under review with a view to its systematic development and reform: Law Commission Act 1965. In particular, the Law Commission must consider the need for codification of law, the elimination of anomalies, the repeal of obsolete and unnecessary enactments, the reduction of the number of separate enactments and generally the simplification and modernisation of the law.

(b) Codification

Codifying Acts promulgate in codified form a body of law which was previously contained either in case law or in piecemeal enactments together with case law. The Bills of Exchange Act 1882 and the Sale of Goods Act 1893 are important examples of codifying Acts.

(c) Consolidation

Consolidation Acts are passed in order to draw together into a single statute any body of law which was previously scattered between a number of Acts. This is essentially a tidying process. The characteristic of consolidating legislation is that no new law is made by it. Consolidation Bills are not, therefore, subject to parliamentary debate in the usual way. A special procedure is followed to ensure that there is no substantial departure from existing law during consolidation. This procedure is now set out in the Consolidation of Enactments (Procedure) Act 1949. Where consolidation is recommended by the Law Commission there is an appropriate procedure available to Parliament. This takes into account any amendments which have been recommended.

Examples of consolidating Acts are: the Solicitors Act 1974, the Sale of Goods Act 1979, the Supreme Court Act 1981, the County Courts Act 1984 and the Companies Act 1985.

(d) Finance Acts

No tax may be levied without the sanction of Parliament. This is a fundamental principle of law and government. The annual Finance Act incorporates the details of the latest budget proposals of the Chancellor of the Exchequer. A Money Bill may receive the Royal Assent without the consent of the Lords provided that it has been passed by the Commons and sent to the Lords at least a month before the end of the Parliamentary Session and has not been passed without amendment by the Lords within a month.

2.3 DELEGATED LEGISLATION

Parliament may delegate the legislative power to any subordinate body. Regulations may thus be made and promulgated without the time-consuming procedures attending the passage of a Bill through Parliament. Delegated legislation must be *intra vires*, i.e., promulgated within the powers conferred by Parliament. Any purported delegated legislation which is beyond the powers conferred by Act of Parliament is void. It is *ultra vires* – beyond the powers.

Effective control of delegated legislation is a serious modern parliamentary problem. The detailed social control exercised by government results in a vast amount of delegated legislation. It would be impossible for all this detail to be included in Acts of Parliament. In theory, all delegated legislation is subject to the inspection and control of Parliament, but it is doubtful whether effective control over the whole range is possible.

The most common form of delegated legislation is the ministerial promulgation of Statutory Instruments. Orders in Council and the Rules of the Supreme Court are further examples.

2.4 AUTONOMIC LEGISLATION

Where an autonomous body has the power to legislate, its legislation is called autonomic. The power to legislate must be sanctioned by the courts and Parliament. The doctrine of *ultra vires* applies to autonomic legislation – it must be within the sanctioned powers. Any autonomic legislation beyond the sanctioned powers is void. Examples of bodies with autonomic powers are the Church of England, most professional bodies, trade unions and employers' associations. It is worth noting that the rules and regulations made by autonomic bodies affect the public in their dealings with those bodies although, strictly, the rules and regulations are binding only on the members.

The Order in Council for Crown Colonies is a special case. It is made under the prerogative jurisdiction of the Crown and, accordingly, the doctrine of *ultra vires* does not apply.

2.5 INTERPRETATION AND CONSTRUCTION OF STATUTES

Where the words of a statute are clear and unambiguous when read as a whole, the courts must apply the statute. The process of arriving at a clear meaning is called the interpretation of the statute. This involves the reading of the statute (together with its schedules, if any) and nothing else. Words and phrases must be interpreted according to the definitions contained in the statute itself and in the Interpretation Act 1978.

Only in case of ambiguity or uncertainty is the court entitled to refer to extrinsic aids such as the long title, headings, side notes or the provisions of other statutes. Only in case of ambiguity or uncertainty does the court resort to the rules of construction and the further rules known as the presumptions.

(a) The rules of construction

(i) The literal rule.
The basis of the literal rule is that the intention of Parliament is to be found in the ordinary and natural meaning of the words in the statute. This approach has been criticised by the Law Commission on the grounds that it assumes an unattainable perfection in draftsmanship and that it ignores the limitations of language. The literal rule will not be applied if it produces a manifest absurdity.

(ii) The golden rule
This is a rider to the literal rule. It covers the case where the ordinary meaning of the words is at variance with the intention to be collected from the statute as a whole. It also covers the case where the literal rule leads to a manifest absurdity. By the golden rule, the court may modify the language so far as is necessary to avoid the inconvenience, but no further: *Beck* v. *Smith* (1836).

(iii) The mischief rule.
It is an ancient rule that a judge may look at the mischief in order to discover the intention of Parliament. The principle is as follows: where the words are ambiguous or uncertain, the statute may be construed according to its purpose or policy. Where the court decides to adopt this approach, the rule as explained in *Heydon's* case will be strictly followed. Accordingly, there are four questions to be considered:
(1) what was the common law before the Act? (2) what was the mischief and defect for which the common law did not provide? (3) what remedy Parliament has resolved upon? and (4) the true reason of the remedy?

This rule enables the judge to suppress the mischief and advance the remedy. The relevant case law must be taken into account. The long title and headings may be taken into account, as always, in case of ambiguity or uncertainty.

(b) The presumptions

The further rules of construction are usually expressed as presumptions on the basis that Parliament must be presumed *not* to have intended to make certain kinds of law except by express provision.

(i) Presumption against the alteration of the existing law.
This presumption applies equally to existing case law and existing statute law.

The presumption is that where Parliament intends to repeal statute law, this will be done by express words. It follows that where an Act is inconsistent with a previous Act, the two must be construed and reconciled.

Parliament can alter the rules of common law. Any such alteration must be made expressly because no alteration to the body of case law will be implied from the provisions of an Act of Parliament.

(ii) Presumption that a statute does not bind the Crown.
This presumption springs from the ancient prerogative rights of the Crown but is now a matter of presumed parliamentary intention. In *Tamlin* v. *Hannaford* (1950) Denning L.J. said that 'the Crown is not bound by a statute unless there can be gathered from it an intention that the Crown should be bound'. This rule applies to Crown servants in the course of their duties and to the use of Crown property.

(iii) Presumption against retrospective operation of a statute.
Parliament has the power to make enactments having retrospective effect. This power has been used occasionally to grant rights or indemnities effective before the date of the Act in question. This presumption protects existing rights. These are not affected by statute except to the extent that it is expressly provided for in clear unambiguous terms: *Allen* v. *Thorn Electrical Industries* (1967).

(iv) Presumption of application to the whole of the UK.
Parliament is the Parliament of the United Kingdom and it is, therefore, presumed that its enactments extend to the whole of the United Kingdom, but no further. Where Parliament intends to exclude Scotland or Northern Ireland from the effect of an Act, it must be done expressly. Similarly, where a provision is to affect Scotland or Northern Ireland only, this must be expressed.

2.6 EEC LEGISLATION

Under the Treaty of Rome and its associated treaties, the Council and the Commission of the Communities have certain legislative powers and duties. The legislative instruments having a binding effect are regulations, directives and decisions. The interpretation and construction of the EEC treaty or other EEC instrument must be in accordance with principles laid down by the European Court: European Communities Act 1972, s. 3 (1).

(a) Regulations

Community regulations are binding on Parliament and the courts. They are directly applicable, i.e., they are enforceable without the need for internal legislation. Any rights arising out of regulations are known as 'enforceable community rights': European Communities Act 1972, s. 2 (1).

(b) Directives

There are two kinds of directive – those which are directly applicable and those which are not. In *Van Duyn* v. *The Home Office* (1975), before the Court of Justice of the European Communities, it was argued on behalf of the Home Office that since article 189 of the EEC treaty distinguishes between the effects ascribed to regulations, directives and decisions, it must therefore be presumed that the Council, in issuing a directive rather than making a regulation, must have intended that the directive should have an effect other than that of a regulation and, accordingly, a directive should not be directly applicable. This argument was rejected. It was held in that case that where the community authorities have, by directive, imposed on Member States the obligation to pursue a particular course of conduct, the useful effect of that directive would be weakened if individuals were prevented from relying on it before their national courts and if those courts were prevented from taking it into consideration as an element of Community law. It was held further that article 177 of the EEC treaty, which empowers national courts to refer to the European court any question concerning the validity and interpretation of any act of the Community without distinction, implies furthermore that these acts may be invoked by individuals in the national courts. It is necessary to examine in every case whether the nature, general scheme and wording of the provision in question are capable of having direct effect on the relations between Member States and individuals.

(c) Decisions

The Council and the Commission are each empowered to make decisions which are binding on any specific enterprise, organ or individual to which a decision is addressed.

2.7 PRECEDENT

Where a court decides an issue between plaintiff and defendant, there are three separate elements involved: (1) the facts of the case as proved by the parties; (2) the principle of law applied by the court to those facts; and (3) the resulting decision in favour of one or other of the parties.

cision of the court is binding on the parties to the action. Further, the principle of the decision may become binding on other parties in future cases. The principle becomes part of the common law. This principle is called the *ratio decidendi* of the case. To discover the *ratio decidendi* of a case, you must first look at the facts and then look at the decision of the court on those facts. At this stage you must take into account the relief sought by the plaintiff and the defence and counter-claim (if any) of the defendant. Then you must ask yourself this question: what principle must have been applied to the facts to achieve this decision? The answer to this question is the *ratio decidendi* of the case. The *ratio decidendi* may often be stated in a number of different ways. It may also be stated at different levels of abstraction. It is an important part of the lawyer's craft to be able to state the *ratio* of a case accurately and in the form best suited to the particular argument in which he is engaged.

Where a judge makes a statement of legal principle which is not strictly applicable to the facts before him, the statement is said to be *obiter,* i.e., by the way. *Obiter dicta* are not part of the precedent. Although they are never binding, *obiter dicta* may be used in argument in the same way as persuasive precedent. The persuasive force of any particular *dictum* will depend largely on the reputation of the judge.

2.8 CASE LAW

The *ratio decidendi* of a case may become a precedent to be followed, i.e., applied by the court in any future case. Precedent thus provides a body of judge-made law, sometimes called case law.

The most important bodies of case law are the common law and equity. The common law may be described as the body of case law which has been developed by the courts in their common law jurisdiction. Equity may be described as the body of case law which has been developed by the courts in their equitable jurisdiction. Since the Judicature Act 1893, all judges of the Supreme Court (created by that Act) have jurisdiction to apply both the rules of equity and the rules of common law. Before the Act, the common law judges had no equitable jurisdiction.

The importance of precedent was emphasised by Lord Gardiner L.C. in a statement made on behalf of all the Lords of Appeal in Ordinary in 1966. He said that:

'Their Lordships regard the use of precedent as an indispensable foundation upon which to decide what is the law and its application to individual cases. It provides at least some degree of certainty upon which individuals can rely in the conduct of their affairs, as well as a basis for the orderly development of legal rules.'

2.9 PRECEDENTS MAY BE BINDING OR PERSUASIVE

The authority of a precedent depends upon the status of the court giving the decision. Each court has its place in the hierarchy of courts which make up the system.

(a) The House of Lords

The most authoritative precedents are those of the House of Lords. Its decisions bind the Court of Appeal, all divisions of the High Court and all inferior courts in civil and criminal matters. Until 1966 the House of Lords treated its own former decisions as binding on itself, but this practice was altered after Lord Gardiner's statement in that year. He said that the House of Lords would treat its former decisions as normally binding but that the House would depart from a previous decision should it appear right to do so. Lord Gardiner made it clear that the announcement was not intended to affect the use of precedent elsewhere than in the House of Lords.

(b) The Court of Appeal (Civil Division)

Decisions of the Court of Appeal (Civil Division) are binding on judges sitting alone in any Division of the High Court, on divisional courts and all inferior courts in civil and criminal cases. The Court of Appeal (Civil Division) is bound by the decisions of the House of Lords and, except in certain well defined circumstances, by its own previous decisions. The exceptions are: (1) where the previous decision conflicts with a later House of Lords decision; (2) where the decision is given *per incuriam*, i.e., the result of oversight or error; and (3) where the decision conflicts with another previous decision of the Court of Appeal, in which case the court is free to choose which it will follow: *Young* v. *Bristol Aeroplane Co.* (1944).

(c) Court of Appeal (Criminal Division)

Decisions of the Court of Appeal (Criminal Division) are binding on all criminal courts in criminal cases. The Criminal Division is bound by decisions of the former Court of Criminal Appeal. Decisions of the Civil Division are also binding, but subject to the three exceptions laid down by the House of Lords in *Young* v. *Bristol Aeroplane Co.* (1944) (see (b) above).

(d) The High Court of Justice

With regard to civil cases, divisional courts are bound by Court of Appeal and House of Lords decisions and by their own previous decisions. A High Court judge sitting alone is bound by the decisions of divisional courts of his own division. Decisions of High Court judges sitting alone are binding on inferior courts but are not binding on other High Court judges. Such decisions may operate as persuasive precedents.

With regard to criminal cases, the divisional court of the Queen's Bench Division is bound by the Court of Appeal (Criminal Division) and by its own decisions which are, of course, binding on all inferior courts when trying criminal cases.

(e) The Court of Justice of the European Communities

By s. 3 (1) of the European Communities Act 1972, in any legal proceedings within the United Kingdom, questions as to the validity, meaning and effect of the Treaty of Rome must be determined in accordance with the jurisprudence of the European Court of Justice. This provision governs the treatment to be accorded to all other Community treaties and Community instruments. To this extent the courts of the United Kingdom are bound by the decisions of the European Court (see Chapter 3.6).

2.10 LAW REPORTING

Any system based on precedent must rely heavily on the availability of law reports of significant cases. A law report is a published account of the proceedings of a case made for the purpose of being used as a precedent in later cases. Ideally it will contain: (1) a statement of the facts; (2) the argument of each side; and (3) the decision of the court.

The history of law reporting falls into three distinct periods as follows:

(a) Year Books

Law reporting began with the Year Books which are, as the name indicates, annual compilations. The Year Books were compiled anonymously - probably by members of the Bar. The earliest Year Books date from the late thirteenth century and were written in Norman French. They were used in manuscript form until the invention of printing. By the sixteenth century several abridgements (summaries) of the Year Books were available in print and these tended to replace the Year Books used by the practising Bar. By this time, the language was a mixture of French and English. For some unknown reason the Year Books came to an abrupt end in the year 1535.

(b) The private reports

After the Year Books came the era of privately published reports, usually named after the reporter. Between the mid-sixteenth century and 1865, a very large number of private reports were produced, varying enormously in style, content, accuracy and authority. The most convenient way to find a private report is to look it up in the English Reports in which the bulk of private reports have been collected in 176 volumes.

(c) Modern law reporting

The modern era of law reporting began in 1865 with the establishment of the Council of Law Reporting. The Council was under the general control of the Inns of Court and the Law Society through their represen-tatives in the Council. Reports published by the Council are called 'the Law Reports'. The Law Reports represent an attempt by the legal profes-sion to exercise some control over the style and accuracy of law reporting. The Law Reports are not, however, official in the same sense as documents emanating from government departments. The reporters are barristers, who must be present in court at the time of the hearing of any case being reported. Judgements are set out in full and the judges are given the opportunity to check and revise reports of their own judgements before publication.

The Law Reports enjoy the highest standing among the several other series of modern law reports. These others may be cited in court only when the case in question is not reported in the Law Reports. Probably the greatest advantage of the Law Reports over other present-day series is their accuracy and completeness with regard to the arguments of counsel.

To overcome and effect of delay in publication of the Law Reports, the Council publishes the Weekly Law Reports. These are published as soon as possible after the hearing and include all cases to be published later in the Law Reports. The Weekly Law Reports do not include the arguments of counsel, but are otherwise complete. They have been published since 1953.

The Council of Law Reporting became incorporated in 1870 and was later renamed the Incorporated Council of Law Reporting. It has no monopoly of the business of law reporting and there are, accordingly, several series of reports published commercially. These other reports often include cases which do not appear in the Law Reports. The fact that they survive commercially indicates that there is a need for them.

Of those published today, the best known are the All England Reports, Lloyd's List Reports and the Solicitor's Journal summary reports. The Times Law Reports ceased publication in 1952 and The Times newspaper summary reports continue to be published as an integral part of the paper.

2.11 SUBSIDIARY SOURCES OF LAW

Legislation and judicial precedent are the two main sources of law. Parliament and the judiciary are virtually the exclusive law-making authorities. It is only in extremely rare cases that counsel needs to look elsewhere than in legislation or law reports to find authority for a rule which he wishes to use in argument. Nevertheless, the picture is not complete without some account of the two subsidiary sources which are (a) local custom and (b) books of authority.

(a) Local custom

Most local customs have been swept away by legislation or have fallen into disuse. The custom of *gavelkind* was brought to an end by the Administration of Estates Act 1925. The same Act ended the custom of *Borough English*. Some local customs, however, remain and will be upheld today. The most usual examples are rights of way and rights of common. It has been held that the fishermen of a particular village were entitled to dry their nets on privately owned land. In other cases, it has been held that villagers could hold horse races or fairs on private land and that they could pass to church over private land.

Anyone wishing to claim the benefit of a local custom must be able to prove that the custom has certain characteristics. He must prove that the custom (1) is certain, (2) is not unreasonable, (3) has been in existence since time immemorial, i.e., since the year 1189, (4) has continued without interruption and (5) is restricted to a particular locality, usually the jurisdiction of an ancient local court.

(b) Books of authority

There are certain ancient texts which contain the earliest statements of the common law. These are of value as a subsidiary source of law, particularly for the period before the modern era of law reporting. These ancient texts enjoy an intrinsic authority as a binding source of law in contradistinction to modern texts stating a principle which the court may be persuaded to adopt in the absence of binding authority. An example of a statement taken from a modern text is Pollock's definition of consideration, adopted by the House of Lords in *Dunlop* v. *Selfridge* (1915). Modern texts may never be cited in court against a precedent or a statute.

The ancient books of authority which function as a source of law are those of Glanville, Bracton, Littleton, Coke and Blackstone.

(i) Glanville.
Ranulph de Glanville produced the first treatise on English law in the early twelfth century. It was called *Tractatus de Legibus et Consuetudinibus Angliae* (Treatise on the laws and customs of England) or *de Legibus* for short. Although *de Legibus* is no more than an account of procedures in the King's court, it enjoyed great authority by reason of Glanville's high office as the chief justiciar of Henry II.

(ii) Bracton.
Henry of Bracton was a judge in the time of Henry III (1216-1272). His treatise bore the same title as that of Glanville but it was a longer and immensely more detailed work. From the mid-thirteenth century down to the time of Coke it was regarded as a source of law of first importance.

(iii) Littleton.
Sir Thomas Littleton, a judge of the common pleas, wrote his *Treatise on Tenures* in 1481 as an instructional text. This work attained a great reputation for its accuracy and authority on matters concerning real property.

(iv) Coke.
Sir Edward Coke (pronounced *cook*) was a great common law judge, law reporter and parliamentarian in the time of James I (1603-1625). He wrote his *Institutes of the laws of England* on retirement from active public life at the age of eighty. He died in 1633. It was characteristic of Coke as a common lawyer that he did not allow himself to recognise the virtues and the authority of equity. The *Institutes* were much cited in the common law courts as a direct source of law for two centuries and more after his death. Coke's eminence and influence as a common lawyer remain unmatched.

(v) Blackstone.
Sir William Blackstone's elegantly written *Commentaries on the laws of England* were published in 1765. The *Commentaries* comprised four books covering the whole field of English law with specially detailed treatment of crime and tort in Books III and IV. The *Commentaries* were conceived and published as a comprehensive text for students; yet the status of a book of authority was achieved. Although in England the *Commentaries* did not equal the *Institutes* in influence, they had a special place in the development of the common law in the United States of America in the first half of the nineteenth century.

New editions of the *Commentaries* continued to be published for a century by which time the modern era of law reporting had dawned. Good law reporting signalled a decline in the significance of books of authority as a source of law. Blackstone's was the last book of authority.

SUMMARY

1 Legislation and precedent are the main sources of law. Local custom and books of authority are subsidiary sources of law.

2 Legislation may be in the form of an Act of Parliament or in the form of delegated legislation. By the doctrine of Parliamentary sovereignty there is no limit to the legislative power of Parliament.

3 The purpose of legislation may be reform, codification, consolidation or tax collection.

4 The process of arriving at a clear meaning of a statutory provision is called *interpretation*. It involves reading the statute as a whole and nothing else.

5 In case of ambiguity or uncertainty the court may resort to extrinsic aids, the rules of construction and the presumptions.

6 The interpretation and construction of the EEC treaty or other EEC instrument must be in accordance with principles laid down by the European Court. Regulations, directives and decisions must be considered as separate categories of instrument for this purpose.

7 The underlying principle applied by a judge in reaching his decision is called the *ratio decidendi* of the case. This may become a precedent to be followed in later cases. Precedent forms a body of judge-made law (case law). The common law and equity are the two great bodies of case law.

8 A precedent may be binding or persuasive according to the relationship between the court in which the *ratio* originated and the court applying it as a precedent. This relationship is governed by the hierarchy of the system of courts.

9 Law reports are vital to a system of law based on precedent. The history of law reporting includes the Year Books, the private reports and modern law reporting from 1865.

EXERCISES

1 Explain carefully what is meant by (a) legislation and (b) judicial precedent.

2 By what stages does a Bill become enacted law?

3 'Parliament is sovereign'. Explain this statement with regard to the effect of legislation. In your answer mention the different kinds of statute.

4 How do the judges interpret and construe legislation?

5 What are regulations, directives and decisions? What rules govern their interpretation and construction?

6 Explain very carefully what you understand by the expression *ratio decidendi.*

7 Distinguish between binding and persuasive precedents. What has this to do with the hierarchy of the courts?

8 Explain the need for law reports. What is the difference between the Law Reports and the private reports? What are the Year Books? Why are the years 1535 and 1865 important in the history of law reporting?

9 What are the subsidiary sources of law? Explain carefully why it is seldom necessary to resort to a subsidiary source today. Were the subsidiary sources of law more important in times past?

CHAPTER 3

THE SYSTEM
OF COURTS

3.1 INTRODUCTORY MATTERS

The hierarchical structure of the system of courts in England and Wales can be understood only if it can be seen that the Supreme Court of Judicature is central to it. Essentially, appeals lie from the inferior courts to the Supreme Court and from the Supreme Court to the House of Lords. Within the structure of the Supreme Court itself, appeals lie from the Crown Court to the Court of Appeal.

In this chapter, the courts are treated separately, first with regard to their respective constitutions and, secondly, with regard to their respective jurisdictions.

With regard to jurisdiction, s. 49 of the Supreme Court Act 1981 reaffirms that every court exercising jurisdiction in England and Wales in any civil cause or matter must continue to administer law and equity on the basis that, wherever there is any conflict or variance between the rules of equity and the rules of the common law, the rules of equity must prevail.

3.2 THE HOUSE OF LORDS

(a) Constitution

The High Court of Parliament was first mentioned in the preamble to the Statute of Westminster I in the year 1275, since when it has been a court of common law, the judicial function being exercised by the House of Lords.

Until 1876, all peers were entitled to sit and vote in judicial sessions regardless of their lack of knowledge and experience of the law. The Appellate Jurisdiction Act 1876 provided for the creation of legally

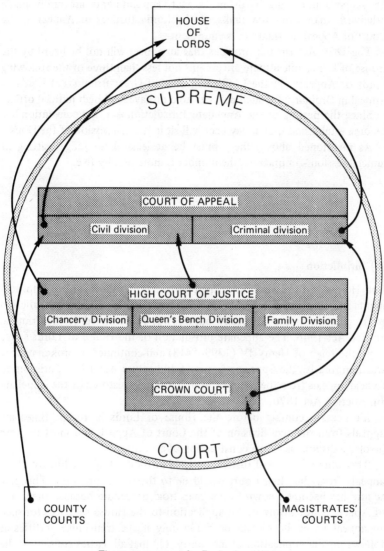

The court structure for England and Wales.
(Appeals are indicated by arrows.)

qualified life peers, styled 'Lords of Appeal in Ordinary' to be appointed by Her Majesty the Queen.

The 1876 Act provides that a person will not be appointed as a Lord of Appeal in Ordinary unless he has been, for a period of not less than two years, the holder of high judicial office, or has been, for not less than

15 years, a practising barrister. In fact, appointments are rarely made otherwise than from the ranks of the Lords Justices of Appeal in the Court of Appeal, or their Scots equivalent.

The 1876 Act further provides that an appeal will not be heard by the House of Lords unless there are present not less than three of the following Lords of Appeal: (1) the Lord Chancellor of Great Britain; (2) Lords of Appeal in Ordinary; (3) such peers as hold or have held high judicial office.

Since the passing of the Appellate Jurisdiction Act, the convention has become established that no lay peer will sit in judicial session of the House.

As mentioned above, there must be at least three judges sitting in judicial session - in practice, the number is more usually five.

(b) Jurisdiction

The House of Lords has an ancient jurisdiction with regard to impeachments and claims of peerage. There was also an ancient criminal jurisdiction to try peers for treason or felony, but this was discontinued by the Criminal Justice Act 1948. The appellate jurisdiction of the House of Lords stems from the reign of Henry IV (1399-1413) and continued unbroken until it was removed by the Supreme Court of Judicature Act 1873. Jurisdiction to hear appeals from the Court of Appeal was fully restored by the Appellate Jurisdiction Act 1876.

Most cases coming before the House of Lords in recent times are appeals from the civil division of the Court of Appeal, and most of these involve a dispute as to the construction of a statute.

The Administration of Justice Act 1969 introduced a procedure by which appeals from the High Court would lie to the House of Lords. This procedure has become known as the 'leap frog' procedure because the Court of Appeal is not involved. An application to the House of Lords for such an appeal to be heard can be made only if the trial judge certifies as follows on the application of any party: (1) that all parties consent to the procedure; (2) that a sufficient case for appeal to the House of Lords has been made out; (3) that a point of law of general public importance is involved which either (a) relates wholly or mainly to the construction of an Act of Parliament or a Statutory Instrument and has been fully argued in the proceedings and fully considered in the judgement of the trial judge, or (b) is one in respect of which the judge is bound by a decision of the Court of Appeal or the House of Lords and which was fully considered by the Court of Appeal or the House of Lords as the case may be.

When the trial judge issues such a certificate, the application to the House of Lords is determined without a hearing.

By section 33 of the Criminal Appeal Act 1968, appeal lies from the criminal division of the Court of Appeal to the House of Lords. Such appeal lies at the instance of either the defendant or the prosecutor. Leave to appeal must be obtained from either the Court of Appeal or the House of Lords, and will not be granted unless it is certified by the Court of Appeal that a point of law of general public importance is involved. Leave will be granted only if it then appears to the Court of Appeal or the House of Lords, as the case may be, that the point in question is one which ought to be considered by the House of Lords.

3.3 THE SUPREME COURT: CONSTITUTION

The Supreme Court is central to the system of courts in England and Wales. It was created by the Judicature Act 1873 and is now governed by the Supreme Court Act 1981, which consolidated the relevant legislation in force in 1981.

The Supreme Court of England and Wales consists of the Court of Appeal, the High Court of Justice and the Crown Court. The Lord Chancellor, who is traditionally the head of the judiciary, is now constituted president of the Supreme Court by the 1981 Act.

(a) The Court of Appeal

(i) The Judges.
The Court of Appeal consists of ex-officio judges and not more than eighteen ordinary judges. The ex-officio judges are as follows:

(*a*) the Lord Chancellor;
(*b*) any person who has been Lord Chancellor;
(*c*) Lords of Appeal in Ordinary with certain qualifications;
(*d*) the Lord Chief Justice;
(*e*) the Master of the Rolls;
(*f*) the President of the Family Division;
(*g*) the Vice-Chancellor.

Previous Lord Chancellors and Lords of Appeal in Ordinary do not sit in the usual course but only at the request of the Lord Chancellor and with their own consent.

The ordinary judges of the Court of Appeal are styled 'Lords Justices of Appeal'.

A court usually consists of three judges, but for certain types of action, specified in ss. 54 and 55, a court is duly constituted, in both civil and criminal divisions, if it consists of two judges.

(ii) Divisions of the Court of Appeal.

There are two divisions of the Court of Appeal, namely, the criminal division and the civil division: Criminal Appeal Act 1966. The Lord Chief Justice is president of the criminal division and the Master of the Rolls is president of the civil division. The criminal division hears criminal appeals in the exercise of the jurisdiction conferred by the Criminal Appeal Act 1968 and the Criminal Justice Act 1972. The civil division hears appeals (*inter alia*) from any judgement or order of the High Court.

(b) The High Court

(i) The Judges.

The High Court consists of:

- (*a*) the Lord Chancellor;
- (*b*) the Lord Chief Justice;
- (*c*) the President of the Family Division;
- (*d*) the Vice-Chancellor; and
- (*e*) not more than eighty puisne judges of the High Court.

The puisne judges are styled 'Justices of the High Court'. The word 'puisne' is pronounced 'puny' and means junior or lower in rank, i.e, as compared with the Lords Justices of Appeal and other senior members of the judiciary.

(ii) Divisions of the High Court.

There are three Divisions of the High Court, namely:

- (*a*) the Chancery Division, consisting of the Lord Chancellor, the Vice-Chancellor and a number of puisne judges attached by direction of the Lord Chancellor;
- (*b*) the Queen's Bench Division, consisting of the Lord Chief Justice (president) and a number of puisne judges attached by direction of the Lord Chancellor; and
- (*c*) the Family Division, consisting of the President of the Family Division and a number of puisne judges attached by direction of the Lord Chancellor.

The High Court is one court. Any order or judgement emanating from any of the Divisions is an order or judgement of the High Court and should not be regarded as an order or judgement of any particular Division. The

Lord Chancellor is nominal president of the Chancery Division which, in practice, is headed by the Vice-Chancellor.

It should be noticed that puisne judges are attached to a Division by direction of the Lord Chancellor. Judges may be transferred from one Division to another by direction of the Lord Chancellor subject to the consent of the judge and the concurrence of the senior judge of the Division from which it is proposed to transfer him.

(iii) The Patents, Admiralty and Commercial Courts.
These are the three specialist courts which take their place within the divisions of the High Court. The Admiralty Court and the Commercial Court have long been part of the Queen's Bench Division. The Patents Court was constituted by the Patents Act 1977 as part of the Chancery Division.

(c) The Crown Court

The Crown Court was established by the Courts Act 1971 to be part of the Supreme Court together with the Court of Appeal and the High Court. The jurisdiction of the Crown Court is exercisable by:

- (*a*) any judge of the High Court; or
- (*b*) any Circuit judge or Recorder; or
- (*c*) in certain cases, a judge of the High Court, Circuit judge or Recorder sitting with not more than four justices of the peace,

and such persons are judges of the Crown Court when they are exercising the jurisdiction of that court.

When the Crown Court sits in the City of London in the Old Bailey it is known as the Central Criminal Court. The Lord Mayor or any Alderman is entitled to sit as a judge of the Central Criminal Court with any judge of the High Court or any Circuit judge or Recorder.

(d) The appointment of judges

Whenever the office of Lord Chief Justice, Master of the Rolls, President of the Family Division or Vice-Chancellor is vacant, Her Majesty the Queen may, by letters patent, appoint a qualified person to that office on the advice of the Prime Minister.

Subject to the statutory upper limit on numbers, Her Majesty may from time to time by letters patent appoint qualified persons as Lords Justices of Appeal or as puisne judges of the High Court. No person is qualified for appointment as a puisne judge of the High Court unless he is a barrister of at least ten years' standing. No person is qualified for appointment as a

Lord Justice of Appeal unless he is a barrister of at least fifteen years' standing or a judge of the High Court.

All judges of the Supreme Court hold office during good behaviour, subject to a power of removal by Her Majesty on an address presented to her by both Houses of Parliament.

3.4 THE SUPREME COURT: JURISDICTION

(a) The Court of Appeal

The Court of Appeal is a superior court of record. This means, in practice, that it has wide powers to deal with contempt of court. The Supreme Court Act 1981 preserves the previously exercised jurisdiction of the Court of Appeal, including the pre-1875 appellate jurisdiction of the superior courts of common law and equity.

Since 1966 the Court of Appeal has been divided into two divisions – a civil division and a criminal division: Criminal Appeal Act 1966.

(i) Civil jurisdiction.
The civil division exercises all the jurisdiction which was exercisable before the 1981 Act. This includes appeals from the High Court, the county courts, the Restrictive Practices Court, the Employment Appeal Tribunal and various other tribunals. The parties to a County Court action may, before judgement, enter into a binding agreement not to appeal.

(ii) Criminal division.
The criminal division of the Court of Appeal has succeeded to the jurisdiction of the Court of Criminal Appeal: Criminal Appeal Act 1966. The criminal division hears appeals against conviction by the Crown Court and also appeals against sentences of that court.

(b) The High Court

The Supreme Court of Judicature Acts of 1873 and 1875 (as consolidated by the Acts of 1925 and 1981) have conferred on the High Court the original jurisdiction of the superior courts of common law and the Court of Chancery. When the High Court was first established, it consisted of five divisions: there are now three, namely, the Chancery Division, the Queen's Bench Division and the Family Division. Jurisdiction is conferred on the High Court and, in theory, the jurisdiction is exercisable to its full extent by each Division, but section 61 and Schedule 1 of the 1981 Act provide for the distribution of High Court business between the three Divisions as follows:

(i) Chancery Division.
To this Division are assigned all causes and matters relating to:

(*a*) the sale, exchange or partition of land, or the raising of charges on land;

(*b*) the redemption or foreclosure of mortgages;

(*c*) the execution of trusts;

(*d*) the administration of the estates of deceased persons;

(*e*) bankruptcy;

(*f*) the dissolution of partnerships or the taking of partnership or other accounts;

(*g*) the rectification, setting aside or cancellation of deeds or other instruments in writing;

(*h*) probate business, other than non-contentious or common form business;

(*i*) patents, trade-marks, registered designs or copyright;

(*j*) the appointment of a guardian or a minor's estate, and all causes and matters involving the exercise of the High Court's jurisdiction under the enactments relating to companies.

(ii) Queen's Bench Division.
To this Division are assigned:-

(*a*) applications for writs of habeas corpus, except applications made by a parent or guardian of a minor for such a writ concerning the custody of the minor;

(*b*) applications for judicial review;

(*c*) all causes and matters involving the exercise of the High Court's Admiralty jurisdiction or its jurisdiction as a prize court; and

(*d*) all causes and matters entered in the commercial list.

The 1981 Act preserves the power of the High Court to issue orders of mandamus, prohibition and certiorari, by which administrative bodies and inferior tribunals are compelled to exercise their powers and to act within their powers. These orders are part of the supervisory jurisdiction of the High Court, which also includes the issue of the ancient writ of habeas corpus.

(iii) Family Division.
To this Division are assigned:

(*a*) all matrimonial causes and matters (whether at first instance or on appeal);

(*b*) all causes and matters (whether at first instance or on appeal) relating to:

1. legitimacy;
2. the wardship, guardianship, custody or maintenance of minors (including proceedings about access), except proceedings solely for the appointment of a guardian of a minor's estate;
3. affiliation or adoption;
4. non-contentious or common form probate business;

(*c*) applications for consent to the marriage of a minor;

(*d*) proceedings on appeal from an order or decision to enforce an order of a magistrates' court made in matrimonial proceedings or with respect to the guardianship of a minor.

(c) The Crown Court

The Crown Court is a superior court of record. It was established in 1972 by the Courts Act 1971, which conferred on it the jurisdiction of the courts of assize and quarter sessions. All proceedings on indictment must be brought before the Crown Court, which also has jurisdiction to hear appeals on a wide variety of cases from magistrates' courts.

3.5 OTHER COURTS

(a) County Courts

The law relating to County Courts has been consolidated in the County Courts Act 1984.

(i) Constitution.
A County Court is a court of record. England and Wales are divided into districts and a County Court is held in each district. The Lord Chancellor, by order, specifies the place and times of each County Court's sittings.

The Lord Chancellor assigns one or more circuit judges to each district. For this purpose, any circuit judge is capable of sitting in any district.

(ii) Jurisdiction.
A County Court has jurisdiction in actions founded in contract or tort where the debt, demand or damage claimed does not exceed the County Court limit.

If the parties to an action which would, if commenced in the High Court, have been assigned to the Queen's Bench Division, agree to submit to the jurisdiction of a County Court, then, provided the agreement is in writing and signed by the parties, that County Court will have jurisdiction. This provision does not apply to the Admiralty jurisdiction of the High Court.

County Courts have jurisdiction in actions for the recovery of land where the net annual value for rating of the land does not exceed the County Court limit.

The County Court also has jurisdiction in probate proceedings where the estate of the deceased is less than the County Court limit.

A County Court has all the jurisdiction of the High Court to hear and determine the following:

(a) proceedings on the administration of the estate of a deceased person where the estate does not exceed in amount or value the County Court limit;

(b) proceedings with regard to trusts where the estate or trust fund does not exceed in amount or value the County Court limit;

(c) proceedings for the foreclosure or redemption of any mortgage where the amount owing in respect of the mortgage does not exceed the County Court limit;

(d) specific performance where the value of the property does not exceed the County Court limit;

(e) partnership dissolution where the whole assets do not exceed in amount or value the County Court limit;

(f) proceedings for relief against frauds or mistake, where damage sustained does not exceed in amount or value the County Court limit. The County Court limit may be varied from time to time by Statutory Instrument. The present limit is £5,000 for actions in contract or tort and £30,000 for actions in equity.

(b) Magistrates' Courts

By s. 148(1) of the Magistrates' Courts Act 1980, 'magistrates' court' means any justice or justices of the peace acting under any enactment or by virtue of his or their commission or under the common law. The appointment of justices of the peace is regulated by the Justices of the Peace Act 1979, which provides for their appointment on behalf and in the name of Her Majesty by the Lord Chancellor. The 1979 Act also makes provision for the appointment of stipendiary magistrates from the ranks of barristers and solicitors of not less than seven years' standing. Stipendiary magistrates sit alone and have the same powers as two justices of the peace sitting together. There are some twenty thousand magistrates in England and Wales, each appointed to a particular area. Justices of the peace are not required to have any legal qualification, although the clerk to the magistrates in each court is a qualified barrister or solicitor.

The jurisdiction of magistrates' courts is provided for in the Magistrates' Courts Act 1980. This jurisdiction is both criminal and civil.

mittal proceedings. The function of examining justices may be
harged by a single justice sitting in open court. Evidence is
g. en in the presence of the accused and the defence may question
witnesses. If a magistrates' court enquiring into an offence as
examining justices is of opinion, on consideration of the evidence
and of any statement of the accused, that there is sufficient evidence
to put the accused on trial by jury for any indictable offence, the
court must commit him for trial. When the accused is committed
for trial, the place of the trial must be specified - usually a sitting
of the Crown Court.

If the court decides not to commit the accused, he must be
discharged.

(b) *Summary trials*. Magistrates' courts are courts of summary jurisdiction
for minor offences. Certain offences are triable only summarily, while
others are triable either way, i.e., summarily or by indictment in the
Crown Court. (An indictment is the document containing the formal
accusation.)

On the summary trial, the court must state to the accused the
substance of the information laid against him and ask him whether
he pleads guilty or not guilty. If the accused pleads guilty, the court
may convict him without hearing evidence. If the court hears the
evidence, it must convict the accused or dismiss the information. The
sentence imposed by the court may not exceed six months, except
that a total of twelve months' imprisonment may be imposed in
the case of consecutive sentences for offences triable either way.

An accused person convicted by a magistrates' court may appeal
to the Crown Court against conviction, sentence or both.

(ii) Civil jurisdiction

Magistrates' courts have jurisdiction to hear and decide complaints. A com-
plaint is usually for an order for the payment of a sum recoverable summarily
as a civil debt, or for the variation of the rate of any periodical payments
previously ordered. There is also a jurisdiction to make decisions in what
are known as 'domestic proceedings', i.e., proceedings under a variety of
statutes dealing with maintenance orders, guardianship of minors, adoption
and child care. The 1980 Act contains provisions controlling the reporting
of domestic proceedings.

Appeals from decisions in domestic proceedings will lie with the Family
Division of the High Court. Other appeals will, in general, lie with the
Crown Court. In some cases, however, there may be an appeal to the
Queen's Bench Division on a point of law by way of case stated.

(c) Employment Appeal Tribunal

(i) Constitution.

The Appeal Tribunal was created by the provisions of the Employment Protection Act 1975 which were re-enacted in the Employment Protection (Consolidation) Act 1978. The Appeal Tribunal consists of:

- (*a*) judges nominated from time to time by the Lord Chancellor from among the judges of the High Court and the Court of Appeal;
- (*b*) at least one Scots judge from the Court of Session nominated by the Lord President of that Court;
- (*c*) other members appointed by Her Majesty on the joint recommendation of the Lord Chancellor and the Secretary of State. Members so appointed will have special knowledge or experience of industrial relations as representatives of either workers or employers.

Although the Appeal Tribunal enjoys the services of very senior judges, it is not a constituent part of the Supreme Court.

(ii) Jurisdiction.

The Employment Appeal Tribunal can dispose of appeals from Industrial Tribunals in matters of unfair dismissal, redundancy payments, equal pay, sex descrimination and race relations. The procedure adopted should be simple and speedy.

(d) The Restrictive Practices Court

This court was established by the Restrictive Trade Practices Act 1956 and is now governed by the consolidating Restrictive Practices Court Act 1976. It consists of five judges nominated from the Supreme Court (or the Scots or Northern Ireland equivalent) and not more than ten appointed members. The appointed members must be persons appearing to the Lord Chancellor to be qualified by virtue of their knowledge of or experience in industry, commerce or public affairs.

For the hearing of any proceedings the Court must consist of a presiding judge and at least two other members, except that in the case of proceedings involving only issues of law, the Court may instead consist of a single member being a judge.

The Restrictive Trade Practices Act 1976 confers jurisdiction, on the application of the Director General of Fair Trading, to declare whether or not any restrictive agreement is contrary to the public interest. Any agreement is void to the extent declared to be against the public interest.

(e) The Judicial Committee of the Privy Council

The Judicial Committee was created by, and is governed by, the Judicial Committee Act 1833 as amended. It consists of the Lord President of the Council, the Lord Chancellor, ex-Lord Presidents, the Lords of Appeal in Ordinary and those members of the Privy Council who hold high judicial office. Hearings are before not less than three members, although the number is usually five.

The Privy Council is the Sovereign in Council and, therefore, the jurisdiction is in the form of Advice tendered to the Sovereign, which is then implemented by an Order in Council. Appeal lies from the Supreme Courts of all the British colonies and Protectorates. It also lies from those independent Commonwealth countries which have not, by legislation, prevented such appeals.

The Judicial Committee also hears appeals from ecclesiastical and medical tribunals.

3.6 THE EUROPEAN COURT

When the United Kingdom became a member of the European Community on 1 January 1973, the House of Lords ceased to be the final court of appeal in regard to certain types of appeal. It will be seen, however, that in the great majority of cases the position of the House of Lords remains unaffected.

(a) Constitution

The European Court consists of eleven judges and five Advocates-General. It is the duty of the Advocates-General to assist the court by presenting reasoned conclusions on cases brought before it. Where a case is submitted by a Member State or one of the Community institutions, the Court must sit in plenary session. In other cases, however, the Court may sit in groups of three or five judges.

(b) Jurisdiction

The European Court has jurisdiction to deal with cases arising between Member States and institutions of the Community. It has a further jurisdiction which relates the European Court to the system of courts in the United Kingdom, namely, under Article 177 of the European Economic Community Treaty. By this Article, if a case comes before the final appellate court of a Member State, and raises a question of the interpretation of the EEC Treaty, that court must refer the matter to the European Court and is bound to apply the ruling of the European Court to that case. Where such questions arise before any other court of a Member State, the judge is not bound to refer to the European Court – he has a discretion to do so if he sees fit. If a trial judge decides to interprèt the Treaty himself, he must do so according to the principles laid down by the European Court: European Communities Act 1972, s. 3.

Article 177 operates within English law by virtue of the governing provisions of the European Communities Act 1972 which provide that legal effect be given to the EEC Treaty.

Thus, in England, on questions of interpretation or validity, the European Court is supreme. If such a question arises before the House of Lords, the House is bound to refer it to the European Court and, having done so, must follow the European Court's ruling in that particular case. English courts other than the House of Lords have a discretion whether to refer to the European Court on any such question.

(c) The impact of the European Court on English Law

The relationship of the European Court to the English system of courts and to English law was explained in a well known passage in the judgement of Lord Denning M.R. in *H.P. Bulmer Ltd* v. *J. Bollinger S.A.* (1974):

'The first and fundamental point is that the Treaty concerns only those matters which have a European element, that is to say, matters which affect people or property in the nine countries of the Common Market besides ourselves. The Treaty does not touch any of the matters which concern solely England and the people in it. These are still governed by English law. They are not affected by the Treaty. But when we come to matters with a European element the Treaty is like an incoming tide. It flows into the estuaries and up the rivers. It cannot be held back. Parliament has decreed that the Treaty is henceforward to be part of our law. It is equal in force to any statute. . . . Any rights or obligations created by the Treaty are to be given legal effect in England without more ado.'

In the same judgement, Lord Denning sought to answer the question: By what courts is the Treaty to be interpreted? He said:

'It is important to distinguish between the task of *interpreting* the Treaty – to see what it means – and the task of *applying* the Treaty. On this matter in our courts the English judges have the final word. They are the only judges who are empowered to decide the case itself.

They have to find the facts, to state the issues, to give judgement for one side or the other, and to see that the judgement is enforced.

Before the English judges can apply the Treaty, they have to see what it means and what is its effect. In the task of *interpreting* the Treaty, the English judges are no longer the final authority. . . . The supreme tribunal for *interpreting* the Treaty is the European Court of Justice at Luxembourg. Our Parliament has so decreed.'

Lord Denning then went on to quote from section 3 of the European Communities Act 1972, which provides that for the purposes of all legal proceedings any question as to the meaning or effect of any of the Treaties, or as to the validity, meaning or effect of any Community instrument, shall be treated as a question of law.

3.7 JURIES

The essential feature of trial by jury is that questions of law are decided by the judge and questions of fact are decided by the jury. The statutory rules governing juries and jury service are consolidated in the Juries Act 1974.

(a) Jury service

The general rule is that every person is qualified to act as a juror in the Crown Court, the High Court and County Courts if (1) he is registered as a parliamentary or local government elector and is not less than eighteen nor more than sixty-five years of age, and (2) he has been ordinarily resident in the United Kingdom for any period of at least five years since attaining the age of thirteen: Juries Act 1974, s. 1.

Persons ineligible or disqualified for jury service, or excusable as of right are, respectively, listed in Schedule 1 to the 1974 Act. Those ineligible include (1) the judiciary and others concerned with the administration of justice, e.g., barristers, solicitors and the police, (2) the clergy and (3) the mentally ill. Those disqualified on criminal grounds are specified in the Juries (Disqualification) Act 1984. Finally, members of either House of Parliament and members of the armed forces are excusable as of right.

(b) Majority verdicts

The ancient common law rules governing juries required a unanimous verdict but the position is now relaxed by modern statutory provisions which allow a majority verdict to be given. By s. 17(1) of the 1974 Act, the general rule is that a verdict of a jury in proceedings in the Crown

Court need not be unanimous if (1) in a case where there are not less than eleven jurors, ten of them agree on a verdict, and (2) in a case where there are ten jurors, nine of them agree on a verdict. Section 17(2) of the same Act provides that, in general, the verdict of a County Court jury (eight jurors) need not be unanimous if seven of them agree on a verdict.

(c) Juries in criminal cases

The procedure for indictable offences (3.3 and 3.5 above) is a preliminary hearing before a magistrates' court followed by trial by jury. In contrast, non-indictable offences are tried by a magistrate without a jury.

(d) Juries in civil cases

The use of a jury in a civil case – rare in modern times – is governed by section 69 of the Supreme Court Act 1981. By section 69(1), where, on the application of any party to an action to be tried in the Queen's Bench Division, the court is satisfied that there is in issue either (1) a charge of fraud against that party, or (2) a claim in respect of libel, slander, malicious prosecution or false imprisonment, the action must be tried with a jury unless the court is of opinion that the trial requires a prolonged examination of documents or any scientific or local investigation which cannot conveniently be made with a jury.

3.8 THE LEGAL PROFESSION

(a) The division of the profession

The outstanding characteristic of the legal profession in England and Wales is that it is divided into two distinct branches, namely, the Bar and the solicitors' profession. The origins of this division can be traced back to the fourteenth century when professional advocates first began to practise. The division was confirmed when the Inns of Court refused to admit practising attorneys to membership. Attorneys, like present-day solicitors, dealt directly with the lay clients, instructing counsel – as barristers may be styled – where the services of an advocate was required in the Royal Courts. In the Court of Chancery the function equivalent to that of the attorney was performed by persons who became known as 'solicitors'. As membership of the Inns of Court was not available to attorneys and solicitors they formed their own professional society in the early eighteenth century. This society was the origin of the Law Society.

No person may practise law unless he is a member of an Inn of Court or a member of the Law Society, i.e., he must be a barrister or a solicitor.

(b) Proposals for fusion of the profession

The question whether the two branches of the legal profession should be fused has been much discussed in recent years. The prevailing view seems to be that fusion might lead to a decline in the standard of advocacy in the superior courts.

The divided nature of the profession need not adversely affect individual legal careers because, subject to regulations which are generally regarded as reasonable, solicitors may become barristers if they so wish and barristers may become solicitors. It is not possible for any person to be both a barrister and a solicitor at one and the same time.

Where a barrister who previously spent a period as a solicitor seeks any office which requires a minimum period of practice at the Bar, he may count his time as a solicitor as if he was then at the Bar: Barristers (Qualification for Office) Act 1961, s. 1.

(c) Solicitors

The Law Society is the governing body of the solicitors' profession. The Society's objects are defined in the incorporating Charter as 'promoting professional improvement and facilitating the acquisition of legal knowledge'.

The statutory provisions governing solicitors and the Law Society are now reduced to a single code by the consolidating Solicitors Act of 1974. This Act deals with (1) qualification and the right to practise, (2) professional conduct and discipline and (3) remuneration.

By s. 2(1) of the 1974 Act the Law Society, with the concurrence of the Lord Chancellor, the Lord Chief Justice and the Master of the Rolls may make training regulations for persons seeking to be admitted as solicitors. By section 6, the Law Society must keep a roll of all solicitors. By section 50, a solicitor is an officer of the Supreme Court of Judicature. Accordingly, a solicitor's full style and title is 'solicitor of the Supreme Court'.

Solicitors may practise in partnership: barristers may not. The larger partnership firms may give the opportunity to some solicitors to specialise, e.g., in commercial law or tax matters.

Solicitors are engaged by lay clients and, when they think fit, will instruct counsel. Counsel will always be instructed when there is the likelihood of litigation in the High Court. Apart from preparing for litigation, solicitors may act as general legal advisers to individuals and to companies. They draft contracts of all kinds, conveyances of land, settlements and wills. Solicitors have a right of audience in magistrates' courts, County Courts, and, in certain matters, in the Crown Court.

The legal assistants who are employed by solicitors are called 'legal executives'. Their professional body is the Institute of Legal Executives which controls such matters as training, examination and admission of legal executives as well as their professional standards and conduct.

(d) Barristers

A student wishing to be called to the Bar must join one of the Inns of Court. These are the Middle Temple, the Inner Temple, Gray's Inn and Lincoln's Inn. The student must then satisfy the examination requirements of the Council of Legal Education after which he will be required to serve for a year in pupillage with an experienced barrister.

Barristers form themselves into groups, each group working from a set of rooms known as 'chambers'. Each set of chambers has a clerk who will deal with solicitors wishing to brief any member of the chambers. Although barristers are grouped in this way they practise as individuals – not in partnership.

Barristers, unlike solicitors, have a right to plead in the High Court, the Court of Appeal and the House of Lords. They may draft documents of any kind and write legal opinions. They may be engaged (or briefed) by solicitors only – not by lay clients directly. Successful barristers of ten years or more in standing may apply to 'take silk'. In other words, they may apply to become Queen's Counsel. A Queen's Counsel may be referred to informally as a 'silk' after the material from which his court gown is made. Appointments are made by H.M. the Queen on the advice of the Lord Chancellor. A Queen's Counsel does not draft pleadings, this being left to a junior barrister, who will usually appear in court with the silk. It follows that Queen's Counsel are briefed only in cases of considerable importance.

Appointments to the High Court judiciary are made from the ranks of barristers and Queen's Counsel only.

SUMMARY

1   The Supreme Court is central to the system of courts in England and Wales.

2   By the Appellate Jurisdiction Act 1876 appeals from the Court of Appeal to the House of Lords must be heard by not less than three of the following Lords of Appeal – the Lord Chancellor, Lords of Appeal in Ordinary, such peers as hold or have held high judicial office.

3   The 'leap frog' procedure was introduced by the Administration of Justice Act 1969.

4   The Criminal Appeal Act 1968 provides for appeal from the Criminal

44

division of the Court of Appeal to the House of Lords at the instance of the defendant or the prosecutor.

5   The Supreme Court consists of the Court of Appeal, the High Court of Justice and the Crown Court.

6   The two divisions of the Court of Appeal were created by the Criminal Appeal Act 1966.

7   There are three Divisions of the High Court, namely, the Chancery Division, the Queen's Bench Division and the Family Division.

8   The Patents, Admiralty and Commercial Courts are specialist courts which take their place within the Divisions of the High Court.

9   The Supreme Court Act 1981 governs the constitution and jurisdiction of the Supreme Court.

10   The distribution of High Court business between the three Divisions is carried out according to s. 61 of the 1981 Act and Schedule 1.

11   The Crown Court was established in 1972 by the Courts Act 1971.

12   The law relating to County Courts has been consolidated in the County Courts Act 1984.

13   The Lord Chancellor assigns one circuit judge or more to each County Court district.

14   A County Court has jurisdiction in actions founded in contract or tort where the debt, demand or damage claimed does not exceed the County Court limit.

15   The appointment of Justices of the Peace is regulated by the Justices of the Peace Act 1979.

16   The criminal jurisdiction of a magistrates' court includes committal proceedings and summary trials.

17   The Employment Appeal Tribunal was created by the Employment Protection Act 1975.

18   The Restrictive Practices Court is now governed by the Restrictive Practices Court Act 1976.

19   The Judicial Committee of the Privy Council was created by, and is governed by, the Judicial Committee Act 1833 as amended.

20   Legal effect was given to the EEC Treaty by the European Communities Act 1972.

21   If a case comes before the House of Lords which raises a question of the interpretation of the EEC Treaty, the House is bound to refer the matter to the European Court and is also bound to apply the ruling of the European Court to that case.

EXERCISES

1   What are the 'Lords of Appeal in Ordinary'?

2 How must the House of Lords be constituted for the hearing of an appeal?

3 What jurisdiction has the House of Lords?

4 Explain in detail the special procedure for appeal to the House of Lords which was introduced by the Administration of Justice Act 1969.

5 What courts make up the Supreme Court and what is the constitution of each?

6 Summarise the rules governing the distribution of business to the different Divisions of the High Court.

7 Write a short note on the appointment of judges of the Supreme Court.

8 Summarise the criminal jurisdiction of the Court of Appeal, the High Court and the Crown Court.

9 What civil jurisdiction has the Supreme Court?

10 How are County Courts constituted?

11 Give a detailed explanation of the jurisdiction of the County Courts.

12 What is the jurisdiction of the magistrates' courts? What is a summary trial?

13 Explain the constitution and jurisdiction of the Employment Appeal Tribunal. Mention whether the Appeal Tribunal is part of the Supreme Court.

14 What is the function of the Restrictive Practices Court?

15 Write a note on the Judicial Committee of the Privy Council.

16 What is the constitution and jurisdiction of the European Court?

17 How do the provisions of the EEC Treaty affect, or become part of, English law?

18 Construct a diagram which shows the hierarchy of courts and, at the same time, the central position of the Supreme Court.

19 What is the essential feature of a trial by jury?

20 How does the work of a barrister differ from that of a solicitor?

CHAPTER 4

BASIC LEGAL CONCEPTS

4.1 INTRODUCTORY MATTERS

Law is about rights and duties, usually in relation to property of some kind. The only entities which have the capacity of exercising rights or undertaking duties are those which the law recognises as having personality. All human beings have personality in the eyes of English law, but so have certain other entities known as corporations. These are persons created under the law, in other words, artificial persons. Human beings are, of course, natural persons.

The above statement contains a number of key legal concepts: rights, duties, capacity, persons, corporations, property. These concepts, and some others, namely, obligation, liability, personalty, realty, possession and ownership occur frequently in textbooks, reports and legal discussion.

The purpose of this chapter is to consider the meaning of these basic concepts so as to clear the way forward in the study of law.

4.2 PERSONS

(a) Definition

A person in law is an entity which is capable of enjoying rights and undertaking duties. In contra-distinction, a thing is the subject of rights and duties. Personality is the characteristic of a legal person for rights and duties can exist only in relation to persons.

Persons may be either natural or artificial. A natural person is a human being. An artificial person is a corporation created under the law.

(b) Corporations

A corporation has a personality distinct and separate from those natural persons who, from time to time, constitute it. A corporation sole is formed by a succession of solitary natural persons, for example the Bishop of London. The present Bishop is in law the same person as all his predecessors when acting in his official capacity. Perhaps the best example of a corporation sole is the Crown. A corporation sole is capable of perpetual existence.

Corporations aggregate are classified according to their mode of creation, namely, (1) by charter, (2) by statute and (3) by registration under the Companies Acts. Chartered corporations are the creation of the Royal Prerogative and are only rarely formed in modern times. Statutory corporations are created by Act of Parliament. It is an expensive process to form a corporation by private Act of Parliament as compared with the simple process of registration according to the requirements of the Companies Acts. Most statutory corporations formed in recent times are those created by Public Acts for the purpose of running nationalised industries. With regard to registered companies, the requirements for registration vary according to whether the company in question is a private or a public limited company.

All corporations aggregate are capable of perpetual existence as the membership changes from time to time, always with the possibility of new members joining as others leave.

A corporation of any kind may be called by its ancient description – a body politic.

(c) Capacity

Capacity is an incident of personality. It denotes the extent of a person's capability of being subject to duties and obligations, on the one hand, and of enjoying rights and benefits, on the other. In contract law, for example, all natural persons who are sane and sober have full contractual capacity, while minors, insane and drunken persons have only a limited contractual capacity.

The contractual capacity of a corporation stems from the manner of its creation.
(Chapter 12.4(f)). A chartered corporation has virtually the same full capacity as a natural person, while statutory and registered companies are restricted by the terms of the creating statute or the Memorandum of Association, respectively.

(d) Unincorporated associations

People group themselves together otherwise than by the formation of corporations for many and various purposes in life. The main examples of unincorporated associations are trade unions and employers' associations, partnerships and clubs. In none of these cases does the group of people - the association - enjoy the advantages which derive from a separate legal identity. This advantage is enjoyed only by corporations.

(i) Trade unions.
Although trade unions may not be incorporated, they have many advantages over most other kinds of unincorporated associations.

Thus a trade union is capable of making contracts, trade union property is vested in trustees for the union and, subject to trade union immunity to actions in tort, a trade union is capable of suing and of being sued in its own name in proceedings relating to any kind of cause of action.

A judgement against a trade union is enforceable against the assets of that trade union.

(ii) Partnership.
Partnerships are governed by the Partnership Act 1890 and the law of agency (see Chapter 15). In general, every partner is an agent of the firm and his other partners for the purpose of the business of the partnership. The acts of every partner who does any act for the carrying on in the usual way business of the kind carried on by the firm bind the firm and his partners. Every partner is liable jointly with the other partners for all debts and obligations of the firm incurred while he is a partner.

(iii) Clubs.
Clubs and associations are formed by their members for almost any kind of lawful purpose. The rules of a club may be regarded as of contractual force as between individual members. A club cannot contract in its own name, so that when a club officer or member purports to contract on behalf of the club, he is either bound personally or has contracted as agent on behalf of each and every member, according to the facts and the rules of agency.

4.3 RIGHTS AND DUTIES

(a) Definition

A right may be described as some liberty attaching to a person, by which he may act or not act in any particular manner or enjoy the possession or ownership of property, and for the infringement of which the law provides a remedy. In short, a right is a liberty attaching to a person which is protected by the law.

On the other side of the coin, where a person enjoys or exercises a right, he does so by virtue of another person (or persons) owing and performing a duty toward him. For example, if A contracts to buy a table from B for the price of £100 and B delivers it to A, then B will have a right to recover the price in accordance with the agreement. In this case B's right to the money is correlative to A's duty to pay. Similarly, in the law of tort where parties are in such proximity that a duty of care is owed by X to Y, then Y may be seen as enjoying a right which is correlative to X's duty. Y has a right not to be injured by X's negligence.

Rights *in rem* may be distinguished from rights *in personam,* and primary rights may be distinguished from secondary rights.

(b) Rights in rem

A right *in rem* is a right lying in the land or thing itself, and exercisable against the whole world. A right *in rem* in one person is correlative of a duty owed to him by the whole world. For example, if a person owns the freehold of a house and has not given any part of his right of ownership to another person, the whole world owes him a duty not to disturb him in the possession and enjoyment of his house.

(c) Rights in personam

In the case of a right *in personam,* the correlative duty attaches to another person; for example, a right which a contract gives to one party is correlative to a duty in identical terms owed by the other contracting party.

(d) Primary and secondary rights

Primary rights are those which arise in favour of a person in contract, tort, property or any other branch of the law. Secondary rights are those which exist solely for the protection and enforcement of primary rights. For example, where a contracting party fails to perform in accordance with the contract, he has violated the primary right of the other party. In this event, there arises immediately a secondary right in that other party to be compensated in money. If it becomes necessary to sue, the court will award compensation in the form of damages to the aggrieved party (see Chapter 10.6(a)).

A person's secondary rights sometimes include measures to protect a primary right short of actual enforcement of the primary right by the court. Thus there are rights of self-help and self-protection available in the law of tort, e.g., in cases of trespass to the person or to goods as well as in conversion and detinue (Chapter 6.5).

(e) Other terms

So far in this chapter we have mentioned the terms person, capacity, rights and duties in their relationship one to another. There are some further terms which should now be considered shortly:

(i) Obligations.
An *obligation* exists where parties are in a relationship of right and correlative duty. Although the term covers the right and the duty, it is commonly used to denote duty only.

(ii) Liabilities
A person is under a *liability* (or is *liable*) when he owes a duty or an obligation to another. In this case, the sense of the word 'liability' or 'liable' can, however, be used in a different sense to meet the case where the duty or obligation is potential. For example, where a guarantor guarantees a debt, he makes himself immediately liable to the creditor, but he will incur an actual duty to pay the creditor only if and when the debtor is in default, the debtor being primarily responsible and the guarantor only secondarily so.

(iii) Powers.
A *power* is a special kind of right to act in a particular way. A power may be discretionary or it may be coupled with a duty to act. Powers are public or private. For an example of a public power, consider the Director General of Fair Trading who is given wide powers in regard to the new system of consumer credit by the Consumer Credit Act 1974 (Chapter 18.1(b)). Consider further the powers of the Lord Chancellor over the appointment of judges and the administration of the County Courts under the County Courts Act 1984 (Chapter 3.5(a)).

Private powers are those which are exercisable by private persons. These may be conferred by statute, as in the case of executors of the estate of a deceased person under the Administration of Estates Act 1925. Private powers may also be conferred by the parties themselves by contract. For example, in a building contract it is provided that the architect will have the power to issue binding instructions in certain specified matters to the employer's contractor.

4.4 PROPERTY

The word 'property' has two meanings. First, and most important, it means that which is the subject of rights, i.e. land or things of all kinds. Secondly, it means a right equivalent to ownership in land or in a thing.

(a) 'Property' as the subject of rights

Property in this sense means land or things which are capable of being owned by a person. Property is either real property or personal property or, as lawyers sometimes say, realty or personalty.

(b) Real property

Ownership of land was protected by *real* actions, that is to say, actions by which restitution of the land *in specie* could be enforced. Since land was the only kind of property which was recoverable *in specie* by a real action, interests in land have for centuries been known as real property.

Real property law stems from feudal law by which real actions were available only to tenants who were 'seised' of the land, i.e. who were entitled to the land for an indefinite period of time as compared with any tenant who held for a definite term of years. The latter, if dispossessed, could in early times bring only a personal action for damages. In theory, no one could own land, for it could be held only by way of tenancy, ultimately of the Crown, the pinnacle of the feudal hierarchy. The entity which could be regarded as subject to ownership was the 'estate'. An 'estate' was an abstraction which the law placed between the tenant and the land. Tenants holding land for an indefinite period, the 'freeholders', owned what was called an estate in fee simple. This estate is the nearest thing to absolute ownership of land permitted by English law.

(c) Terms of years

Terms of years - what we would now call leaseholds - were regarded as estates less than freehold. Leaseholds were called *chattels real* because, although they were not strictly real property, they 'savoured of the realty'. The want of a sufficiently indeterminate duration constituted leaseholds as chattels, i.e. personalty.

(d) The effect of the Law of Property Act 1925

This Act, which was part of the great reforming legislation of 1925, provides that the only estates which are capable of being conveyed or created at law are:

 (*a*) an estate in fee simple absolute in possession;
 (*b*) a term of years absolute.

The Act also specifies those interests or charges which are capable of subsisting in or over land, such as easements and rights of entry.

(e) Pure personalty

Personal property excluding leaseholds may be called pure personalty. Property of this kind is sometimes called chattels personal - a term which nowadays covers all kinds of property other than realty and leaseholds. Pure personalty can comprise things in action and things in possession, according to whether ownership is ultimately enforceable by legal action or, on the other hand, by taking actual physical possession (see Chapter 18). Things in action include debts and other contract rights, patents, copyrights, company shares and negotiable instruments. The law governing things in action stems from Roman Law, the customs of merchants and the general common law of contract and tort.

(f) 'Property' as the right of ownership

This is the second meaning of the word 'property'. To take an example – in a contract for the sale of goods, it is intended that the ownership in the goods will pass from the seller to the buyer. As a matter of convention, the word 'property' is used to denote the rights of ownership. Lawyers speak of the 'property' in the goods and discuss the rules governing the passimg of the 'property' from the seller to the buyer (Chapter 16.3).

4.5 OWNERSHIP

(a) Absolute ownership

Ownership is the concept which relates a person to property over which he has exclusive control, subject only to the general law. A person can have ownership of any kind of property, real or personal, e.g., land, shares in a company, rights under contract, bills of lading, negotiable instruments, and so on.

In legal theory, all land is held ultimately from the Crown, and all owners are thus tenants, but the owner of a fee simple absolute in possession is as close to absolute ownership as the law allows.

An absolute owner has the right to possess the property, the right to use it, the right to destroy it and the right to transfer it to another person.

Where persons other than the owner enjoy rights of user in the property, the owner has restricted ownership only, for example, where the owner's rights to land are subject to another person's right of way over that land or to the rights of the general public, as in the case of a public footpath or bridleway.

(b) Co-ownership

Where two or more persons are entitled to the ownership of the same thing or land concurrently, there is co-ownership. All co-owners are entitled to use and enjoy the property which is, itself, not divided, no co-owner being entitled to any specific part of it. The rights of each co-owner are subject to the rights of the other, or others. Joint tenancy and tenancy in common are examples of co-ownership.

(c) Beneficial ownership

Where a person holds the legal title to property of any kind for the benefit of another person, the legal owner is only nominally an owner and the rights of user and enjoyment belong to the beneficial owner. The legal owner is called a *trustee* and the beneficial owner is called the *beneficiary*. The concept of the separation of nominal ownership from beneficial ownership is the basis of the law of trusts.

4.6 POSSESSION

(a) What constitutes possession

To exercise possession over property, a person must (1) have actual or potential physical control of the propery, (2) have the intention to exercise control and (3) ensure that there are external and visible signs of the fact of his possession. These requirements must be fulfilled whatever kind of property is in question, real or personal. Obviously, the measures required to exercise control and to show possession will vary according to the nature of the property.

(b) Consequences of possession

The possessor of property has a presumptive title to that property, for possession raises the presumption that the possessor is the true owner. Thus the person in possession is protected by the law except against a claimant who can show a better title. This is what is meant by the old saying that 'possession is nine points of the law'. (See also the torts of trespass to land and to goods and the tort of conversion below: Chapter 6.3 and 6.4.)

In most cases, the person in possession of property is either the owner or a person authorised by the owner. The person in possession may or may not have rights of user and enjoyment, according to the agreement with the owner. For example, in a contract of sale of goods, the seller may deliver the goods to the buyer on the basis that title does not pass until some future event, e.g., payment of the price. In this case, until payment, the buyer is in possession with all rights of user and enjoyment, while the seller remains the owner until the price is paid. To take a further example, if the owner of goods delivers them to a warehouseman for storage, the duties of the warehouseman will be contained in the express and implied terms of a contract with the owner. In the normal course of events, the warehouseman will have no rights of user and enjoyment of the property. His duties are to keep the property secure and to dispose of it according to the instructions of the owner. For a final and simple example from the law of real property, when the holder of a fee simple grants a lease to a tenant, the tenant will have the right of possession according to the terms of the lease. The effect of the lease is to separate ownership from possession, i.e., the owner retains ownership and the lessee is entitled to actual possession, and to the use and enjoyment of the property.

(c) Bailment

The essential meaning of 'bailment' is the delivery of goods. The person who delivers the goods is called the bailor and the person to whom they are delivered is called the bailee. The intention of the parties is always that the goods will be returned to the bailor or delivered to some other person designated by him. The bailee is, thus, always in possession of goods which he does not own. The bailor may or may not have ownership, according to the circumstances.

There are several kinds of bailment, e.g. (1) where goods are deposited with the bailee to keep for the use of the bailor; (2) where goods are lent free of charge to a friend to be used by him; (3) where goods are delivered to a carrier who has contracted to carry them for a consideration; (4) where goods are delivered to a carrier who has undertaken to carry them free of charge; (5) where goods are delivered by way of pawn, i.e. as security for money lent by the bailee to the bailor; (6) where goods are hired by the bailee for his own use; (7) where goods are delivered to a bailee who has contracted to do something to them for a consideration; (8) where goods are delivered to a bailee who has undertaken to do something to them free of charge.

The bailee's duty to take care of the goods bailed to him varies according to the circumstances of the bailment. The extent of the duty may be expressed in a contract, or it may be implied as the presumed intention of the parties. Where the bailment is for the benefit of the bailee alone, he must take great care of the goods. On the other hand, where the bailment is for the benefit of the bailor alone, the bailee is liable only for negligence. Where, however, the bailment is for the benefit of both parties – and this is usually the case – the bailee is bound to exercise reasonable care of the goods.

SUMMARY

1   A person in law is an entity which is capable of enjoying and enforcing rights and undertaking duties and obligations; a thing is the subject of rights and duties.

2   A natural person is a human being; an artificial person is a corporation created under the law.

3   A corporation has a personality distinct and separate from those natural persons who, from time to time, constitute it.

4   Corporations may be sole or aggregate. A corporation sole is comprised by a continuous succession of solitary natural persons. It is capable of perpetual existence.

5   Corporations aggregate may be formed by charter, by statute or by registration.

6   Corporations aggregate are capable of perpetual existence as the membership changes from time to time, always with the possibility of new members joining as others leave.

7   Capacity is an incident of personality. It denotes the extent of a person's capability of being subject to duties and obligations and of enjoying and enforcing rights.

8   Unincorporated associations such as trade unions, partnerships and clubs do not exist as entities separate from their members.

9   Trade unions may make contracts in their own name, and (subject to the immunity to actions in tort), a trade union is capable of being sued in its own name in proceedings relating to any kind of cause of action.

10   A right may be described as some liberty attaching to a person, by which that person may act or not act in any particular manner or by which that person may enjoy the possession or ownership of property, and for the infringement of which the law provides a remedy.

11   A right is correlative to a duty.

12   A right *in rem* is a right in land or a thing and is exercisable against the whole world. A right *in personam* is a right in respect of which the correlative duty attaches to another person.

13   Primary rights are those which arise in contract, tort, property or any other branch of the law: secondary rights are those which exist solely for the protection and enforcement of primary rights.

14   'Property' has two meanings, (1) the subject of rights and (2) the right of ownership.

15 An 'estate' is an abstraction – the subject of ownership – which feudal law placed between the owner and the land.

16 Ownership of land was protected by *real* actions by which the restitution of the land *in specie* could be enforced. For centuries, land has been known as real property or realty.

17 Real actions were available only to tenants who were 'seised' of the land, i.e., who were entitled to hold the land for an indefinite period of time.

18 Tenants who held land for a definite period of time could only bring personal actions for damages if they were dispossessed.

19 The basic classification of 'property' is (1) realty, (2) pure personalty and (3) chattels real.

20 By the Law of Property Act 1925 there are only two estates capable of existing at law (1) a fee simple absolute in possession and (2) a term of years absolute.

EXERCISES

1 Explain fully what is meant by 'person' in law.

2 What is 'capacity'?

3 Compare unincorporated associations with corporations.

4 Give a careful definition of a 'right'.
Illustrate your definition with examples.

5 Distinguish between rights *in rem* and rights *in personam*.

6 What is a secondary right?

7 Give the two meanings of the word 'property'.

8 Explain what is meant by (1) realty, (2) pure personalty and (3) chattels real.

9 Is absolute ownership of land possible in English law?

10 What do you understand by the expression 'restricted ownership'?

11 What is beneficial ownership?

12 Does co-ownership involve the division of property?

13 There are three constituent elements in possession. What are they?

14 'Possession is nine points of the law.' Discuss this old saying.

15 Give three common examples of bailment and explain the duty owed by the bailee in each case.

PART II
BRANCHES OF LAW

CRIMINAL LAW

5.1 INTRODUCTORY MATTERS

(a) Definition of a crime

In *Board of Trade* v. *Owen* (1957) the House of Lords adopted the definition of a crime given in *Halsbury's Laws of England,* namely, as follows: *'A crime is an unlawful act or default which is an offence against the public and renders the person guilty of the act liable to legal punishment'.* This definition is in terms of a definable act for which there is a definable punishment. The province of the criminal law is, thus, to define each crime, to facilitate the procedures for establishing guilt or innocence of the accused and to establish the punishments available for the guilty.

(b) *Actus reus* and *mens rea*

It is a fundamental doctrine of the criminal law that the act itself does not constitute guilt unless the mind is guilty. The act or deed which is an element of a crime is part of the *actus reus* and the essential mental element is called the *mens rea.*

(i) Actus reus.
The meaning of *actus reus* is wider than merely the act or deed of the accused. Reference must be made to the definition of the crime in question to discover all the factual elements contained there. The totality of these elements, including the deed itself, constitute the *actus reus.*

Consider the traditional definition of murder as given by Coke: 'When any man of sound memory, and of the age of discretion, unlawfully killeth within any county of the realm any reasonable creature *in rerum natura* under the king's peace, with malice aforethought, either expressed by the party or implied by law, so as the party wounded, or hurt, etc., die of the sound or hurt, etc., within a year and a day after the same'.

From this definition, the *actus reus* comprises the following elements,

(1) 'any man of sound memory and the age of discretion' i.e., any person of capacity; (2) kills; (3) 'within any county of the realm' – the geographical limitation which has now been much widened by statute; (4) 'any reasonable creature in *rerum natura*', i.e. any human being; (5) 'under the king's peace', i.e. entitled to the protection of the law from violence; (6) 'die of the wound or hurt, etc., within a year and a day after the same'. It will be seen that the *actus reus* of murder is wider than the mere act of violence which caused the death of a person.

If the prosecution is unable to prove every element of the *actus reus* of the crime in question, no crime has been committed and the accused can go free.

(ii) Mens rea.

This denotes the mental element of a common law crime. It involves either an intention or a recklessness in carrying out a criminal act. *Mens rea* is an essential element and its existence must be proved by the prosecution or the defendant will be found not guilty.

The *mens rea* in the traditional definition of murder given in *(i)* above is, 'with malice aforethought, either expressed by the party or implied by law'. In other words, the deed of the accused must have been accompanied by an intention to kill or do grievous bodily harm to the victim.

There is a presumption that proof of *mens rea* is essential in every prosecution and this presumption may be displaced only by the express words of a statute defining or dealing with the offence.

In *Sweet* v. *Parsley* (1970), for example, the accused was charged with a statutory crime, namely, with being concerned with the management of premises used for the purpose of smoking cannabis. In fact, the unlawful use of drugs had taken place in a farmhouse let by her to others and without her knowledge. It was held by the House of Lords that the conviction in this case should be quashed for there was no evidence to show *mens rea* which, in this case, was the requirement of proof that the accused knew that her premises were being used for the smoking of cannabis.

(c) General defences

General defences are those which are applicable to offences generally. Special defences are those which are applicable each to a specific crime. Special defences are usually to be found in the statute which defines the crime in question. The general defences are mistake, insanity, intoxication, compulsion and automatism.

(i) Mistake.

If the accused is able to show that, when the act took place, he was under a mistake such as to negate intention or recklessness, there will be no *mens rea* and, therefore, no crime. Mistake will not be a defence where the crime is one of strict liability, i.e, where no *mens rea* need be proved against the accused. Mistake as to the law is no defence for ignorance of the law is no excuse.

(ii) Insanity.

'Insanity' for the purposes of the criminal law is not the same as insanity from the medical point of view. The defence of insanity is governed by the M'Naghten rules which were given to the House of Lords by the judges in answer to questions put to them by the House after the much criticised verdict in *R. v. M'Naghten* (1843). The main rule requires the defence to prove that, at the time of the act, the accused was labouring under such a 'defect of reason, from disease of the mind', as not to know the nature and quality of the act he was doing or, if he did know it, that he did not know that what he was doing was wrong. 'Wrong' means contrary to law.

In every trial there is a presumption of sanity; the defence succeeds only where this presumption is rebutted.

It is no defence for the accused to show that he acted under an irresistible impulse.

(iii) Intoxication.

There are three ways in which drunkenness may affect criminal liability. First, it may produce a state of mind which comes within the M'Naghten rules; although intoxication is not medical insanity, there would be a good defence. Secondly, intoxication may negative *mens rea* generally or, where appropriate, some specific form of *mens rea* applicable to some particular offence. Thirdly, drunkenness may be taken into account where the defence pleads mistake.

(iv) Compulsion.

The criminal law has long recognised the defence of compulsion, i.e., that the act of the accused was performed involuntarily as the result of something done by another person. Compulsion may take any of the following forms: duress by threats, necessity, obedience to orders and marital coercion.

(a) *Duress by threats* is sometimes called duress *per minas* or menace. To form a good defence it must be shown that the duress was a threat of a serious nature such as a threat to life or of serious bodily harm. A threat to damage property will not suffice. Duress is not a general defence where the accused is charged with murder.

(b) *Necessity* may be raised as a general defence where the accused can show that his act prevented the occurrence of something more evil. In *R. v. Dudley and Stephens* (1884) some shipwrecked mariners in an open boat ate one of their companions. In their defence it was shown that, but for this act, they probably would have starved to death. The defence of duress by necessity failed in the charge of murder brought against them.

(c) *Obedience to orders,* military or otherwise, may be relevant in deciding whether there is *mens rea* in any case. Obedience to orders will not constitute a good defence if the act in question is manifestly illegal.

(d) *Marital coercion.* Under the modern criminal law, a wife who is able to prove that her offence was committed in the presence of, and under the coercion of, her husband, has a good defence.

5.2 OFFENCES AGAINST THE PERSON

Most crimes can be categorised as either offences against the person or as offences against property. Offences against the person include murder, manslaughter, assault and unlawful wounding.

(a) Murder

The traditional definition of murder has been referred to in Section 5.1(b) above. It might be restated in modern terms as follows: murder occurs when any person of capacity kills within the jurisdiction any human being with malice aforethought, the death occurring within a year and a day from the act causing the death.

This definition includes the *actus reus* and the *mens rea* of murder, the latter being denoted by the expression 'malice aforethought', which must be regarded as a technical term when used in connection with murder. Broadly, it means that the accused intended by his act to kill or to cause serious bodily harm to the victim.

The same malice aforethought must be proved in cases where the killing is done in the course of, or furtherance of, some other offence: Homicide Act 1957, s.1. This statutory rule applies even to a killing done in the course of resisting arrest.

In a controversial decision of the House of Lords, *DPP* v. *Smith* (1961), it was laid down that the accused could be convicted of murder if it could be shown that the death or serious bodily harm was, as a result of an objective assessment, the natural and probable result of the accused's act. The effect of this decision was modified by the Criminal Justice Act 1967, s. 8, which provides that —

A court or jury, in determining whether a person has committed an offence:

(a) shall not be bound in law to infer that he intended or foresaw a result of his actions by reason only of its being a natural and probable consequence of those actions but

(b) shall decide whether he did intend or foresee that result by reference to all the evidence, drawing such inferences from the evidence as appear proper in the circumstances.

In other words, the court or jury must determine from the evidence what the accused actually thought at the time of his act.

Malice aforethought was again considered by the House of Lords in *Hyam* v. *DPP* (1975). In this case, the accused had set fire to a house in order to frighten one of the persons sleeping in it. That person escaped from the conflagration but two others died of asphyxia. On being found guilty of murder, the accused appealed to the Court of Appeal, where the appeal was dismissed. Leave to appeal to the House of Lords was given by the Court of Appeal which certified that the case involved the following point of law of general public importance, namely, the question 'Is malice aforethought in the crime of murder established by proof beyond reasonable doubt that when doing the act which led to the death of another the accused knew that it was highly probable that that act would result in death or serious bodily harm?'

It was held by the House of Lords that in order to establish malice aforethought it is sufficient to prove that, when the accused performed the relevant act, he knew that it was probable that it would result in grievous bodily harm to somebody, even though he did not desire to bring that result about. It was held further that 'grievous bodily harm' means 'really serious bodily harm' and is not limited to harm of such a nature as to endanger life. The appeal was, therefore, dismissed.

A later case, *R.* v. *Cunningham* (1981) gave the House of Lords an opportunity to consider and approve the principle in *Hyam,* namely, that to prove malice aforethought, it is sufficient for the Crown to establish an intention to cause grievous bodily harm, even though such intention might fall short of an intention to kill or to endanger life.

The death penalty was abolished by the Murder (Abolition of Death Penalty) Act 1965. By this Act, any person found guilty of murder must be sentenced to imprisonment for life, but the court may recommend a minimum period of imprisonment to be served by the convicted person before release on licence.

(b) Manslaughter

There are two kinds of manslaughter: (1) where the accused killed with malice aforethought, but under provocation or with diminished responsibility (voluntary manslaughter); and (2) where the accused killed unlawfully but without malice aforethought (involuntary manslaughter).

The *actus reus* for manslaughter is the same as that for murder.

(i) Provocation

By the Homicide Act 1957, s. 3:

> Where on a charge of murder there is evidence on which the jury can find that the person charged was provoked (whether by things done or by things said or by both together) to lose his self-control, the question whether the provocation was enough to make a reasonable man do as he did shall be left to be determined by the jury; and in determining that question the jury shall take into account everything both done and said according to the effect which, in their opinion, it would have on a reasonable man.

(ii) Diminished responsibility.

By the Homicide Act 1957, s. 2:

> Where a person kills or is party to the killing of another, he shall not be convicted of murder if he was suffering from such abnormality of mind (whether arising from a condition of arrested or retarded development of mind or any inherent causes or induced by disease or injury) as substantially impairs his mental responsibility for his acts and omissions in doing or being party to the killing.

(iii) Voluntary manslaughter.

The expression 'voluntary manslaughter' denotes a killing which would have been murder (with both *actus reus* and *mens rea* proved) but where the accused has been able to prove either provocation or diminished responsibility.

(iv) Involuntary manslaughter.

The expression 'involuntary manslaughter' denotes an unlawful killing done without malice aforethought. There are two cases to consider. It is manslaughter if death results from an unlawful and dangerous act on the part of the accused. It is also manslaughter if death results from an extreme degree of carelessness or negligence on the part of the accused. In some cases these two grounds may overlap. In *R. v. Lamb* (1967), for example, the Court of Appeal quashed the conviction where the accused had pointed a loaded revolver in jest at his friend and, because neither of them understood the mechanism of the gun, did not expect the bullet to be fired when the trigger was pulled. Expert evidence had shown the mistake to be understandable.

(c) Assault and battery

'An assault is any act which intentionally – or possibly recklessly – causes another person to apprehend immediate and unlawful personal violence.' Although 'assault' is an independent crime and is to be treated as such, for practical purposes today 'assault' is generally synonymous with the term battery, and is a term used to mean the actual or intended use of unlawful force to another person without his consent. See *Fagan* v. *Metropolitan Police Commissioner* (1968).

> 'Where an assault involved a battery, it matters not ... whether the battery is inflicted directly by the body of the offender or through the medium of some weapon or instrument controlled by the action of the offender. ... To constitute this offence, some intentional act must have been performed; a *mere* omission to act cannot amount to an assault. . . . For an assault to be committed, both the elements of *actus reus* and *mens rea* must be present at the same time. The *'actus reus'* is the action causing the effect on the victim's mind. The *'mens rea'* is the intention to cause that effect. It is not necessary that *mens rea* should be present at the inception of the *actus reus;* it can be superimposed on an existing act. On the other hand, the subsequent inception of *mens rea* cannot convert an act which has been completed without *mens rea* into an assault.'

In *Fagan*, the appellant, while parking his car under the direction of a police officer, stopped with one wheel on the officer's foot. The officer told the appellant to get off his foot and received an abusive reply. The appellant then switched off the ignition. He did not start the engine and move the car until the officer had told him several times to move. By a majority, a divisional court dismissed the appeal on the ground that the appellant's act became criminal from the moment the intention was formed to produce the apprehension which was flowing from the continuing act, i.e. keeping the wheel on the officer's foot.

An assault is regarded as the more serious if it is upon a police officer. By s. 51 of the Police Act 1964, any person who assaults a constable in the execution of his duty is guilty of an offence.

(d) Offences against the Person Act 1861

Certain offences involving unlawful injury are provided for in the 1861 Act. They are as follows:

(i) Assault occasioning actual bodily harm.
Section 47 of the 1861 Act provides for this offence. The *actus reus*

must include some hurt or injury caused by the assault. The *mens rea* is the same as in the case of common assault (see section 4.2(c) above).

(ii) Wounding with intent.
Section 18 of the 1861 Act as amended provides that:

> Whosoever shall unlawfully and maliciously by any means whatsoever wound or cause any grievous bodily harm to any person with intent to do some grievous bodily harm to any person, or with intent to resist or prevent the lawful apprehension or detainer of any person shall be liable to imprisonment.

The prosecution must prove *mens rea* which includes either an intent to cause very serious injury or an intent to resist arrest.

To prove a 'wound', it is necessary for the prosecution to show that the entire thickness of the victim's skin has been broken. Any injury which does not break the skin is not a 'wound'. 'Grievous bodily harm' means any really serious bodily harm.

The world 'maliciously' in a statutory crime postulates foresight of consequence and requires either an actual intention to do the particular kind of harm which, in fact, was done or recklessness whether such harm should occur or not. There is no requirement for the prosecution to show ill-will toward the victim: *R.* v. *Cunningham* (1957).

(iii) Wounding or inflicting grievous bodily harm.
Section 20 of the 1861 Act provides that: 'Whosoever shall unlawfully and maliciously wound or inflict any grievous bodily harm upon any other person, either with or without any weapon or instrument' will be liable to imprisonment. This offence may be called 'unlawful wounding' or 'malicious wounding'.

5.3 OFFENCES AGAINST PROPERTY

In this section all statutory section references are to the Theft Act 1968 unless otherwise stated.

(a) Theft

The basic definition of theft is given in section 1(1) of the Theft Act 1968, which provides that — '*A person is guilty of theft if he dishonestly appropriates property belonging to another with the intention of permanently depriving the other of it . . .*' From this provision it is clear that the *actus reus* of theft is the appropriation of property belonging to another. The *mens rea* of theft is that the accused must have acted dishonestly and with the intention of permanently depriving the owner of the property in question. It is not material whether the appropriation is made with a view to gain, or is made for the thief's own benefit: s. 1(2).

In *R.* v. *Ghosh* (1982) the Court of Appeal clarified the meaning of 'dishonesty' for the purpose of the Theft Acts 1968 and 1978. In that case it was held that the jury should be directed that the accused acted dishonestly if (1) his act would be regarded as dishonest by the ordinary standards of reasonable and honest people and (2) the accused himself realised that his act was dishonest by these standards. If this test is satisfied it is immaterial that the accused does not regard his act as dishonest.

(i) Property.
By s. 4(1) 'property' includes money and all other property, real or personal, including things in action and other intangible property.

(ii) Appropriation.
By s. 3(1) any assumption by a person of the rights of an owner amounts to an appropriation, and this includes, where he has come by the property (innocently or not) without stealing it, any later assumption of a right to it by keeping or dealing with it as owner.

(b) Robbery

By section 8(1) a person is guilty of robbery if he steals, and immediately before or at the time of doing so, and in order to do so, he uses force on any person or puts or seeks to put any person in fear of being then and there subjected to force.

(c) Burglary

Burglary may be committed in either of two ways.

By section 9(1)(a) a person is guilty of burglary if he enters any building or part of a building as a trespasser and with intent to commit any of the following offences: stealing anything in the building or part of the building; inflicting grievous bodily harm on any person in it; raping of any woman in it or doing unlawful damage to the building or anything in it.

By section 9(1)(b) a person is guilty of burglary if having entered any building or part of a building as a trespasser he steals or attempts to steal anything in the building or that part of it or inflicts or attempts to inflict on any person in it any grievous bodily harm.

(d) Aggravated burglary

By section 10(1) a person is guilty of aggravated burglary if he commits any burglary and at the time has with him any firearm or imitation firearm, any weapon of offence, or any explosive.

(e) Fraud under the Theft Act 1968

The following offences, which are indictable and arrestable, are among those which exist by virtue of the 1968 Act.

(i) Obtaining property by deception.

By section 15 a person who by any deception dishonestly obtains property belonging to another, with the intention of permanently depriving the other of it, will on conviction be liable to imprisonment.

(iii) Obtaining a pecuniary advantage by deception.

By section 16(1) a person who by any deception dishonestly obtains for himself or another any pecuniary advantage will on conviction of indictment be liable to imprisonment.

(iii) False accounting.

The offence of false accounting may be committed in either of two ways:

First, by section 17(1) (a), where a person dishonestly, with a view to gain for himself or another or with intent to cause loss to another destroys, defaces, conceals or falsifies any account or any record or document made or required for any accounting purpose.

Secondly, by section 17(1) (b), where a person dishonestly, with a view to gain for himself or another or with intent to cause loss to another, in furnishing information for any purpose, produces or makes use of any account, or any record or document made or required for any accounting purpose, which to his knowledge is or may be misleading, false or deceptive in a material particular.

SUMMARY

1   A crime is an unlawful act or default which is an offence against the public and renders the person guilty of the act liable to legal punishment: Halsbury, adopted by the House of Lords in *Board of Trade* v. *Owen* (1957).

2   The totality of the factual elements contained in the definition of an offence is called the *actus reus.*

3   *Mens rea* is the mental element of an offence.

4   There is a presumption that the prosecution must prove *mens rea* in every case, but this presumption may be displaced by the express words of a statute dealing with any particular offence.

5   There are general defences for offences generally and certain special defences appropriate to specific offences only.

6   The general defences are, mistake, insanity, intoxication and compulsion.

7   Most crimes can be categorised either as offences against the person or offences against property.

8   Murder occurs when any person of capacity kills within the jurisdiction any human being with malice aforethought, the death occurring within a year and a day from the act causing the death.

9   In order to establish malice aforethought it is sufficient to prove that, when the accused performed the relevant act, he knew that it was probable that that act would result in grievous bodily harm to somebody, even though he did not desire to bring that result about.

10   Grievous bodily harm means really serious harm. It is not limited to harm of such a nature as to endanger life.

11   There are two kinds of manslaughter - voluntary and involuntary.

12   Voluntary manslaughter occurs where the accused is charged with murder and the *actus reus* and *mens rea* are both proved but the defence is able to prove either provocation or diminished responsibility.

13   Involuntary manslaughter occurs where there is an unlawful killing done without malice aforethought.

14   'An assault is any act which intentionally - or possibly recklessly - causes another person to apprehend immediate and unlawful personal violence.'

15   The Offences against the Person Act 1861 provides for the following offences involving unlawful injury to the person: (1) assault occasioning actual bodily harm, (2) wounding with intent and (3) wounding or inflicting grievous bodily harm.

16   The word 'maliciously' in a statutory crime postulates foresight of consequence and requires either an actual intention to do the particular kind of harm which, in fact, was done or recklessness whether such harm should occur or not.

17   A person is guilty of theft if he dishonestly appropriates property belonging to another with the intention of permanently depriving the owner of it.

18   A person is guilty of robbery if he steals, and immediately before or at the time of doing so, and in order to do so, he uses force on any person or puts or seeks to put any person in fear of being then and there subjected to force.

19   Section 9 of the Theft Act 1968 contains two definitions of burglary.

20   The Theft Act 1968 creates several arrestable and indictable fraud-related offences.

EXERCISES

1   Give an authoritative definition of a crime.

2   Explain *actus reus* and *mens rea*.

3   Write a short account of the general defences to prosecutions.

4   In every trial there is a presumption of sanity. Explain.

5   Is it a defence for the accused to show that he acted under an irresistible impulse?

6   State and explain the traditional definition of murder.

7   How was the decision of the House of Lords in *DPP* v. *Smith* (1961) modified in its effect by the Criminal Justice Act 1967?

8   What is the importance of *Hyam* v. *DPP* (1975)?

9   What is the rule about malice aforethought where a killing is done in the course of some other offence?

10   Is it correct to say that it is sufficient for the Crown to establish an intention to cause grievous bodily harm, with regard to malice aforethought in cases of murder?

11   Explain fully what is meant by (a) involuntary manslaughter and (b) voluntary manslaughter.

12   Define 'assault'. What is meant by 'battery'?

13   What is 'assault' occasioning actual bodily harm? How does it differ from 'wounding with intent'?

14   What is the offence sometimes called 'malicious wounding'?

15   Define 'theft'.

16   Distinguish between robbery and burglary. What is aggravated burglary?

17   Give some examples of fraud-related offences under the 1968 Theft Act.

THE LAW OF TORTS

6.1 INTRODUCTORY MATTERS

(a) The nature and function of the law of torts

The word 'tort' is Norman French. It means 'twisted' or 'wrung' or, to use a modern word – 'wrong'. A tort is a wrong for which redress is available in the civil courts. The usual action is an action for damages, i.e. money compensation, but, where damages are not appropriate, the equitable remedy of injunction may be available. For example, to walk unlawfully on another's land is trespass – a tort. If the trespasser repeatedly trespasses, doing no damage to the land, there would be little point in claiming money compensation. The appropriate remedy in such a case would be an injunction, i.e, the trespasser would be ordered not to trespass on the plaintiff's land.

The law of torts gives a remedy for many different kinds of civil wrong, giving protection against injury to persons, chattels, land and a number of other interests.

(b) Torts and crime

The purpose of the criminal law is to punish those who are found guilty of crimes by process in the criminal courts. This is quite a different purpose from that of the law of torts which is to compensate those who have suffered loss or injury as a result of another's wrong. Most crimes which cause injury or damage to persons or to property are also torts. It is thus quite possible that a wrongdoer will be tried and punished by the criminal courts as well as sued in tort for compensation by the person who suffered the injury or loss, although it should be noted that some recent statutes have given the criminal courts a power to award restitution or to grant compensation in certain restricted circumstances.

(c) Torts and contract

The law of contract and the law of torts are both concerned with rights and obligations under the civil law. The main difference is that in contract the obligations are created by agreement between the parties and owed by one party to another, whereas in tort the obligations are, in general, owed to the whole world. In contract, the obligations are fixed by the terms of the agreement between the parties; in tort, the obligations are fixed by the law. The main similarity between contract and tort is that the usual remedy is an action for damages.

A breach of contract may also constitute a tort, either against the other contracting party or against a third party, see particularly the case of *Junior Books* v. *Veitchi* (1982).

6.2 TORTS TO THE PERSON

The ancient torts of assault, battery and false imprisonment are forms of trespass to the person.

(a) Assault and battery

Assault and battery are two distinct forms of trespass to the person. An assault occurs when the defendant directly and intentionally or negligently by his conduct causes the plaintiff to fear an immediate physical contact with his person. Where physical contact occurs, there is battery. For example, it would be an assault for the defendant to point a loaded gun at the plaintiff and a battery for a bullet from the gun to hit the plaintiff. Even the pointing of an unloaded gun would be an assault if the plaintiff thought that it might be loaded. The unlawful taking of fingerprints, spitting in the face and striking with the fist are all examples of battery. A threatening act accompanied by words which indicate that no immediate physical contact will occur will not be an assault. This point is illustrated by *Tuberville* v. *Savage* (1669) in which the defendant placed his hand on his sword in an aggressive and threatening manner saying, 'If it were not assize time, I would not take such language from you'. The words indicated that there was no intention to strike the defendant.

(b) False imprisonment

False imprisonment is a form of trespass to the person by which the defendant directly and intentionally or negligently causes the plaintiff to be confined within a limited area. The essence of this tort is that the plaintiff is physically detained. In the *Commentaries, Book III,* Blackstone says: 'Every confinement of the person is an imprisonment, whether it be in a common prison or in a private house, or in the stocks, or even by forceably detaining one on the public streets'. The defendant will not be liable if the plaintiff has contracted to remain in a place until being released by the defendant according to the agreement. In *Herd* v. *Weardale Steel, Coke and Coal Co.* (1913) a miner, who had contracted to work in shifts and to be brought to the surface by his employer at the end of each shift, asked to be taken to the surface before the end of a shift. The request was refused and the miner, who had to stay underground until the end of the shift, sued for damages for false imprisonment. It was held by the Court of Appeal that there was no false imprisonment.

6.3 INTERFERENCE WITH GOODS

(a) The Torts (Interference with Goods) Act 1977

By section 1 of this Act, 'wrongful interference with goods' means:

- (*a*) conversion of goods;
- (*b*) trespass to goods;
- (*c*) negligence so far as it results in damage to goods or to an interest in goods;
- (*d*) any other tort so far as it results in damage to goods or to an interest in goods.

Section 2 of the Act abolishes the tort of detinue and further provides that an action lies for conversion for loss or destruction of goods which a bailee has allowed to happen in breach of his duty to his bailor. By this provision an action for conversion will lie in cases which otherwise would not be conversion. Such actions would have been brought in detinue before its abolition.

(b) Conversion

There is conversion where the defendant intentionally deals with goods in a manner which is inconsistent with the plaintiff's possession or immediate right to possession. This tort thus protects both possession and the right to possession. Conversion does not necessary protect ownership. An owner may sue in conversion only if he was in possession of the goods, or had an immediate right to possession, at the time of the defendant's wrongful dealing. A bailee can protect his right of possession by this tort and so can a bailor at will, i.e. one who has an immediate right to the return of his goods.

Conversion occurs where goods are treated in a manner which is clearly inconsistent with the plaintiff's right of possession. The tort can be committed in many different ways, for example, by taking goods out of the possession of another without justification, by using, destroying or altering the goods and, in some circumstances, the receipt of goods. Statutory conversion occurs where a bailee, in breach of the terms of his bailment, allows his bailor's goods to be lost or destroyed (see (a) above).

(c) Trespass to goods

Trespass to goods occurs where the defendant interferes with goods in the possession of the plaintiff and the interference is direct and either intentional or negligent. It should be noticed that there is an overlap between conversion and trespass. To succeed in trespass, the plaintiff must show that the goods were in his possession; a mere right to possession is not enough. Trespass thus protects a person in possession of goods from the intermeddling with those goods by others. Examples of trespass would be to deflate the plaintiff's car tyres, to kick his dog, to remove a bottle of milk from his doorstep or to go into his house and steal his gold watch.

It is essential that the plaintiff be in possession of the goods at the time of the wrongful interference. To prove his possession, the plaintiff must show (1) that he had actual or potential physical control over the goods, (2) that he had the intention to exercise control and (3) that he ensured that there were external and visible signs of the fact of his possession (see Chapter 4.6(a)).

6.4 TRESPASS TO LAND

The tort of trespass to land protects the person in possession from any kind of direct intrusion. It does not necessarily protect the rights of the owner unless he is the person in possession. The defendant's intrusion must be intentional or negligent and it must be direct. Clearly, trespass to land can take many forms, e.g., walking on the land, throwing a stone at a building, knocking a nail into a wall or putting up a bill-board.

6.5 DEFENCES

The common feature of all the torts discussed above, namely, that the defendant's act was intentional or negligent, is relevant to the kinds of defence that might be available. These will be considered separately.

(a) Consent

The maxim is *volenti non fit injuria*: a person who has freely assented to the conduct of another cannot, if injured by that conduct, recover damages for the injury. Consent may take either of two forms. First, there is consent proper, i.e. where the plaintiff has given his assent to the defendant's conduct, which otherwise would have been tortious. For example, where the defendant is on the plaintiff's land after the plaintiff has granted a right of way to him, the defendant commits no trespass while exercising his right of way: if sued, his defence would be that the plaintiff consented. Secondly, there is a defence more appropriate to negligence which is usually known as the 'assumption of risk' (see Chapter 7.5(b)).

A very common form of consent with regard to trespass to the person is to be found in most physical sports. A cricketer, for instance, cannot recover damages when he is hit on the head by a ball driven in his direction by a batsman; a rugger player cannot complain if he is hurt by a tackle which is within the rules of the game; similarly, a boxer cannot complain if he is punched in the eye.

When a hospital patient is about to submit to a surgical operation, it is usual for the hospital authorities to require him to sign a form of consent to the operation. Such a form is evidence of consent which might be useful to the authorities in the event of an action against them by the patient.

(b) Self-defence

In an action for trespass to the person it is a good defence for the defendant to show that (1) it was reasonable for him to defend himself in the circumstances and (2) that the measures taken in self-defence were no more than were reasonable. In some cases, the defence will be available in an action for trespass to goods, for instance, where the defendant, in defending himself, tears the plaintiff's clothing. This kind of defence is extended to the protection of another person where the circumstances show that it was reasonable, for example, protecting a member of one's own household.

(c) Defence of land or goods

On the same test of reasonableness as in (b) above, a person may defend land or goods in his possession against a person committing a trespass against them. The defence is available only where the defendant is able to show all three elements of possession, which apply equally to land and goods.

(d) Necessity

To take action on the grounds of necessity may involve causing harm to an innocent person. This is to be compared with self-defence, which involves causing harm to a person in default. For instance, a person may take steps to prevent his land from becoming flooded, even though those steps cause a neighbour's land to flood. The defence is available only where the defendant has taken necessary steps in an urgent situation of imminent peril.

(e) Other defences

Further defences to actions for trespass or conversion are:

(i) The recaption of chattels.
It is not a tort to use reasonable force to retake goods which are wrongfully withheld from the person entitled to possession.

(ii) The abatement of a nuisance.
It is a defence to show that entry on to the plaintiff's land was for the purpose of abatement of a nuisance, e.g. to cut down branches over-hanging the defendant's land.

(iii) Lawful discipline or arrest.
It is a defence to an action for trespass to the person or false imprisonment to show that the act was justified by, for example, the right of a parent to punish his child or, in the case of false imprisonment, by the fact that the arrest was lawful.

6.6 OTHER TORTS

Having examined those torts which involve an intentional or negligent act on the part of the defendant, it now remains to consider the following: nuisance, *Rylands* v. *Fletcher*, defamation, deceit and breach of statutory duty. Negligence as a separate tort is of such great importance that the next chapter is devoted to it entirely.

(a) Private nuisance

A nuisance is a substantial interference with an occupier's enjoyment of land, or an interference with his rights over land, or indirectly causing some physical damage to the land. Nuisance can be caused by vibrations, fumes, smells or noise. A nuisance may also be caused by the type of user of adjoining property; for instance, it has been held to be a nuisance to use adjoining premises for prostitution or as a sex shop. Where the plaintiff relies on his right to enjoy the land and premises which he occupies, the locality where the defendant's act was committed must be taken into account: what is a nuisance in one locality may not be a nuisance in another.

The defences to an action for nuisance are as follows:

(i) Prescription

Where the conduct complained of has gone on continuously for more than twenty years, there may be an easement by prescription.

(ii) Statutory authority.

Many modern authorities and companies are authorised by statute to build and construct and to engage in various activities and enterprises. Where the statute is merely permissive, there is no excuse for committing a nuisance. Where, on the other hand, compliance with the statute makes a nuisance inevitable, then there is a good defence to any action for nuisance. However, if the actual nuisance which has been caused is greater in extent than that which was inevitable, the statutory immunity does not apply: *Allen* v. *Gulf Oil Refining Ltd* (1980), a House of Lords case.

(iii) Other defences.

Necessity, consent or defence of property may all, in appropriate circumstances be raised by the defence in an action for nuisance.

Where damages would not be a satisfactory remedy, the court may grant an injunction to prevent the continuance or repetition of the nuisance. Such an injunction may be either in addition to or instead of damages.

(b) Rylands *v.* Fletcher.

The rule in *Rylands* v. *Fletcher* is concerned with the responsibility of a defendant who brings on to his land and accumulates anything which is not naturally there. By this rule, if what is accumulated is likely to do harm if it escapes, the defendant will be liable if it does escape from his land and then interferes with the use of the land of another. In such cases, the plaintiff does not have to prove negligence. In *Rylands* v. *Fletcher* (1866), the judgement of the Court of Exchequer Chamber included the following passage:

> 'We think that the trur rule of law is, that the person who for his own purposes brings on his lands and collects and keeps there anything likely to do mischief if it escapes, must keep it in at his peril, and, if he does not do so, is *prima facie* answerable for all the damage which is the natural consequence of its escape.'

The difference between *Rylands* v. *Fletcher* and nuisance is that the former requires the escape of something tangible, whereas nuisance involves an indirect interference. In the case itself, water escaped from a reservoir on the defendant's land causing the flooding of a mine on neighbouring land. In later decided cases all of the following have been held to be within the rule: electricity, gas, petrol, sewage and caravan dwellers.

It is important to notice that, under the rule. the liability is strict. There is no need to prove negligence.

(c) Deceit

Deceit was defined by Lord Herschell in the case of *Derry* v. *Peek* (1889) as follows:

'First, in order to sustain an action of deceit, there must be proof of fraud, and nothing short of that will suffice. Secondly, fraud is proved when it is shown that a false representation has been made (i) knowingly, or (ii) without belief in its truth, or (iii) recklessly, careless whether it be true or false. Although I have treated the second and third as distinct cases, I think the third is but an instance of the second, for one who makes a statement under such circumstances can have no real belief in the truth of what he states. To prevent a false statement being fraudulent, there must, I think, always be an honest belief in its truth. And this probably covers the whole ground, for one who knowingly alleges that which is false has obviously no such belief. Thirdly, if fraud be proved, the motive of the person guilty of it is immaterial. It matters not that there was no intention to cheat or injure the person to whom the statement was made.'

The essence of this passage is that to prevent a false statement being fraudulent, there must be an honest belief in its truth.

(d) Defamation

The law of defamation protects the reputation of all persons. The rules vary according to whether the tort in question is libel or slander. In general, a defamatory communication of a permanent character is libel and any defamatory communication which is temporary and is not visible, but only audible, is slander. Thus defamatory statements in books and newspapers constitute libel and defamatory statements by word of mouth are slander.

The plaintiff must prove (1) that the statement was defamatory, (2) that it referred to the plaintiff and (3) that the statement was published to at least one person other than the defendant's spouse.

Defamatory material in a film has been held to be libel mainly because the defamatory element was contained in the pictorial part, the sound element being regarded as ancillary to the moving picture: *Youssoupoff* v. *Metro-Goldwyn-Meyer Pictures Ltd* (1934). There is still no clear ruling on whether a film with defamatory material on sound only is libel or slander.

The common law of libel and slander has been modified by statute. The Defamation Act 1952 provides that, for the purposes of the law of libel and slander, the broadcasting of words by means of wireless telegraphy will be treated as publication in permanent form. In this Act 'words' includes pictures. The Theatre Act 1968 provides that words spoken in the course of a theatrical performance are to be treated as publication in permanent form.

Libel is actionable *per se*, i.e. no special damage need be shown.

Slander is generally actionable only on proof of special damage. Exceptionally, however, slander is actionable *per se* when the statement imputes that the plaintiff committed a crime, or has a venereal disease or is slandered in respect of his profession or trade.

(i) What is meant by 'defamatory'.
A defamatory statement has been described as one which is calculated to injure the reputation of another, by exposing him to hatred, contempt or ridicule: *Parmeter* v. *Coupland* (1840). However, this definition needs some extension to make it cover the modern concept of defamation, particularly with regard to the plaintiff's trade or profession. *Sim* v. *Stretch* (1936) took the definition a stage further by suggesting that the test should be whether the words tend to lower the plaintiff in the estimation of right-thinking members of society generally. The problem remains, of course, as to who are the 'right-thinking members of society'. So far, there has been no authoritative general pronouncement from the courts on the matter.

(ii) Defences.
The general defences may be available in an action for defamation and, in addition, there are some defences which are peculiar to defamation, namely, justification, absolute privilege, qualified privilege, fair comment and apology.

(iii) Justification.

It is a good defence to prove that the defamatory statement is true in all material respects. Justification is a good defence even where the statement was made maliciously. The common law requirement of complete justification has been modified by section 5 of the Defamation Act 1952 which provides that:

In an action for libel or slander in respect of words containing two or more distinct charges against the plaintiff, a defence of justification shall not fail by reason only that the truth of every charge is not proved if the words not proved to be true do not materially injure the plaintiff's reputation having regard to the truth of the remaining charges.

(iv Absolute privilege.

On grounds of public policy, statements made by judges in the course of legal proceedings are absolutely privileged. This means that a judge cannot be liable for a defamatory statement made during legal proceedings even if the statement is irrelevant or malicious. This principle of public policy extends to counsel, solicitors and witnesses to an uncertain extent. It is clear, however, that these people do not enjoy absolute privilege in regard to statements which are irrelevant to the proceedings in question.

(v) Qualified privilege.

There are certain occasions where the public interest requires that a person will not be liable for an untrue defamatory statement made without malice. The principle of qualified privilege requires the defendant to prove that the statement was made without malice. The principle is based generally on the public interest and covers, for example, reports of Parliamentary and judicial proceedings. The principle of qualified privilege extends to communications made in the common interest of the parties concerned even though the general public is not directly affected, for example, a reference given to an employer in regard to the suitability of an applicant for employment.

(vi) Parliamentary immunity.

The courts have no jurisdiction over what is said in either of the Houses of Parliament. Nor have the courts jurisdiction over reports and other documents published under the authority of Parliament.

(vii) Fair comment.

Persons in public office must accept honest criticism of their public lives provided that the criticism is not malicious. The defence of fair comment allows journalists and others to make critical statements about public figures. It does not allow criticism of private lives except perhaps in regard to matters of honesty and personal integrity which reflect on the public side of their activities. The statement must be one of honest opinion based on the true facts. It must not be actuated by malice. The burden of proving that the statement deals with a matter of public interest, that the facts are true and that the opinion is honest and without malice, lies on the defendant.

(e) Breach of statutory duty

In order to succeed in an action for breach of statutory duty, the plaintiff must show (1) that a statute creates an interest in him, (2) that the statute requires the interest to be protected against interference and (3) that the defendant interfered with the interest. The name of this tort is thus somewhat misleading with its emphasis on statutory 'duty'. This tort must, indeed, be recognised as entirely different from the breach of duty in the tort of negligence.

The matter was explained by Lord Wright in *L.P.T.B.* v. *Upson* (1949) as follows:

'... a claim for damages for breach of a statutory duty intended to protect a person in the position of the particular plaintiff is a specific common law right which is not to be confused in essence with a claim for negligence. The statutory right has its origin in the statute, but the particular remedy of an action for damages is given by the common law in order to make effective for the benefit of the injured plaintiff his right to the performance by the defendant of the defendant's statutory duty. It is an effective sanction. It is not a claim in negligence in the strict or ordinary sense.'

The most usual actions for breach of statutory duty arise from allegations of breach of duty under a statute or statutory regulations governing some industrial process. The Health and Safety at Work Act 1974 and the many detailed Regulations made under it to govern particular industrial processes replace the various statutes governing mines and factories and other places. For example, if an employer or occupier of industrial premises fails to provide some specific safety requirement such as a guard over dangerous machinery, he will have interfered with the interest of any employee who has to work that machinery. In the event of consequential injury to the employee, the employer will be liable in common law damages to him for breach of statutory duty.

SUMMARY

1   The law of torts gives protection against injury or loss caused by civil wrongs. It gives protection against injury to persons, to goods, to land and a number of other interests.

2   In contract, the obligations are created by agreement between parties. A contractual obligation is thus owed by one party to another. In tort, the obligations are owed to the whole world.

3   The three forms of trespass to the person are assault, battery and false imprisonment.

4   Conversion occurs where the defendant intentionally deals with

goods in a manner which is inconsistent with the plaintiff's possession or immediate right to possession, as the case may be.

5 Trespass to goods occurs where the defendant interferes with goods in the possession of the plaintiff and the interference is either direct and intentional or direct and negligent.

6 Trespass to land is a direct intrusion on land in possession of another, where the intrusion was intentional or negligent.

7 A person who has freely consented to the conduct of another cannot, if injured by that conduct, recover damages for the injury.

8 In an action for damages for trespass to the person, it is a good defence for the defendant to show that it was reasonable for him to defend himself in the circumstances and that the measures taken in self-defence were no more than were reasonable.

9 The difference between the defence of self-defence and the defence of necessity is that in the former case it is a wrongdoer who is harmed, whereas, in the latter, it is an innocent person who is harmed.

10 A private nuisance is a substantial interference with an occupier's enjoyment of land, or an interference with his rights over land, or something *indirectly* causing some physical damage to the land, e.g., by vibrations.

11 By the rule in *Rylands* v. *Fletcher,* a person who accumulates anything on his land which is not there naturally, is strictly liable for damage caused by its escape.

12 Deceit occurs where the defendant has made a false statement without an honest belief in its truth.

13 Libel and slander are the two forms of defamation. In general, a defamatory communication of a permanent character is libel. A defamatory communication which is temporary and is not visible, but only audible, is slander.

14 In an action for damages for defamation the following defences may be available, according to the circumstances: justification, absolute privilege, qualified privilege, fair comment or any appropriate general defence.

15 Breach of statutory duty is proved if the plaintiff can show (1) that a statute creates an interest in him, (2) that the statute requires the interest to be protected against interference and (3) that the defendant interfered with the interest.

EXERCISES

1 What is the derivation of the word 'tort'?

2 Compare the province of the law of torts with that of the law of contract. What is the difference between a tort and a crime?

3 Explain the significance of *Tuberville* v. *Savage* (1669).

4 What is false imprisonment?

5 What is meant by 'wrongful interference with goods'?

6 Explain carefully the difference between conversion and trespass to goods. Are there any similarities?

7 What is the essence of the tort of trespass to land? Give some examples of trespass to land.

8 Explain the significance of *Fowler* v. *Lanning* (1959).

9 As a defence, consent may take either of two forms. Explain.

10 List the remaining defences and comment on each.

11 What is a private nuisance? What defences may be raised in an action for nuisance?

12 What is the rule in *Rylands* v. *Fletcher?* How does this kind of liability differ from liability for nuisance?

13 Why is the case of *Derry* v. *Peek* (1889) so important?

14 Outline the law of defamation. In your answer (a) distinguish between libel and slander, (b) explain the meaning of 'defamatory' and (c) mention any special defences.

15 What is the difference between absolute privilege and Parliamentary immunity?

16 What must the plaintiff show in order to succeed in an action for breach of statutory duty?

CHAPTER 7

THE TORT OF
NEGLIGENCE

The word 'negligence' may sometimes mean no more than the way in which trespass or some other tort is committed: or it may mean an independent tort. This chapter is about the latter meaning of the word and considers something which is called negligence but which is not merely carelessness. It will be seen that negligence is the complex concept of duty of care and the damage which is suffered as a result of a breach of that duty.

7.1 THE GENERAL DUTY OF CARE

Negligence was first recognised as an independent tort in the case of *Donoghue* v. *Stevenson* (1932).* In his speech in this case, Lord Atkin formulated the general principle governing the duty of care in the following passage:

'The rule that you are to love your neighbour becomes in law, you must not injure your neighbour; and the lawyer's question, Who is my neighbour? receives a restricted reply. You must take reasonable care to avoid acts or omissions which you can reasonably foresee would be likely to injure your neighbour. Who, then, in law is my neighbour? The answer seems to be - persons who are so closely and directly affected by my act that I ought reasonably to have them in contemplation as being so affected when I am directing my mind to the acts or omissions which are called in question.'

This passage in Lord Atkin's speech must be treated as a statement of broad principle and not as if it were a statutory definition. Lord Atkin's proposition is so broad and authoritative that it may be regarded as a

*This indicates a case noted in the Case Notes at the end of the Chapter.

statement of common law policy. It has been said that the neighbour principle will apply unless there is some justification for its exclusion. In *Anns* v. *Merton* (1977),* Lord Wilberforce said:

'. . . the position has now been reached that in order to establish that a duty of care arises in a particular situation, it is not necessary to bring the facts of that situation within those of previous situations in which a duty of care has been held to exist. Rather the question has to be approached in two stages. First one has to ask whether, as between the alleged wrongdoer and the person who has suffered damage, there is a sufficient relationship of proximity or neighbourhood such that, in the reasonable contemplation of the former, carelessness on his part may be likely to cause damage to the latter, in which case a *prima facie* duty of care arises. Secondly, if the first question is answered affirmatively, it is necessary to consider whether there are any considerations which ought to negative, or to reduce or limit the scope of the duty or the class of person to whom it is owed or the damages to which a breach of it may give rise.'

It is clear that there are two stages in the establishment of a duty of care. First, is there sufficient proximity between the parties to give rise to a *prima facie* duty of care? This is Lord Atkin's test. Secondly, are there any considerations which ought to negative or reduce the scope of the duty?

The section below considers some of the second-stage limitations on the establishment of the duty of care.

7.2 LIMITS OF THE DUTY OF CARE

Even where proximity can be established by the neighbour test the duty of care might be reduced or eliminated in the following situations:

(a) Omissions

Mere failure to act for the benefit of others is not a breach of the general duty of care. In the case of omissions there cannot be a breach of duty of care unless the omission is of a thing which is commonly done by other persons in like circumstances or, alternatively, the omission is of a thing which is so obviously wanted that it would be unreasonable or imprudent to neglect to provide it: *Moreton* v. *William Dixon Ltd* (1909). However, an omission may exceptionally constitute a breach of duty where the duty arises substantially out of a particular relationship, e.g. employer and employee, carrier and passenger, nominated sub-contractor and building owner. Further, there are special relationships which require one of the parties to act in certain circumstances for the protection of third parties. For example, in *Home Office* v. *Dorset Yacht Co. Ltd.* (1970)* the House of Lords held that three Borstal officers had broken their duty of care to a yacht owner when they failed to take steps to prevent certain boys under their control from escaping and doing damage to a nearby yacht. In the words of Lord Morris: '...the risk of such a happening was glaringly obvious.'

(b) Negligent mis-statements

Until the House of Lords' decision in *Hedley Byrne* v. *Heller* (1963)* there was no liability in negligence for a false statement made carelessly. In that case it was explained that there can be no liability for a negligent mis-statement unless there was a special relationship at the time of the statement which justified a reliance on the statement by the party to whom it was made. In some recent cases there have been difficulties over the meaning of 'reliance' on mis-statements. In *JEB Fasteners Ltd.* v. *Marks, Bloom & Co.* (1983), the Court of Appeal held that there was no 'true reliance' on accounts negligently prepared by the defendants because these accounts had not affected the plaintiff's decision to take over a company. The duty of care may arise even where the negligent mis-statement was one of several factors relied upon: in the *JEB Fasteners* case, Stephenson L.J. said:

> 'As long as a misrepresentation plays a real and substantial part, though not by itself a decisive part, in inducing a plaintiff to act, it is a cause of his loss and he relies on it, no matter how strong or how many are the other matters which play their part in inducing him to act.'

(c) Economic loss

Until the House of Lords' decision in *Hedley Byrne* v. *Heller* (1963), the courts did not allow the recovery of any kind of economic loss as damages for negligence. The reason appears to be that economic loss, unlike physical damage, has a tendency to manifest itself at several removes from the direct effects of a defendant's negligence, thus creating difficulties in applying the foreseeability element. Recent decisions show that economic loss may be recoverable where the proximity test is satisfied and the economic loss is foreseeable. For example, in *Ross* v. *Caunters* (1979) a solicitor was held to be liable for the pecuniary loss caused to an intended beneficiary by the careless drafting of a will.

The importance of the proximity test is further shown by the House of Lords' decision in *Junior Books* v. *Veitchi* (1982).* In this case, the proximity arose from the nomination by a building owner of a sub-contractor who was a specialist in floor-laying. In the construction industry, when a sub-contractor is nominated to the main contractor, that sub-contractor is in a closer relationship with the building owner than those who have been selected by the main contractor. For instance, the amount of each interim payment to a nominated sub-contractor is controlled not by the main contractor but by the building owner's architect. In *Junior Books*, the specialist nominated flooring sub-contractor was held to be liable to the building owner for the economic loss caused by negligence in laying a floor. In *Spartan Steel and Alloys Ltd.* v. *Martin & Co. Ltd.* (1972),* it was held that economic loss was recoverable if it was consequential upon physical damage caused by negligence, but not otherwise.

(d) Occupier's duty of care

It is possible to detect certain special areas of human activity where the law of negligence has taken up an important place. This is particularly so in the case of defective premises, for which the occupier's duty of care is now defined by statute.

The duty of the occupier of premises to those persons who are on them is now governed largely by the Occupiers' Liability Acts 1957 and 1984 which have replaced the common law rules. The Act of 1957 deals with the occupier's duty towards his *visitors* and the Act of 1984 deals with the occupier's duty towards persons other than his visitors. A visitor is a person to whom the occupier has given an invitation or permission to enter or use the premises.

(i) The Occupiers' Liability Act 1957.
By s. 2(1) of the Act:

An occupier of premises owes the same duty, the 'common duty of care' to all his visitors, except in so far as he is free to and does extend, restrict, modify or exclude his duty to any visitor or visitors by agreement or otherwise.

Section 2(2) goes on to provide that:

The common duty of care is a duty to take such care as in all the circumstances of the case is reasonable to see that the visitor will be reasonably safe in using the premises for the purposes for which he is invited or permitted by the occupier to be there.

Section 2(5) incorporates the rule of assumption of risk:

The common duty of care does not impose on an occupier any obligation to a visitor in respect of risks willingly accepted as his by the visitor......

(ii) The Occupiers' Liability Act 1984.
This Act deals with the liability of the occupier of premises to persons other than his visitors. The words 'persons other than his visitors' include trespassers and certain other categories of persons on the premises.

By s. 1(3) of the 1984 Act, the occupier's duty arises if:

(a) he is aware of the danger or has reasonable grounds to believe that it exists;
(b) he knows or has reasonable grounds to believe that the person other than his visitor is in the vicinity of the danger; and
(c) the risk is one against which, in all the circumstances of the case, he may reasonably be expected to offer the person other than his visitor some protection.

The duty is defined in s. 1(4) as follows: 'to take such care as is reasonable in all the circumstances of the case to see that the person other than his visitor does not suffer injury on the premises by reason of the danger concerned.'

The different duties under the 1957 Act and under the 1984 Act should be compared carefully. Notice how much higher is the duty to visitors.

7.3 THE STANDARD OF CARE

Where it is established that the defendant owed the plaintiff a duty of care it is sometimes necessary to consider the appropriate standard of care required by the law. All this may be necessary in order to discover whether the defendant has broken the duty of care. Unless there are special circumstances, the standard of care required of the defendant is that of a reasonable man. The court will ask itself, what would be the standard of care exercised by a reasonable man in the defendant's position when the alleged negligence occurred? It should be noticed that the question whether the defendant did his own best is not relevant to the question of standard of care.

Where the defendant has held himself out as having some special skill, e.g. that of a doctor or an accountant, he will be judged by the standard of care expected from a reasonably competent doctor or accountant, as the case may be.

The standard of care required in any case must be proportioned to the risk of injury involved. Also, in any given situation, there might be a factor which increases the injury which is risked. These two matters are discussed below.

(a) The degree of risk (The greater risk of injury)

There is an inverse relationship between the likelihood that the defendant's conduct will cause harm, on the one hand, and the amount of caution which the law requires from him, on the other. For instance, where the possibility of harm is extremely remote, the duty of care may be discharged even if no special precautions are taken by the defendant; but where there is an obvious likelihood of harm, the duty of care arises and will require care to be taken. The matter was explained by Lord Wright in *Northwestern Utilities Ltd.* v. *London Guarantee and Accident Co. Ltd.* (1936) as follows: 'The degree of care which that duty involves must be proportioned to the degree of risk involved if the duty of care should not be fulfilled.'

In this connection, the two 'cricket ball' cases give a useful illustration. The cases are *Bolton* v. *Stone* (1951) and *Miller* v. *Jackson* (1977). In the former case the plaintiff was injured by a cricket ball hit by a batsman in a nearby cricket ground. Hits of this kind had occurred only half a dozen times in the past thirty years. It was held by the House of Lords that there was no duty of care owed by members of the cricket club because the chance of such an accident was so remote that no precautions could be reasonably expected to be taken by the club. In the latter case, the plaintiffs had bought a house adjacent to a village cricket ground from which balls landed in their garden at the rate of about five in one season. Some of these balls had done minor damage to the house. For this damage the defendants, on their own behalf and on behalf of the other members of the cricket club, were held liable in damages.

(b) The seriousness of the risk (The risk of greater injury)

Where the circumstances are such that the risk of a greater injury is involved, this will be taken into account when deciding the required standard of care. *Paris* v. *Stepney B.C.* (1949) provides an illustration. In this case a workman who had only one good eye was employed as a fitter in the defendant's garage. While he was hammering a piece of metal, a chip flew into his one good eye rendering him totally blind. The defendant employers had not provided the workman with goggles for this operation. It was held by the House of Lords that the following were relevant facts to be taken into account when determining the question whether the employers took reasonable precautions for the workman's safety: (i) the condition of the workman's eyes; (ii) the knowledge of the employers; (iii) the likelihood of an accident happening; and (iv) the gravity of the consequences if an accident should occur.

7.4 CAUSATION AND REMOTENESS

In order to succeed in a claim for negligence the plaintiff must show that the damage or injury which he suffered was caused by the defendant's breach of duty. In establishing this causal connection between the defendant's breach of duty, on the one hand, and the damage suffered, on the other, two important questions arise. First, did the breach of duty cause the damage? Secondly, is any part of the damage too remote? The first is a question of fact. The second is a question of law.

(a) Causation

The plaintiff must bear the burden of proving that, on the balance of probability, the defendant's breach of duty caused the damage. It follows that it is a good defence for the defendant to show that the damage or injury was caused by the plaintiff himself or by a third party. In *McWilliams* v. *Sir William Arrol & Co.* (1962) a steel erector was killed on falling from a tower being constructed in a shipyard. The defendants, the employers, were in breach of their statutory duty to provide safety belts. The widow's action against the employers failed because it was shown that even if safety belts had been provided, the plaintiff's husband would not have worn one.

Similarly, if it can be shown that the damage would have occurred notwithstanding the breach of duty, there will be no liability in negligence. For instance, in *Barnett* v. *Chelsea and Kensington Hospital Management Committee* (1969) the defendants were not liable for a doctor's failure to examine a patient brought into the hospital, for the patient would have died anyway, even with the best of medical attention.

In determining the question of causation, the judges adopt a commonsense attitude to the facts of each case. Where there are two or more arguable causes of the injury, the courts try to pick out that cause which was most closely connected with it. An illustration of this commonsense approach is to be found in *Carslogie S. S. Co.* v. *Royal Norwegian Government* (1952). In this case the plaintiffs' ship was damaged as a result of the default of a ship belonging to the defendants. The damage was repaired temporarily to allow the ship to sail to New York for permanent repairs. On this voyage, the plaintiffs' ship suffered further damage due to storms. The ship went into dry dock and both sets of repairs were carried out concurrently. On the question whether the defendants were liable for loss of profits incurred while the ship was in dry dock, the Court of Appeal found in favour of the plaintiffs but, on appeal to the House of Lords, this decision was reversed.

In the above case, the House of Lords distinguished between the cause of detention of the ship and the cause of the lost profit. The fact was that the ship would have been detained for 30 days even if there had been no collision, for it took 30 days to repair the storm damage. For 10 days out of this period of 30 days, the collision damage was carried out concurrently. Lord Tucker said: 'I am prepared to assume . . . that the collision was *a* cause of the detention, but none the less the detention for repair did not result in any loss of profit'.

(b) Remoteness of damage

The test of remoteness is whether a reasonable man, at the time of the breach of duty, would have foreseen the type and kind of damage which has occurred. If the damage caused by the breach of duty is of such a type and kind, i.e. reasonably foreseeable, the defendant is liable for it. On the other hand, where the damage is of a different type and kind from anything that a reasonable man could, at the time of the breach of duty, have foreseen, he is not liable for it. In *The Wagon Mound* (no. 1) the plaintiff's wharf in Sydney Harbour was destroyed by fire resulting from the careless spillage of oil from the defendants' ship the *Wagon Mound*. At the time of the spillage, the *Wagon Mound* was 200 yards from the plaintiffs' wharf. The plaintiffs, who were engaged in the repair of a ship, the *Corrimal*, halted their welding until assured by authoritative opinion that oil would not ignite when floating on water. Later, however, a spark from a welder fell on to a rag floating with the oil causing it to ignite and to set the oil on fire. This fire eventually destroyed the plaintiffs' wharf. The Supreme Court of New South Wales found in favour of the plaintiffs on the ground that *some* damage was foreseeable, such as fouling. On appeal to the Privy Council, the defendants succeeded because the fire damage was not of a type and kind which was reasonably foreseeable.

Hughes v. *Lord Advocate* (1963) provides a further example of the operation of the foreseeability test of remoteness. In this case, Post Office workmen had left a manhole for the evening, covered with a tent and lighted by a number of paraffin lamps. An eight-year-old boy entered the tent and knocked a lamp into the manhole, thus causing a violent explosion which caused him to fall into the hole and sustain severe burns. In this case it was found as a fact that it was highly unlikely that a paraffin lamp would explode. From this, the defence argued that, since the explosion was not foreseeable, they were not liable for the damage caused, i.e., the boy's burns. The House of Lords took the view that the explosion was simply one of several ways in which burning might be caused by the potentially dangerous lamps. The damage was not different in kind from that which might have been caused if a lamp had spilled to produce a fire in the hole.

In *Doughty* v. *Turner Manufacturing Co. Ltd* (1964) the plaintiff employee was injured in the defendants' factory when an explosion occurred throwing molten metal on him. The explosion was caused by the asbestos cement lid falling into a cauldron. The evidence showed that the explosion was entirely unexpected. Nobody supposed that the lid could not be safely immersed into the bath. It was conceded by the plaintiff's counsel that if the defendants had deliberately immersed the lid as part of their manufacturing process and an explosion had occurred, the defendants would not be liable for any resulting explosion. It followed that the fact that the lid was inadvertently knocked into the bath could not of itself convert into negligence what they were entitled to do deliberately.

(c) Novus actus interveniens

Where something unreasonable, unexpected or unforeseeable breaks the chain of causation between the breach of duty and the resulting damage, the defendant may escape liability. Such an unforeseeable and unreasonable intervening agency is called novus actus interveniens. In *The Oropesa* (1943) the Oropesa was in collision with another ship, the Manchester Regiment, the fault being allocated four-fifths to the Oropesa and one-fifth to the Manchester Regiment. During the rescue operation which followed the collision, the master of the Manchester Regiment left his ship and set off in a lifeboat to confer with the master of the other ship. Due to rough seas, the lifeboat capsized and the plaintiff's son was drowned. The plaintiff claimed against the owners of the Oropesa in negligence. The defence was raised that the chain of causation had been broken by the conduct of the master of the Manchester Regiment. The trial judge and the Court of Appeal decided that the master's conduct was not, in the circumstances, unreasonable or unwarranted, and was not, therefore, *novus actus interveniens*. In that case, Lord Wright said: 'To break the chain of causation it must be shown that there is something which I will call ultroneous, something unwarrantable, a new cause which disturbs the sequence of events, something which can be described as either unreasonable or extraneous or extrinsic.' He went on to say that the behaviour of the master of the Manchester Regiment might be regarded as the natural consequence of the emergency in which he was placed by the negligence of the Oropesa.

In *Haynes* v. *Harwood* (1935) a policeman was injured in stopping bolting horses and a van which had been negligently left unattended by the defendant. It was held that the intervening action of the plaintiff was not unreasonable and that the defendant was liable in negligence for his injuries. What is reasonable might also be regarded as foreseeable. There is no break in the chain of causation where the intervention, looked at as a whole, is reasonable and justifiable and a natural and probable consequence of the defendant's negligence, which ought reasonably to have been foreseen.

7.5 DEFENCES

Although some of the general defences may, as appropriate, be raised in defence to negligence, there are two important special defences, i.e. contributory negligence and voluntary assumption of risk.

(a) Contributory negligence

At common law a defendant to an action for negligence would escape liability if he could prove that there was contributory negligence on the part of the plaintiff. This was clearly an unsatisfactory rule which in some cases could work unfairly. The Law Reform (Contributory Negligence) Act 1945 introduced the principle of shared responsibility. Section 1(1) provides:

> Where any person suffers damage as the result partly of his own fault and partly the fault of any other person or persons, a claim in respect of that damage shall not be defeated by reason of the fault of the person suffering the damage, but the damages recoverable in respect thereof shall be reduced to such extent as the court thinks just and equitable having regard to the claimant's share in the responsibility for the damage.

(b) Voluntary assumption of risk

The maxim *volenti non fit injuria* includes two aspects of risk assumed by the plaintiff. In the first place it means consent, express or implied (6.5(b)). Secondly, it means the assumption of risk voluntarily and knowingly. It is the second of these aspects of the maxim which provides a defence to an action for negligence. Thus, in order to succeed, the defendant must prove as a fact that the plaintiff freely and voluntarily, with full knowledge of the nature and extent of the risk he ran, impliedly agreed to incur it.

SUMMARY

1   Negligence was first recognised as an independent tort in *Donoghue* v. *Stevenson* (1932) in the House of Lords.

2   In *Donoghue* v. *Stevenson* Lord Atkin said:

'The rule that you are to love your neighbour becomes in law, you must not injure your neighbour; and the lawyer's question, Who is my neighbour? receives a restricted reply. You must take reasonable care to avoid acts or omissions which you can reasonably foresee would be likely to injure your neighbour. Who, then, in law is my neighbour? The answer seems to be – persons who are so closely and directly affected by my act that I ought reasonably to have them in contemplation as being so affected when I am directing my mind to the acts or omissions which are called in question.'

3   Lord Atkin's statement is one of broad principle. Its correct application in the 'two-stage' approach to the question of the duty of care was explained in *Anns* v. *Merton* (1977) in the House of Lords.

4   The principle of liability for statements made negligently was proposed by the House of Lords in *Hedley Byrne* v. *Heller* (1963).

5   Economic loss is probably recoverable where the proximity test is satisfied and the economic loss is foreseeable. However, in the *Spartan Steel* case, the Court of Appeal ruled that economic loss is recoverable only where it flows from physical damage.

6   In determining the question whether the defendant exercised an appropriate standard of care the degree of risk and the seriousness of the risk may have to be considered.

7   The plaintiff must show that the damage was caused by the defendant's breach of the duty of care. In determining this question the courts adopt a commonsense attitude to the facts of each case.

8   The defendant is not liable for damage which is too remote. The test of remoteness is whether the damage is of a type and kind which would have been foreseen by a reasonable man.

9   Where something unreasonable, unexpected or unforeseeable breaks the chain of causation the defendant may escape liability. Such an intervening agency is called *novus actus interveniens*.

10   The important special defences to an action for negligence are contributory negligence and voluntary assumption of risk.

CASE NOTES

Anns v. *London Borough of Merton* (1977) H. L.

The plaintiffs were lessees under long leases of flats in a two-storey block. Walcroft Limited, who had completed the building of the block in 1962, were also the owners of the block. In 1972, cracks appeared in the walls and the floors began to tilt. The plaintiffs alleged that these defects were due to inadequate foundations. Local authorities were enabled through byelaws made under the Public Health Act 1936 to supervise and control the construction of foundations of buildings. Byelaws made by a local authority (the council) provided for the inspection of plans and the inspection of work. The council approved plans for the two-storey block in question. These plans showed foundations '3 feet or deeper to the approval of the local authority'. The byelaws did not provide that the council was under a duty to inspect the foundations. The plaintiffs alleged that the foundations were built to a depth of two feet six inches only and not to the depth of three feet required by the plans deposited with the council. The plaintiffs claimed damages against the council for negligence by their approving the foundations or their failure to inspect the foundations.

HELD: (i) The question of the duty of care must be considered in relation to the council's duties, powers and discretions under the Public Health Act 1936; (ii) although the Act and the byelaws did not impose a duty of inspection, it was the council's duty to give proper consideration of the question whether they should inspect or not; (iii) the council were under a duty to take reasonable care to ensure that a builder did not cover up foundations which did not comply with byelaws. A right of action would accrue to a person who was owner or occupier of the building when the damage occurred.

Donoghue v. *Stevenson* (1932) H. L.

The appellant went with a friend into a café, where the friend ordered for her a bottle of ginger beer. This was served in an opaque bottle the contents of which could not be seen inside. The café proprietor opened the bottle and poured some of the contents into the appellant's glass. This she drank and her friend then poured in the rest of the bottle. The appellant alleged that this contained the decomposed remains of a snail which caused her to suffer shock and, later, gastric illness. She brought this action for negligence in the Scottish Court of Session against the manufacturer of the ginger beer. The Scottish Court held that there was no cause of action and the case came before the House of Lords on the question of law alone.

HELD by a majority: the manufacturer of the ginger beer owed a duty of care to the claimant.

Hedley Byrne & Co. v. *Heller & Partners Ltd.* (1963) H. L.

A bank telephoned merchant bankers concerning the financial position of Easipower Limited. This company was a customer both of the bank and the merchant bankers. The bank said that they wanted to know, without responsibility on the part of the merchant bankers, whether the company would be good for an advertising contract for £8,000 to £9,000. Later, the bank wrote to the merchant bankers asking in confidence for an opinion of the respectability and standing of Easipower Limited by stating whether this company was trustworthy to the extent of £100,000 per annum. The merchant bankers replied favourably but they qualified it as being 'without responsibility'. Relying on this statement, a firm of advertising agents placed orders at their own cost for advertising time and space for Easipower Limited. Easipower went into liquidation and the advertising agents lost £17,000 on the advertising contracts for Easipower. The advertising agents sued the merchant bank.

HELD: But for the express disclaimer of responsibility the circumstances might have given rise to a duty of care. Lord Morris said:

> 'It should now be regarded as settled that if someone possessed of a special skill undertakes, quite irrespective of contract, to apply that skill for the assistance of another person who relies upon such skill, a duty of care will arise. The fact that the service is to be given by means of or by the instrumentality of words can make no difference. Furthermore, if in a sphere in which a person is so placed that others could reasonably rely upon his judgement or his skill or upon his ability to make careful enquiry, a person takes it upon himself to give information or advice to, or allows his information or advice to be passed on to, another person who, as he knows or should know, will place reliance upon it, then a duty of care will arise. . .'

Home Office v. *Dorset Yacht Co. Ltd* (1970) H. L.

A party of seven Borstal Boys in the charge of three officers were working on Brownsea Island in Portland Harbour, a busy yachting centre. One night the officers all retired to bed leaving the boys unsupervised. The boys, some of whom had escaped before, left their quarters and boarded a yacht which they subsequently caused to collide with the plaintiff's yacht. The plaintiff claimed damages, alleging that the officers had been negligent.

HELD: The Home Office, through their officers, owed a duty of care to the plaintiff. Lord Morris said:

'. . . a normal or even a modest measure of prescience and prevision must have led an ordinary person, but rather specially an officer in charge, to realise that the boys might wish to escape and might use a yacht if one was near at hand to help them to do so . . . the risk of such a happening was glaringly obvious.'

Junior Books Ltd. v. *Veitchi Ltd.* (1982) H. L.
A building contractor undertook to build a factory for the owners. By a provision in the building contract, the owners' architect nominated a specialist sub-contractor to lay a concrete floor with a special surface. Two years after completion of the work, the floor developed cracks and the owners were faced with the problem of continual maintenance work on it. The owners brought this action against the flooring sub-contractor, alleging that the defects in the floor were due to negligence in laying it. The owners claimed the cost of replacing the floor and the consequential economic loss arising out of (i) moving machinery, (ii) closing the factory, (iii) the payment of wages and overheads and (iv) the loss of profits during the period of replacement. The owners alleged that such replacement costs would be cheaper than the continuous maintenance of the defective floor.

HELD: Since (a) the owners' architect had nominated the flooring sub-contractor as specialists, the relationship was so close as to fall just short of a contractual relationship and (b) the sub-contractor must have known that the owners had relied on his skill and experience and (c) and damage was a direct and foreseeable result of the sub-contractor's negligence in laying a defective floor, it followed that the proximity between the owner and the sub-contractor was sufficiently close to give rise to a duty of care not to lay a defective floor which would cause the owners financial loss.

Rimmer v. *Liverpool City Council* (1984)
The plaintiff was a tenant in a flat which had been designed, built and let by the defendant council. The flat contained a narrow passage in which was a panel of thin breakable glass. The plaintiff complained about the possible danger and the council replied that the panel was standard in that block of flats and could not be changed. Some time later, the plaintiff stumbled and fell in the passage and put out his hand to save himself. His hand went through the glass panel and he was injured. The plaintiff brought this action alleging breach of duty of care by the council.

HELD: Since the council had designed and built the flat it owed a duty of care to the plaintiff. The fact that the plaintiff knew of the danger did not exonerate the council because the plaintiff had not been free to remove or avoid the danger.

Spartan Steel and Alloys Ltd. v. *Martin & Co. Ltd.* (1972) C. A.

The plaintiffs manufactured metal alloys in their factory which worked 24 hours a day. For this purpose, continuous power was needed to maintain the temperature of the furnace. The defendants who were engaged in road works damaged the electricity supply cable with the result that power had to be shut off for 14½ hours. To protect the furnace, the plaintiffs poured oxygen on the 'melt' which was in progress at the time of the power cut. This reduced the value of the melt by £368. Had there been no cut, a profit of £400 would have been made on this melt. Furthermore, the plaintiffs lost a profit of £1,767 which would have been earned during the period of the electricity cut. The plaintiffs claimed damages for all three of these sums. The defendants admitted negligence, but disputed the amount claimed.

HELD: (i) The defendants were liable for the physical damage to the melt and for the loss of profit thus caused because that loss was consequential upon the physical damage: (ii) the defendants were not liable for loss of profit of £1,767 because this was not the consequence of physical damage. Lord Denning said:

'At bottom the question of recovering economic loss is one of policy. Whenever the courts draw a line to mark out the bounds of duty, they do it as a matter of policy so as to limit the liability of the defendants. The time has come to discard the tests which have been propounded in the reported cases and which have proved so elusive. It is better to consider the particular relationship in hand, and see whether or not, as a matter of policy, economic loss should be recoverable.'

Wheat v. *E. Lacon Co. Ltd.* (1966) H. L.

One Wheat, who was lodging in a public house owned by Lacon's, the brewing company, fell down the back staircase and was killed. The handrail ended before the bottom of the stairs and it was dark, there being no bulb in the stairway light. Wheat had made the arrangement for lodgings with the wife of the manager, who was permitted by the company to run a boarding-house business. By the agreement between the manager and the company, the company had the right to enter the premises to inspect the state of repair. Also, by this agreement the manager's occupation of the premises did not create a tenancy. Wheat's widow brought this action against the company under the Fatal Accidents Acts, 1846 to 1908, claiming damages for breach of the common duty of care imposed by

s. 2(1) and (2) of the Occupiers' Liability Act 1957, on the basis that the company was in occupation or control of the back staircase and that Wheat was a visitor within s. 1(2) of the 1957 Act.

HELD: (i) Under the agreement between the company and the manager, the company had not divested itself of the occupation and control of any part of the public house, and the whole of it was in the occupation of their manager who was their employee; accordingly the company was the occupier of the back staircase for the purposes of s. 1(2) of the Occupiers' Liability Act 1957. (ii) Wheat was a 'visitor' to whom the common duty of care was owed by the company under s. 2(1) and (2) of the 1957 Act, but there was not sufficient evidence to enable it to be deduced how the accident happened, and, on the evidence, the staircase, though unlit, was not dangerous to someone using it with proper care, so that no breach of duty on the part of the company to take such care as in all the circumstances of the case was reasonable had been established.

EXERCISES

1   Negligence has long been an element in trespass and other torts. In which case was it first recognised as a separate and independent tort?

2   State accurately Lord Atkin's formulation of the 'neighbour' principle. Explain what is meant when it is said that this statement is one of broad common law policy.

3   In *Anns* v. *Merton* (1977) Lord Wilberforce said that there should be two stages in the approach to the problem of establishing whether a duty of care exists. What are these two stages?

4   Can the mere failure to act constitute a breach of the duty of care?

5   In what circumstances is there a liability for statements made negligently? Mention the concept of 'reliance' in your answer.

6   Explain carefully the problem of including economic loss in the calculation of damages for negligence. Mention any decided cases that you know to be relevant to your answer.

7   What duty of care is owed by the occupiers of premises under the Occupiers' Liability Acts 1957 and 1984?

8   'Unless there are special circumstances, the standard of care required of the defendant is that of a reasonable man.' Comment on this statement.

9   What principles govern the question of the amount of caution required of a defendant?

10   Why is *Paris* v. *Stepney B.C.* (1949) an important case?

11   Problems of causation are questions of fact: problems of remoteness

of damage are questions of law. Explain fully, illustrating your answer
with decided cases.

12 An unforeseeable and unreasonable intervening agency into the
chain of causation is called *novus actus interveniens*. Explain fully, con-
centrating on the requirements of unforeseeability and unreasonableness.

13 What is contributory negligence and what is its effect?

14 In what circumstances may the defendant take advantage of the
principle in the maxim *volenti non fit injuria?*

WORKSHOP

1 In *Home Office* v. *Dorset Yacht Co. Ltd.* (1970) it was held that the
duty of care had been broken by the officers. Why? To whom do you
think the duty was owed?

2 In *Hedley Byrne* v. *Heller & Partners* (1963) the defendants had
qualified their statement with the words 'without responsibility'. What
difference, if any, would it have made had the statement not been qualified
in this way? In what later case was the principle of liability for negligent
statements considered?

3 Read the note on *Spartan Steel and Alloys Ltd.* v. *Martin & Co. Ltd.*
(1972). In this case some of the plaintiff's loss was caused by physical
damage. Some loss was not caused by physical damage. What was the
significance of this difference? What exactly was the physical damage in
this case? What did Lord Denning mean when he said in this case, 'At
bottom the question of recovering economic loss is one of policy'?

4 Consider *Junior Books* v. *Veitchi* (1982). Explain carefully why
the relationship between the parties gave rise to a duty of care. To what
extent was the claimant successful in recovering economic loss? Mention
the principle involved.

5 In *Wheat* v. *E. Lacon & Co. Ltd.* (1966) it was held by the House of
Lords that there was no breach of the duty of care owed to Mr Wheat
under the Occupiers' Liability Act 1957. Why was this decision reached?

6 Consider how the duty of care arose in *Rimmer* v. *Liverpool C.C.*
(1984). Consider further how it was broken.

7 Read the note on *Anns* v. *Merton* (1977). How would you formulate
the *ratio decidendi* of this case?

THE LAW OF REAL PROPERTY

8.1 INTRODUCTORY MATTERS

There are three great influences which have shaped the law of property over the past thousand years or so. First, *the common law,* which gave shape and support to the kind of feudalism imposed by William I after his conquest of the English in 1066. Secondly, the invention of *the trust* which stems from the recognition by the thirteenth century Chancellors of the practice of putting land in 'use', resulting in the separation of nominal and beneficial ownership. The third great shaping force was *the property legislation of 1925* which modernised and simplified much of the unnecessary complexity of the old law.

(a) The common law

In mediaeval times, land was virtually the sole form of wealth. Only the possession of land could give status, wealth and, in some cases, power. The old law was based on the twin doctrines of tenure and of the estate. Through the combination of these doctrines, the kind of feudalism imposed by William I caused the development of customs to suit the needs of a feudal society. These customs, enforced by the King's judges, became the early rules of common law. The concepts of 'tenure' and the 'estate' should be considered separately.

(i) Tenure.
William I regarded himself as the lawful heir to the throne of England. He regarded Harold as a usurper with whom he was forced to do battle in order to recover his rightful crown. He therefore regarded himself as free to deal with the land and the landed nobility of England as he wished. William's first principle was that all land was owned by the Crown. This meant that even the mightiest noblemen were tenants owing service to the Crown in return for their tenancies. Those who held directly of the

Crown were called tenants in chief, and there were about 1500 of them. Some of these were his Norman supporters and some were English noblemen who were allowed to retain a tenancy in their former lands in return for money payments to William. The tenants in chief granted sub-tenancies to lesser noblemen in return for military or other services. This process would be repeated several times, so that there might be half a dozen sub-tenancies existing between the tenant in actual possession and the King as supreme landlord. The process of granting sub-tenancies was called sub-infeudation and the tenure was called mesne tenure. In short, the system of tenure provided the enjoyment and use of the land and its profits to all but the lowest layers of society in return for services of many kinds, including military service – this last service ultimately providing the King with a loyal army. In the event of non-performance of tenurial service, the land could be recovered by the aggrieved intermediate landlord or by the King himself in the event of serious default by any tenant in chief. Military tenure was called knight service and the highest non-military tenure was called sergeanty, the others being socage and copyhold.

King William I permitted the ecclesiastical corporations sole and aggregate to continue holding their land under the two pre-Norman tenures of frankalmoign and divine service, each of which required the tenant to perform certain religious services.

The system of tenure suited the needs of a feudal and agricultural society in which land was the prime source of wealth and influence. During the sixteenth and seventeenth centuries, however, far-reaching social and economic changes were taking place, largely due to the growth of trade and the development of towns and cities. As the grant of tenancies in land became less appropriate as a method of payment for services, so did the system of tenure itself outlive its usefulness. By the Tenures Abolition Act 1660, most tenures were abolished, leaving only copyhold and socage, each of which required agricultural services from the tenant. As a result of the 1925 legislation, socage is the only remaining tenure.

(ii) The 'estate'.
When a tenant was in rightful possession of the land granted to him or inherited by him, he was said to be 'seised' of the land. He had what was known as 'seisin'. These words are pronounced *seezed* and *seezin* respectively. The common law protected seisin (or possession) for, as has been said, it was only the Crown itself who could own land.

The duration of the right of seisin was known as the estate. Although a tenant could not in theory own the land, he could at least regard himself as the owner of this abstraction known as the estate. The characteristic of the freehold estate was that there was no fixed duration for the tenant's right of seisin. Freeholders usually held their land for life. Occasionally, a tenant would hold his land for an uncertain period other than his own life. Estates less than freehold were those which were of certain duration, or capable of being made certain, for example, a grant of a term of years, or a tenancy from year to year. As to terminology, it should be noticed that it was only the freeholders who had *seisin:* tenants with estates less than freehold had *possession.* A freeholder was *seised* of his land: a tenant for a fixed term of years was *possessed* of his land.

Where wrongful dispossession occurred, a freeholder would have an action *in rem* to recover his seisin, but a tenant with an estate less than freehold would have an action *in personam* only.

(b) Equity and the trust

The doctrines of tenure, seisin and the estate were suited to the relatively simple social and economic order of the early middle ages, but the rigid pattern of possible interests in land allowed by the common law was not entirely suited to the more sophisticated requirements of the later middle ages and beyond.

During the thirteenth century it became possible to separate the nominal ownership of land from the beneficial ownership by virtue of the invention of the 'use'. A tenant could formally transfer his estate to a transferee on the undertaking from the transferee that he would hold the estate not for his own enjoyment and benefit, but for the enjoyment and benefit of another (or others) named by the transferor. Such a beneficiary was called the *cestui que use* - pronounced *setty que use* ('use' with a soft 's'). Where land was transferred by A to B for the use of C, B would be the rightful owner of the land in the eyes of the common law and his rights would be enforced by the courts of common law; but if C petitioned the Chancellor, he could obtain a decree forcing B to hold the land for the benefit of C. C, the *cestui que use,* was entitled to the enjoyment and the profit from the land, and his beneficial rights were protected by the Chancellor's court. It should be noticed that at no point in this process was there any denial of B's nominal right as common law owner of the estate in the land. In this illustration, the decree of the Chancellor acted on the conscience of the legal transferee, compelling him to behave in accordance with his undertaking to the transferor, i.e., to hold for the enjoyment and benefit of the *cestui que use.* The modern equivalent of the use is the trust, under which the trustees have the legal ownership of property for the benefit of the *cestui que trust,* or beneficiary. In the plural, the term is *cestuis que use* or *cestuis que trust,* as the case may be.

The key to the relationship between legal title, on the one hand, and equitable title, on the other, is the doctrine of the *bona fide* purchaser. *The bona fide purchaser for value of the legal estate without notice of any equitable interest* takes the legal estate free from the equitable interest.

(c) The legislation of 1925

The reforming legislation of 1925 comprised the following statutes: the Settled Land Act, the Trustee Act, the Law of Property Act, the Land Charges Act and the Administration of Estates Act. These Acts came into force on 1 January 1926. The main purpose was to simplify the law and, consequently, to simplify the practice of conveyancing. The principal simplifications were (1) the abolition of copyhold, thus reducing all tenures to one common form, namely, socage, and (2) the assimilation of the law governing leaseholds with that governing freeholds and (3) the introduction of registered conveyancing.

It is now necessary to consider in outline the estates and interests which may exist under the 1925 regime, both at law and in equity.

(i) Legal estates

The only estates in land which are capable of subsisting or of being conveyed or created at law are:

(*a*) an estate in fee simple absolute in possession, and

(*b*) a term of years absolute: s. 1(1), Law of Property Act 1925.

The legal estate is the basis of conveyancing and, by section 1(1) of the Law of Property Act 1925, the term of years is treated in the same way as the fee simple. These two estates are considered below in section 8.2.

(ii) Legal interests.

By s. 1(2) of the Law of Property Act 1925, the only interests or charges in or over land which are capable of subsisting or of being conveyed or created at law are:

(*a*) an easement, right or privilege in or over land for an interest equivalent to an estate in fee simple absolute in possession or a term of years absolute;

(*b*) a rentcharge in possession issuing out of or charged on land being either perpetual or for a term of years absolute;

(*c*) a charge by way of legal mortgage;

(*d*) rights of entry exercisable over or in respect of a legal term of years absolute, or annexed, for any purpose, to a legal rentcharge.

An *easement* is a privilege exercisable by a landowner A over the owner of adjacent land B to compel that owner B to do, or refrain from doing, something on his own land, or to allow the other landowner A to do something on the land in question. In this example, A is the dominant owner and his land is the dominant tenement; B is the servient owner and his land is the servient tenement. Examples of easements are a right to light, a right to support, a right of way and rights regarding party walls and fences.

(iii) Equitable interests.
By s.1(3) of the Law of Property Act 1925, all estates, interests and charges in or over land, other than those specified in s.1(1) and (2), will take effect as equitable interests. For example, a life interest or a future interest can exist only as an equitable interest.

(iv) Settlements.
The purpose of a settlement is usually to create a series of beneficial interests in favour of members of the settlor's family. The interests may be in real or personal property and the instrument creating the settlement may be a deed or a will.

The 1925 legislation provides for two methods of settlement. First is the strict settlement under the Settled Land Act 1925. This is a method used by settlors who wish to keep lands and buildings *in specie* in the family, from one generation to another. The other method is the trust for sale under the Law of Property Act 1925. This method is sometimes called the trader's settlement because there is usually no desire to keep lands or buildings 'in the family', the purpose of the settlement being to provide the settlor's family and their descendants with an income for their lives.

These two methods of settlement are considered below in section 8.3.

(v) Registered conveyancing.
The Land Registration Act 1925 set in motion a system of registration of title which now applies to most parts of England and Wales. It is the intention of the 1925 legislation that, ultimately, all legal estates will be registered. A system of registered conveyancing has gradually come to replace the former system of unregistered conveyancing. Interests may be entered on the register of the title to which they appertain. These will be registered either as 'over-riding' interests or as 'minor' interests. Over-riding interests bind the registered proprietor of the legal estate regardless of whether they are entered on the register: examples are *profits à prendre*, legal easements, leases for not more than twenty-one years (longer leases are all registrable) and any rights of persons in actual occupation of the land. Purchasers for value of the legal estate will take free from minor interests unless they are entered on the register, in which case they are binding. Examples of minor interests are restrictive covenants, equitable easements and all rentcharges.

8.2 THE FEE SIMPLE ABSOLUTE IN POSSESSION

The 'fee simple absolute in possession' is the statutory expression (s.1(1) of the Law of Property Act 1925) for one of the two legal estates in land permitted by the modern law. It is necessary to consider the three elements of the expression, namely, 'fee simple', 'absolute' and 'in possession'.

(a) Fee simple

The fee simple has always stood as the most extensive estate since all other estates are derivable from it or mergeable into it. It is an estate of inheritance, i.e., it denotes that the tenant in fee simple and his heirs hold the land for ever. The word 'simple' denotes that the land passes to the tenant's heirs general, and not to a particular class of descendants. As a comparison, consider the *fee tail*, which passed on an intestacy to a restricted category of descendants. The modern equivalent is the *entailed interest*.

(b) Absolute

An estate is absolute when it extends in time without any condition to defeat or determine it. In other words, there must not be contained in the terms of the grant a condition which might take effect to bring the tenant's ownership of the estate to an end and pass and transfer it to another owner. The absolute estate should be contrasted with the determinable estate, i.e. an estate the grant of which contains words which raise the possibility of the estate coming to an end. The classic example of a determinable estate is given by Blackstone. In the *Commentaries*, Book II, Chapter 7, he writes:

'A base or qualified fee, is such a one as hath a qualification subjoined thereto, and which must be determined whenever the qualification annexed to it is at an end. As, in the case of a grant to A and his heirs, tenants of the manor of Dale; in this instance, whenever the heirs of A cease to be tenants of that manor, the grant is entirely defeated.'

The Law of Property Act contains an important qualification to this principle of determinability. Section 7(2) provides that a fee simple vested in a corporation is to be regarded as absolute notwithstanding that it is liable to determine on the dissolution of the corporation.

(c) In possession

'Possession' in this context has a wider meaning than mere physical possession for, by s. 205 of the Law of Property Act 1925, the word includes the receipt or the right to receive rents and profits.

8.3 LEASEHOLDS AND OTHER INTERESTS

(a) Leaseholds

A leasehold will be a legal estate if it is within s. 1(2) of the Law of Property Act 1925, i.e. if it is a 'term of years absolute'. Any lease which does not satisfy this definition will exist as an equitable interest by virtue of s. 1(3) of the Act. The essential point is that the lessor must grant a definite term of years. It must be expressed as a fixed period of time. The duration can be of any length; indeed, 999 years is not uncommon.

The period could be even longer, for there is no upper limit. A term of years is absolute notwithstanding that the lease might possibly come to an end by lawful notice to quit. A tenancy for a year or for a fraction of a year is regarded as a term of years; similarly a tenancy from year to year.

Section 1(5) is an important provision with regard to leases. It provides that a legal estate may subsist concurrently with or subject to any other legal estate in the same land in like manner as it could have done before January 1926. It follows that there can be two or more legal estates subsisting concurrently in the same land. If, for example, A, owner of a fee simple absolute in possession, grants to B a term of years in the same piece of land, both A and B will be estate owners in the same land. By the same token, B could grant a term of years absolute to C, so that he too would have a legal estate in the same land as do A and B.

(b) Other interests

Mortgages, licences, easements, profits, rentcharges and restrictive covenants are all interests which characteristically give to a person rights in land which is owned by another, sometimes called rights *in alieno solo*. These interests may be legal or equitable. They are legal if created by deed and are expressed to subsist for a duration equivalent to that of one of the legal estates under section 1 of the Law of Property Act 1925 (8.1(c) above). It should be remembered that by section 1(3) of the Act, all interests and charges in or over land, other than those specified in section 1, will take effect as equitable interests.

(i) Mortgages.
There are two parties to a mortgage agreement – the mortgagor and the mortgagee. By the agreement, the mortgagor agrees to give property to the mortgagee as security for an advance of money. The mortgagee's interest in the mortgagor's property terminates on the repayment of the sum advanced.

A legal mortgage may be effected by lease to the mortgagee where the mortgagor owns the fee simple, or by a sub-lease, where the mortgagor is a leaseholder. Alternatively, a legal mortgage may be most simply effected by a charge by deed expressed to be by way of legal mortgage: ss. 1(2)(c) and 85 of the Law of Property Act 1925. This is usually regarded as the simplest method of effecting a legal mortgage.

An equitable mortgage might be effected where the parties show an intention to enter into a mortgagor and mortgagee relationship without complying with the requirements of the Law of Property Act 1925. *Equity looks to the intent rather than to the form.* Furthermore, where the borrower agrees to execute a legal mortgage in respect of money already advanced to him, there will be an equitable mortgage in favour of the lender. *Equity looks on that as done which ought to be done.* Where the security for the advance is itself equitable, then the mortgage will necessarily be equitable too.

It is fundamental in every type of mortgage, legal and equitable, that the mortgagor has an equity of redemption. One element in the equity of redemption is that the mortgagor has an inviolable right to redeem his property on repayment of the money advanced to him. This right cannot be excluded by agreement. There are only four ways in which the right to redeem can ultimately be lost: namely (1) lapse of time under the Limitation Act 1980; (2) an independent *subsequent* contract by which the mortgagor releases his right to redeem to the mortgagee; (3) where the mortgagee obtains a foreclosure order from the court; or (4) where he is able to exercise the power of sale given by the Law of Property Act 1925, s. 101.

(ii) Licences.
A licence enables the licensee to enter on the licensor's land, usually for an agreed purpose. Essentially, a licence is a permission to enter where otherwise the entry would have been unlawful. It is possible to distinguish three kinds of licence.

(a) *A bare licence* is a gratuitous permission to enter on land or premises and may be revoked without notice.

(b) *A contractual licence* arises where, in accordance with the express or implied terms of a contract, one party is entitled to enter on the land or premises of the other party, e.g. a contract to see a film in a cinema. In the event of revocation contrary to the terms of contract, the aggrieved party will have his remedy in contract, i.e. either damages or an injunction to restrain the breach or threatened breach. In *Winter Garden Theatre* v. *Millennium Productions* (1948), the House of Lords made it clear that if, on the true construction of the contract, the licence was intended to be irrevocable then, whenever appropriate, an injunction should be granted to prevent the revocation of the licence in breach of contract. Whether an injunction is a suitable and appropriate remedy depends on the facts of each case and the discretion of the court. It is obvious, however, that where it is intended that the licensee should stay only for a short while on the premises of the licensor, an injunction is not a suitable remedy in case of breach of revocation of the licence.

(*c*) *A licence coupled with an interest* occurs where the licensee has been granted an interest in the land of another person and is given permission to enter in order to enjoy it. Examples of such an interest are the cutting of timber or the pursuit of game. The licence must be seen as something different from and separate from the grant of the interest. It is not part of the interest – it is auxiliary to it. In the event of the licence being wrongfully revoked so that the licensee is denied the opportunity to enjoy his interest in the land, an injunction will normally be available to prevent the revocation of the licence. It would appear that the injunction is available even where the parties have contracted with regard to the interest, but have not yet executed the grant under seal.

(iii) Easements.

An easement is usually described as a privilege without a profit. That is to say, it confers a right attaching to the dominant land (8.1(c) above) but this right does not extend to the taking of any of the natural produce from the servient land. The essential point about an easement is that it is a right attaching to a piece of land – the right being exercisable over the land of another person. Easements may be positive or negative.

A positive easement enables the dominant owner to enter upon the servient land and behave in a stipulated manner, e.g. to walk or drive across the land, to erect and maintain a signboard or a light. A negative easement restricts the activities of the servient owner on his own land; for example, an easement of support will prevent him from removing earth or other support to the dominant land, while an easement of light will prevent him from building freely if it would cause an interference with light to the dominant land and its buildings.

Any right over land which does not have all four of the following elements is not an easement – an easement comprises all four: (1) There must be a dominant land and a servient land. (2) The servient land must accommodate the dominant land. (3) The dominant and servient owners must be different persons. (4) The easement must be capable of forming the subject-matter of a grant, i.e., it must be capable of definition and not uncertain, and there must be a capable grantor and grantee respectively.

The most usual easements are: rights of way, rights to light, rights in connection with streams and underground water, rights of support and the right to erect overhead telephone wires. The right to have a fence maintained by an adjoining owner has been described as a right in the nature of an easement: *Crow* v. *Wood* (1971).

(iv) Profits à prendre.

A *profit à prendre* is a right which, like an easement, attached to the dominant land, but enables the dominant owner to enter the servient land and take something from that land which is capable of ownership. It is the taking of something from the land which distinguishes a profit from an easement. There are endless possibilities as to what may be taken from the land: it could be the soil itself, crops, timber, animals, fowl, fish or turf. The taking of water, however, is regarded as an easement.

(v) Rentcharges.

A rentcharge is the sum payable where there is no tenure between the creditor and the debtor from whose land it issues. This is to be compared with the more usual rent service, which is the rent payable by a tenant to his landlord. All rentcharges will be extinguished by the year 2037 under the Rentcharges Act 1977. For the purpose of this Act, 'rentcharge' means any annual or other periodic sum charged on or issuing out of land, except: (*a*) rent reserved by a lease or tenancy; or (*b*) any sum payable by way of interest: s.1.

(vi) Restrictive covenants.

A restrictive covenant is an agreement (other than a lease) by which the owner of the servient land agrees with the owner of the dominant land that he will, in some specified manner, restrict the use of his land. The restrictive covenant is a device often used when part of an owner's lands are sold. The land which is sold can be made subject to whatever restrictive covenants are necessary to preserve the views and other amenities of the land retained. The important questions which arise in this connection are concerned with whether the restrictive covenants are binding with regard to the land after the sale of either the dominant or the servient land, or both. If the restrictions constitute a legal easement, or are contained in an executed lease, the covenant remains binding and enforceable between the successors in title to the original parties to the agreement. The covenant is then said to 'run with the land'.

8.4 THE STRICT SETTLEMENT AND TRUST FOR SALE

It has already been mentioned (8.1(*c*) (*iv*) that the modern law permits the settlement of property on a succession of beneficiaries in either of two ways, namely, by a strict settlement or by a trust for sale. Strict settlements are governed by the Settled Land Act 1925 and trusts for sale are governed by the Law of Property Act 1925.

(a) The strict settlement

There is a settlement under the Settled Land Act whenever land is limited to a series of persons by way of succession. The simplest example would be where land is granted to A for life, with remainder to B in fee simple. By section 4 of the Act, every settlement of a legal estate in land *inter vivos*, i.e. between living persons, must be effected by two deeds, namely, a vesting deed and a trust instrument. The Act also provides for exceptional cases where these two documents are not necessary.

(i) The vesting deed.

The purpose of the vesting deed is to vest the fee simple in the person who is to have the present enjoyment of the land, usually the head of the family. This person is called the *tenant for life*. The deed mentions the names of the trustees of the settlement. The tenant for life has considerable powers of dealing with the land conferred on him by the Act, e.g. lease and sale.

(ii) The trust instrument.

The purpose of the trust instrument, as its name implies, is to declare the trusts of the settlement and to appoint the trustees.

(iii) Settlement by will

Where the settlor settles property by will, the vesting deed and the trust instrument are, obviously, not appropriate. In this case, the settlor's personal representatives, on whom devolve the settlor's legal estate, hold the estate on trust to convey it to the tenant for life. This conveyance is called the vesting assent and it serves the same purpose as the vesting deed in the case of a settlement *inter vivos*. The settlor's will serves the same purpose as the trust instrument of an *inter vivos* settlement.

(iv) The tenant for life.

The person of full age who is beneficially entitled for the time being under a settlement to possession of settled land for his life is the tenant for life of that land. Where the person who would otherwise be the tenant for life is a minor, the legal estate in the settled land is vested in the trustees of the settlement.

The Settled Land Act confers wide powers of dealing with the land upon the tenant for life. The powers are sufficient to enable him to manage the land economically and efficiently. By section 107 of the Settled Land Act, it is provided that a tenant for life must, in exercising any power under the Act, have regard to the interests of all parties entitled under the settlement for whom he is deemed to be a trustee.

From the profits of the land, the tenant for life is usually expected to raise money for 'portions' in favour of the other beneficiaries. This often takes the from of a lump sum on reaching full age. This form of settlement enables the family lands to be kept under the control of the head of the family for the time being as tenant for life while, at the same time, providing for the needs of the other members of the family.

(v) The trustees of the settlement.
Capital money arising as a result of the tenant for life exercising a statutory power, e.g. of sale, must be paid to the trustees of the settlement. It is the duty of the trustees of the settlement to ensure that the capital money is invested or applied strictly in the manner prescribed by the Settled Land Act. In this sense they may be regarded as the 'watchdogs' of the settlement.

(b) The trust for sale

A statutory trust for sale under the Law of Property Act is an immediate binding trust for sale with or without a power at discretion to postpone the sale: s. 205, Law of Property Act 1925. Although a trust for sale is 'immediate and binding', there is always an implied power to postpone the sale unless the trust expresses a contrary intention.

Where the sale of land is postponed by the trustees, they enjoy wide statutory powers of dealing with and managing the land. The proceeds of any sale or any other capital money must be paid to at least two trustees or to a trust corporation, as the trust instrument provides.

Trusts for sale may be created by two instruments: first, a conveyance of the land to the trustees on trust for sale; secondly, a trust instrument setting out in detail the trusts on which the trustees hold the legal estate.

As soon as a trust for sale comes into operation, the legal estate is vested in the trustees and the interests of the beneficiaries are interests in the proceeds of sale. This is automatic and is known as the *equitable doctrine of conversion.* The equitable interests of the beneficiaries are shifted away from the land and attach to the proceeds of sale. This means that a purchaser from the trustees is able to take a conveyance of the land quite free from the equitable interests of the beneficiaries.

SUMMARY

1 The three great influences which have shaped the law of property are (1) the common law doctrines of tenure and the estate, (2) the invention of the trust and (3) the reforming legislation of 1925.

2 The first principle of tenure is that all land is held of the Crown. Those who held directly of the Crown were called tenants in chief. The tenants in chief granted sub-tenancies to lesser noblemen in return for services, military or otherwise. This system of tenure suited the needs of a feudal and agricultural society in which land was the prime source of wealth and influence.

3   When a tenant was in rightful possession of the land granted to him or inherited by him, he was said to be seised of the land. He had seisin. The duration of the right of seisin was known as the estate. Although a tenant could not own land, he could regard himself as the owner of this abstraction – the estate in the land.

4   The characteristic of the freehold estate was that there was no fixed duration for the tenant's right of seisin. Freeholders usually held their land for life. Estates of less than freehold were those of a fixed period of time.

5   During the thirteenth century it became possible to separate the nominal ownership of land from the beneficial ownership by means of the use. The modern equivalent of the use is the trust.

6   The purpose of the reforming legislation of 1925 was to simplify the law and the practice of conveyancing.

7   Section 1(1) of the Law of Property Act 1925 provided that the only estates in land which are capable of subsisting or of being conveyed or created at law are (a) an estate in fee simple absolute in possession, and (b) a term of years absolute.

8   The only interests or charges in or over land which are capable of subsisting or of being conveyed or created at law are those set out in section 1(2) of the Law of Property Act.

9   By section 1(3) of the Law of Property Act, all estates, interests and charges in or over land, other than those specified in section 1(1) and (2), will take effect as equitable interests.

10   'Fee simple' denotes an estate of general inheritance, i.e., it does not pass to a particular class of descendants as does, e.g., a fee tail.

11   An estate is 'absolute' when it extends in time without any condition to defeat or determine it.

12   'Possession' in the context of a fee simple absolute has a wider meaning than mere physical possession for, by s. 205 of the Law of Property Act 1925, the word includes the receipt or the right to receive rents and profits.

13   Mortgages, licences, easements, profits, rentcharges and restrictive covenants are rights *in alieno solo*. They are legal interests if they are created by deed and expressed to subsist for a duration equivalent to that of one of the legal estates under s. 1 of the Law of Property Act 1925. All other interests are equitable.

14   By s. 4 of the Settled Land Act 1925 every settlement of a legal estate in land *inter vivos* must be effected by two deeds, namely a vesting deed and a trust instrument.

15   Where a settlement is made by will, the settlor's personal repre-

sentatives hold the estate on trust to convey it to the tenant for life. The settlor's will serves the same purpose as the trust instrument.

16 The person of full age who is beneficially entitled for the time being under a strict settlement to possession of settled land for his life is the tenant for life of that land. The Settled Land Act confers wide powers of dealing with the land on the tenant for life.

17 Capital money arising as a result of the tenant for life exercising a statutory power, e.g., of sale, must be paid to the trustees of the settlement.

18 A statutory trust for sale under the Law of Property Act 1925 is an immediate binding trust for sale with or without a power at discretion to postpone the sale. There is an implied power to postpone sale unless the contrary is expressed in the trust.

19 As soon as a trust for sale comes into operation, the legal estate is vested in the trustees and the interests of the beneficiaries are interests in the proceeds of sale. This is automatic and is known as the equitable doctrine of conversion.

EXERCISES

1 Explain how the common law doctrine of tenure suited the needs of English society in the middle ages.

2 What is meant by 'seisin'?

3 What is the characteristic of the freehold estate in terms of seisin?

4 'It was only the freeholders who had seisin.' Comment on this statement and expand it.

5 In case of dispossession, a freeholder would have an action *in rem* to recover his seisin; but a tenant with an estate of less than freehold would have an action *in personam* only. Explain why.

6 Explain how land was put in use. What were the wider implications of the invention of the use?

7 What is the doctrine of the bona fide purchaser?

8 How were the rights of beneficial owners protected in, say, the fifteenth century?

9 What was the purpose of the property legislation of 1925?

10 What legal estates in land are capable of subsisting today?

11 What legal interests in land are capable of subsisting today?

12 How would you define an equitable interest in land? Give some examples.

13 What is an easement?

14 Define carefully a fee simple absolute in possession. Be particularly careful to explain the meaning of 'absolute'.

15 Explain what is meant by 'a term of years absolute'.

16 What is a mortgage? Are there legal and equitable mortgages? If so, what is the difference?

17 There are three kinds of licence. What are they?

18 What four elements together comprise an easement?

19 What is a *profit à prendre?*

20 Explain carefully the difference between a strict settlement and a trust for sale. Mention how they are created. Who is the tenant for life? What are the functions of the trustees in each kind of settlement? Why is a trust for sale sometimes called a 'trader's settlement'?

21 On reflection over this chapter, assess the significance, in the long term development of the law over the past thousand years, of (1) the doctrine of tenure and the estate, (2) the invention of the use and (3) the legislation of 1925.

CHAPTER 9

COMPANY LAW

(All references are to the Companies Act 1985 unless otherwise indicated.)

9.1 INTRODUCTORY MATTERS

(a) Corporate personality

This chapter is concerned with the most familiar kind of corporation aggregate, namely, the company formed by registration under the Companies Acts. The concept of legal personality was discussed in Chapter 4.2(b) where it was explained that a corporation has a legal personality which is separate and distinct from those persons who from time to time constitute its membership. The result is that a corporation aggregate can enjoy and enforce rights and, by the same token, may become subject to duties and obligations which are enforceable against it. All corporations are capable of perpetual succession.

Salomon v. *Salomon & Co. Ltd* (1897) is the leading case which shows very clearly the principle of separate corporate personality. In this case before the House of Lords, the appellant was one Aron Salomon who had, for about thirty years, carried on a wholesale boot business under the name of A. Salomon & Co. Salomon then formed a limited company to carry on this business. The subscribers to the memorandum of association were Salomon, his wife and daughter and his four sons, thus complying with the statutory requirements then in force. The nominal capital of the company was £40,000 divided into £1 shares. The total number of shares issued was 20,007. Salomon held 20,001 shares, and one share each was held by the members of his family as signatories of the memorandum. The company was named Salomon & Co. Limited.

(At this stage it is necessary to understand that we are concerned with two persons: first, Aron Salomon and secondly, A. Salomon & Co. Limited. Although there is a similarity in names, there are two separate and distinct legal persons.) Salomon's business was sold to the company for £38,782, which was a substantial over-valuation of the business known to all members of the company, i.e., Salomon's family and, therefore, perfectly lawful. At the first meeting of the directors, that is to say, Salomon and two of his sons, it was resolved to pay to Salomon £6,000 in cash and £10,000 in debentures, i.e., a debt of £10,000 due from the company to Salomon. This debt was secured by a floating charge on the assets of the company, that is to say, a charge which did not attach itself to any specific property of the company until an order was made by the court of the liquidation of the company. In the liquidation, the debts outstanding to unsecured creditors amounted to £7,333, and the liquidator claimed in the action (1) to have Salomon's debentures delivered up and cancelled and (2) that Salomon should repay all amounts which had been paid to him by the company. It was held by the House of Lords that, since the company was properly constituted by registration under the Companies Act in force at the time, the company was a separate legal person. It followed that Salomon's debentures should be paid by the company in preference to the sums due to the unsecured creditors. It was also decided that there were no grounds on which Salomon could be forced to repay sums paid to him by the company.

(b) Limited liability

By section 1(2) of the Companies Act 1985, companies may be limited by shares or by guarantee or they may be unlimited. It is fundamental to company law that it is the liability of the members to the company itself that is being referred to in section 1(2). The general rule is that, in the case of a limited company, a shareholder cannot be called upon to contribute more to the company than the amount still unpaid on his shares. Where the shares are fully paid up (and this is by far the most usual position) the company and its creditors have no claim against the shareholders who are protected by their limited liability.

(c) Kinds of registered company

All companies are either public or private. In England and Wales there are about 5,000 public companies and 800,000 private companies.

(i) Public companies.
Section 1(3) of the Companies Act 1985 defines a public company as a

company limited by shares or limited by guarantee and having a share capital, being a company:

(*a*) the memorandum of which states that the company is to be a public company; and

(*b*) in relation to which the statutory requirements of registration as a public company have been complied with.

By section 1(4), it is prohibited to form any new companies limited by guarantee and having a share capital. It would seem that this type of company - never numerous - will dwindle in number in the course of time.

(ii) Private companies.
Section 1(3) defines a private company as a company which is not a public company.

9.2 PUBLIC COMPANIES

(a) Formation of a company

Any two or more persons associated for a lawful purpose may, by subscribing their names to a memorandum of association and otherwise complying with the requirements of the Act, form a company: s. 1(1).

(i) The memorandum of association.
Section 2 states the required contents of the memorandum to be as follows:

(*a*) *The name of the company.* In the case of a public company, the name must end with the words 'public limited company' and, in the case of a private company, with the words 'limited'. These expressions may be abbreviated to 'p.l.c.' or 'Ltd' as the case may be: ss. 25 and 27.

(*b*) *A statement that it is to be a public company* (if such is the case).

(*c*) *The domicile of the company,* which will be either England, Scotland or Wales.

(*d*) *The objects of the company.*

(*e*) *The limitation of liability of members.* This will usually be by shares.

(*f*) *The amount of share capital* which must be divided into shares of a fixed amount.

(ii) The articles of association.
The articles are the internal regulations for the management of a company.

As a matter of comparison, the memorandum may be regarded as the basic constitution of a company.

By s. 7 a company limited by shares may register articles; a company limited by guarantee or an unlimited company must register articles. Where articles are registered they must be signed by the same persons who subscribed the memorandum of association.

Where articles are not registered, Table A will govern the internal management of the company. (Table A is a model form of articles for public or private companies limited by shares.)

By section 14(1) the memorandum and articles bind the company and its members to the same extent as if they had been signed and sealed by each member, and contained covenants on the part of each member to observe all the provisions of the memorandum and of the articles.

(iii) Registration.

By section 10, the memorandum and articles, if any, must be delivered to the registrar of companies for England and Wales if the registered office of the company is in England and Wales and the registrar must retain and register them.

In addition to the memorandum and articles (if any), the following documents must also be registered:

(a) A statement containing particulars of the directors and company secretary, together with their consents to act, and specifying the proposed address of the company's registered office. This statement must be signed by the subscribers of the memorandum.

(b) A statement of capital.

(c) A statement of compliance signed by a solicitor or a director or secretary.

When the registrar is satisfied that all statutory requirements have been satisfied he must, by section 13(1), certify that the company is incorporated. This certificate is known as the certificate of incorporation and the company is formed on the date given in it.

(iv) Commencement of business.

A private company may commence trading as soon as it is incorporated but a public company cannot do so until its trading certificate has been issued.

By section 117, the registrar will issue a trading certificate when he has received a statutory declaration signed by a director or the secretary stating: (1) that the nominal value of the allotted share capital is not less than the authorised minimum; (2) the amount paid up on the allotted share capital; (3) details of preliminary expenses; and (4) any amount paid or benefit given to any promoter and his consideration for it.

(v) The statutory books.

The documents which a company must keep are known as the statutory books. Most of these are required to be kept at the company's registered office.

The list of statutory books is as follows:

(*a*) the register of members;
(*b*) the register of directors and secretaries;
(*c*) the register of directors' interests in shares and debentures;
(*d*) directors' service contracts;
(*e*) the minute books of meetings (general meetings and directors' meetings);
(*f*) the register of charges;
(*g*) the register of interests in shares;
(*h*) the accounting records.

(b) Capital

Capital may be regarded as the money obtained by a company through the issue of shares. Sometimes the expression 'share capital' is used. It is now necessary to see how a public company may raise share capital from the public, how shares are allotted and how dividends become payable to the shareholders.

(i) Raising share capital.

There are three methods of raising share capital from the public, namely, by the issue of a prospectus, by an offer for sale and, finally, by placing.

A prospectus is defined in s. 744 as 'any prospectus, notice, circular, advertisement, or other invitation offering to the public for subscription or purchase any shares or debentures in a company'. The contents of every prospectus are strictly prescribed by the Act for the protection of investors. In particular, the minimum subscription must be stated. This is the amount which, in the opinion of the directors, must be raised in order to provide for (1) the price of any property to be paid for out of the issue; (2) preliminary expenses and underwriting commission; (3) the repayment of any money borrowed in respect of (1) or (2) above; and (4) working capital.

Directors, promoters and company officers concerned with the preparation and issue of a prospectus must be careful to comply with the detailed statutory requirements regarding its contents, particularly as to completeness and factual accuracy. Failure to comply can give rise to criminal or civil liability.

Although a prospectus has been described as 'offering' to the public, it is not strictly a contractual offer. It is an invitation to treat. The offer is made by the investor when he fills in the coupon in the newspaper advertisement and sends it to the company, offering to take shares in it.

Where those responsible for the issue do not wish to involve themselves in the immense amount of work and responsibility regarding a prospectus they may, alternatively, sell the shares to an issuing house which will then make an offer to sell to the public. An issuing house is a finance house specialising in this sort of activity. It makes a profit by selling new shares to the public at a slightly higher price than that paid to the company. The 'offer for sale' is the document published by the issuing house, usually in the newspapers, and this document is deemed to be a prospectus. Thus the investing public is protected as if there had been a prospectus.

Finally, a company may raise capital from the public by placing shares with a broker who will then circularise his clients with details of the issue. The broker is merely the agent of the company authorised to find buyers for the shares.

(ii) The allotment of shares.

By section 738, 'In relation to an allotment of shares in a company, the shares shall be taken ... to be allotted when a person acquires the unconditional right to be included in the company's register of members in respect of those shares'. There are, of course, other methods of gaining membership of a company of which the most usual is purchase from an existing member.

In the case of capital being raised by means of a prospectus or offer for sale, it is the applicant who makes the contractual offer to buy, as has been stated earlier. Usually the offer is made in the application form included in the newspaper advertisement, so that under the rules of offer and acceptance the company (as offeree) is able to accept or reject share applications.

There are numerous stringent provisions in the Act governing allotment. Of all these provisions, the most far-reaching is that contained in section 80, which applies equally to public and private companies. In general, directors may not allot shares unless they are authorised to do so by either a general meeting or by the articles. The authority thus given may never endure for more than five years. It must contain a statement of the maximum amount of securities authorised to be allotted and the date when the authority is to expire. This strict rule governing the authority to allot does not apply to the shares taken by subscribers to the memorandum or to shares allotted under a share scheme for employees.

(iii) Pre-emption rights.

Section 89 of the Act precludes a company from allotting new shares for cash until each present shareholder has been given an opportunity to obtain a proportion of the total new allotment equal to the proportion of shares already held by him. Where there is any contravention of any of the detailed provisions governing the pre-emption rights of existing shareholders, the company and the responsible company officers are liable, jointly and severally, to compensate any person to whom an offer should have been made.

(iv) Classes of shares.

The share capital of a company may comprise shares each of which carries identical rights. It is quite usual, however, for a company to issue shares carrying different rights from any of those previously issued. The rights attaching to each category of shares are called class rights. The rights of the shareholders in each class will usually be stated in the memorandum or the articles, as well as in the relevant prospectus or offer for sale, and may vary with regard to any of the following matters: (1) voting at company meetings, (2) dividend entitlement and (3) rights with regard to return of capital and surplus assets in the event of liquidation of the company.

Broadly, there are three kinds of shares, namely, preference shares, ordinary shares and deferred shares.

(a) *Preference shares.* These have the great advantage of a fixed preferred dividend, i.e., a dividend payable to the preference shareholders of a fixed percentage before any dividend may be paid to the ordinary shareholders. Preference shares are regarded as a safe investment in difficult or uncertain times.

(b) *Ordinary shares.* After the preference shareholders have been paid their fixed percentage dividend, the remaining profits for distribution will go to the ordinary shareholders. If the memorandum or articles provide that the preference shareholders are to have a prior right to the return of their capital in the event of liquidation, then the surplus assets, if any, will be distributed among the ordinary shareholders. Ordinary shares often constitute the 'equity share capital'.

(c) *Deferred shares.* These are a special kind of share normally issued only to promoters or directors. Where deferred shares are issued, the ordinary shares will usually carry a fixed dividend and, after this has been paid, any surplus profit to be distributed will be paid by way of dividend to the deferred shareholders. The issue of deferred shares changes the entire nature of the ordinary shares which cannot then be regarded as the equity share capital, for the balance of risk of loss and chance of profit lies with the deferred shares. Deferred shares are, for this reason, rarely issued.

(v) Dividends.

The way in which a company declares and pays dividends is usually contained in the articles. Often the articles provide that the shareholders cannot increase the amount recommended by the directors. Table A contains such a provision.

The general rule is that dividends are payable only out of profits. Where no profit has been made, no dividends are payable. By s. 263 of the Act, there is a prohibition on any company, public or private, from making any distribution of assets except out of profits available for the purpose. The section goes on to provide that these are the company's *accumulated realised profits less its accumulated realised losses.*

(vi) Debentures.

A debenture is a document by which a company undertakes to repay money which has been lent to it. The loan may be on the part of a single lender or it may be one of a series by which a large number of lenders are able to lend on the same terms. Debentures are usually issued in a series and expressed to be secured by a charge on the company's assets. The charge may be fixed on some particular asset, e.g., a building, or it may be a 'floating charge' on the company's ever-changing movable assets, e.g., its stock in trade. Each debenture must be regarded as an entity in itself. For instance, when a number of debentures from the same series are transferred, there occurs a separate transfer for each separate debenture. There can be no transfer of a part of the debt evidenced by a debenture.

Sometimes, however, a loan is raised by the company in return for debenture stock certificates. Debenture stock is normally divisible into loan stock units of an amount fixed by the company. Any number of units can then be transferred, in accordance with the holder's wishes.

The holders of debentures and debenture stock are entitled to receive interest from the company according to the relevant terms of issue. This interest is quite different in nature from dividends. In particular, interest is payable out of the company's funds regardless of whether profits have been made or not.

(vii) Stock.

By s. 121 of the Act, a company may convert any of its fully paid shares into stock. Thus, on conversion, 1,000 £5 shares will become £5,000 worth of stock. Stock, like debenture stock, can be transferred in any amounts required, whereas shares can be transferred only as so many shares, each one an entity. In other words, each share must be transferred as a whole share – it cannot be subdivided.

(viii) Purchase of shares by a company.

A company may freely purchase shares in other companies and, indeed, there is normally no prohibition on companies holding shares in each other. Where, however, a company proposes to buy its own shares, then problems arise because the result of such a purchase would be a reduction of capital. There would be a similar result where a company lent money to any person for the purchase of its own shares and that person failed to repay it.

At common law, a company may not own shares in itself. The rule has now been given statutory force by s. 143(1) of the Act. The section provides that no company limited by shares or limited by guarantee and having a share capital may acquire its own shares whether by purchase, subscription or otherwise. Section s. 143(2) provides for a single exception to the prohibition, namely, an acquisition by way of gift to the company. Section 143 has been extended by s. 151 of the Act which prohibits the giving of financial assistance by any company for the purpose of the acquisition of shares in that company. This prohibition is subject to a number of complex statutory exceptions.

(c) The operation of a company

(i) Directors.

Every public company must have at least two directors and every private company must have at least one: s. 282 of the Act. A sole director may not also be the company secretary: s. 283.

A director is an officer of the company and may act as agent for it but, as a director, he is not an employee of the company. There is no prohibition, however, on a director entering into a contract of employment with the company or a contract for services, e.g., a consultancy agreement. Where any such agreement is expressed to endure for a period exceeding five years, it must be approved by the company in general meeting: s. 319.

By s. 10 of the Act, a statement regarding the registered office and the directors must be registered on incorporation (9.2(a) (*iii*) (*a*)). The directors named in this statement are deemed to have been appointed the first directors of the company. Subsequent directors are appointed in accordance with the articles or Table A if it applies. In the case of a public company the directors must be elected individually; two or more directors cannot be elected on a single vote unless the meeting has first passed a resolution, without any dissent, to vote on them together.

There are a number of provisions in the Companies Acts which require directors to notify the company of their interests, direct and indirect, in shares and debentures of the company. These interests must be registered by the company and by paras. 25 and 26 of Schedule 13 any person may inspect or require a copy of the register of directors' interests from the company on payment of a nominal fee. All payments to directors must be disclosed in company accounts in the form prescribed by the Companies Act.

Apart from compliance with the complex and detailed requirements of the Act, directors have two basic non-statutory duties towards the company, namely, (1) the requirement of good faith and (2) a duty of care. The first of these is very strict in English law. Directors must act in good faith for the benefit of the company. It must be emphasised that this duty is owed to the company and not to the individual shareholders or any class of them.

(ii) Company meetings.

There are three kinds of meetings of shareholders, namely, (1) annual general meetings, (2) extraordinary general meetings and (3) class meetings.

(*a*) *Annual general meetings.* By s. 366 of the Act, every company must hold a general meeting as its annual general meeting once in each calendar year. The notices calling an annual general meeting must specify it as such. The ordinary business of an annual general meeting comprises: (1) declaring a dividend; (2) considering the accounts, the directors' report and the auditors' report; (3) the election of directors; and (4) the appointment of the auditors.

The contents of the published accounts, the directors' report and the auditors' report are strictly controlled by the Act.

(*b*) *Extraordinary general meetings.* The directors *may* at any time they think fit convene an extraordinary general meeting, i.e., a general meeting other than the annual general meeting. The directors *must,* by s. 368 of the Act, convene an extraordinary general meeting on the requisition of members holding not less than one-tenth of the paid-up capital carrying the right to vote. The business of an extraordinary general meeting may comprise any business which is required by the Companies Act or articles to be done by general meeting.

(*c*) *Class meetings.* Where shareholders of a particular class of shares wish to hold a meeting, e.g. to discuss some proposed variation of their class rights, they may hold their meeting without any other member being present.

(*d*) *Resolutions.* Decisions of the shareholders at meetings are termed resolutions. There are three types of resolution which vary as to the majority required and the period of notice necessary.

(i) *ordinary* resolutions require a simple majority and the period of notice must be not less than 14 days;

(ii) *special* resolutions require a 75 per cent majority and the period of notice must be not less than 21 days;

(iii) *extraordinary* resolutions require a 75 per cent majority and the period of notice must be not less than 14 days.

(iii) Annual return.

By s. 363 of the Act every company limited by shares must make an annual return to the registrar containing the following information:
(1) the address of the registered office; (2) the address where registers of members and debenture holders are kept; (3) a summary of shares issued (in prescribed form showing those issued otherwise than for cash); (4) total indebtedness in respect of registrable charges; (5) a list of members and their holdings; and (6) particulars of directors and secretary.

The annual return must be submitted within 42 days after the date of the annual general meeting.

(iv) Accounts.

By s. 224 of the Act, any company may give notice to the registrar within six months from incorporation specifying a date on which the company's accounting reference period is to end. This date is known as the 'accounting reference date'. Where a company does not give such notice to the registrar, its accounting reference date will be 31 March.

By s. 241 of the Act the directors of every company must, in respect of each accounting reference period, deliver to the registrar the following accounting documents: (1) the profit and loss account; (2) the balance sheet; (3) the auditors' report; (4) the directors' report and (5) group accounts where the company has subsidiaries: s. 239.

The Companies Acts do not require the publication of accounts – merely that they be filed with the registrar. Where, however, a company chooses to publish its accounts, the requirements of the Act ensure that the accounts, as published, are adequate and not misleading if abridged.

(v) Auditors.

By s. 384 of the Act, the directors may appoint the first auditors at any time before the first general meeting at which the accounts are laid before the company. Section 384 also provides for the appointment of one or more subsequent auditors at each general meeting where the accounts are laid before the company.

The main duty of an auditor is to show in his report the true financial position of the company as shown in the company's books. The requirements for his report are set out in detail in ss. 236 and 237 of the Act. In order to prepare the report, an auditor must check the cash in hand and the bank balance and verify the existence and safe custody of any securities. An auditor must be honest and carry out his duties with reasonable skill and care. An auditor is not concerned with management of the company or with policy matters; nor is he responsible for checking stock unless there are circumstances which raise his suspicions.

(vi) Unfair prejudice and insider dealing.
These are two areas in which company legislation is designed to protect the interests of shareholders.

By s. 459 of the Act, any member of a company may apply to the court by petition for an order under this section on the ground that the affairs of the company are being or have been conducted in a manner which is *unfairly prejudicial* to the interests of some part of the members (including at least himself) or that any actual or proposed act or omission of the company would be so prejudicial. If the court is satisfied that any petition under s. 459 is well-founded, it may make such order as it thinks fit.

'Insider dealing' is a general term meaning any dealing in securities by a person who has inside information which would affect the price if it were generally known. Under the Act there are numerous punishable offences with regard to insider dealing, or procuring another person to deal, or communicating information for the purpose of dealing. The prescribed penalties for these offences include prison sentences of up to two years.

(d) Winding up

There are several ways in which a company may be dissolved. Of these, the most common are: (1) when defunct companies are struck off the register by the registrar and (2) by winding up (liquidation). Although striking off the register is by no means uncommon, it is outside the scope of this book, which is concerned only with winding up as a means of dissolution.

There are three methods of winding up, namely, (1) compulsory winding up (i.e. by the court); (2) members' or creditors' voluntary winding up; and (3) winding up subject to the supervision of the court.

(i) Compulsory winding up
By s. 517, a company may be wound up by the court if:

(*a*) the company has passed a special resolution to that effect;
(*b*) a public company, registered as such on its original incorporation, has not been issued with its trading certificate within a year from registration (9.2(a) *(iv)*);
(*c*) the company is an old public company within s. 1 Companies Consolidation (Consequential Provisions) Act 1985;
(*d*) the company does not commence business within one year from incorporation or suspends business for a year;
(*e*) the number of members is reduced below two;
(*f*) the company is unable to pay its debts;
(*g*) the court is of the opinion that it would be just and equitable for the company to be wound up.

The process of winding up on any of the above grounds is begun by a petition usually presented by one of the following: the company itself on passing a special resolution, a creditor or a contributory, i.e., a person liable to contribute towards the company's assets in a winding up. Contributories are, in the main, the holders of shares which are only partly paid up. The holder is liable to pay to the company the amount not yet paid on each share.

On hearing the petition, the court has wide powers: it can make any order it thinks fit. If a winding up order is made, the commencement of the winding up is the time of the presentation of the petition (unless previously the company had passed a resolution for voluntary winding up, in which case the winding up is deemed to have commenced on the date of the resolution). The commencement of winding up is a significant date with important legal and financial consequences.

Where a winding up order is made, a statement of the company's affairs must be made in the prescribed form to the official receiver by one of the directors or the secretary. The official receiver is an official of the Department of Trade and Industry who is attached to the court.

The liquidator is appointed by the court. Wide statutory powers are conferred on the liquidator to enable him to conclude the dissolution of the company. In short, he must call in the assets of the company and use them to pay the debts of the company in strict order of priority. When the liquidator has completed his duties, he may apply to the court for a dissolution order – this completes the process and the company is dissolved from the date of the order.

(ii) Voluntary winding up.
By s. 572(1), a company may be wound up voluntarily:

(a) when the period, if any, fixed for the duration of the company by the articles expires, or the event, if any, occurs, on the occurrence of which the articles provide that the company is to be dissolved, and the company in general meeting has passed an ordinary resolution requiring the company to be wound up voluntarily;

(b) if the company resolves by special resolution that the company be wound up voluntarily;

(c) if the company resolves by extraordinary resolution to the effect that it cannot by reason of its liabilities continue its business, and that it is advisable to wind up.

Section 577(1) provides that where it is proposed to wind up a company voluntarily, the directors or, in the case of a company having more than two directors, the majority of them may, at a meeting of the directors make a statutory declaration that they have made a full inquiry into the affairs of the company, and that they have formed the opinion that the company will be able to pay its debts in full within the period specified in the declaration. This period must not exceed twelve months.

Where there is a declaration of solvency under s. 572(1), the winding up process will be controlled by the members of the company – it will be 'a members' voluntary winding up'; but where there is no declaration of solvency, the winding up will be under the control of the creditors – it will be a 'creditors winding up'.

(iii) Winding up subject to the supervision of the court.
By s. 606, when a company has passed a resolution for voluntary winding up, the court may make an order that the voluntary winding up shall continue subject to the supervision of the court, and with liberty for creditors, contributories, or others, to apply to the court. This type of winding up is extremely rare.

(e) Lifting the veil of incorporation

The fundamental rule of corporation law is that a corporation aggregate is a person separate and distinct from those natural persons or other corporations which comprise its membership. It follows that any claim against the corporation aggregate will be met by the corporation and not the individual members or any of them; any liability or responsibility of the corporation is that of the corporation and not that of any individual member.

In cases where the corporate device is operated as a mere sham to provide a façade for acts of certain members or directors, the law may provide an exception to the principle of separate legal personality by allowing the so-called 'veil of incorporation' to be lifted to reveal the true actors. However, this will be allowed only in exceptional circumstances. For example, under the Act, the Department of Trade and Industry may investigate membership (s. 442); as regards the company's debts, in certain circumstances, members may become liable (ss. 24 and 630); and by ss. 239 and 241, group accounts must be laid before the holding company in the annual general meeting, thus treating a group of companies as a single entity.

9.3 PRIVATE COMPANIES

(a) Definition

The definition of a private company given in s. 1(3) of the Act is, 'a company which is not a public company' (9.1(c) above). One of the results of recent legislation is the increase in the number of points of difference between private and public companies. There is now such a difference between the two kinds of company that, for practical purposes, they may be regarded as different kinds of corporation.

130

(b) Points of difference between public and private companies

Some of the more important points of difference are set out below.

(i) Directors
  (*a*) The statutory minimum is one in the case of a private company and two in the case of a public company.
  (*b*) Two or more directors of a private company can be appointed by a single resolution while in the case of a public company a separate resolution on the appointment of each director is normally required.

(ii) Capital
  (*a*) In the case of a private company trading may be commenced as soon as it is incorporated; a public company cannot commence trading until it has obtained its trading certificate.
  (*b*) In the case of a private company it is an offence to offer shares or debentures to the public.
  (*c*) Non-cash consideration for shares in a private company is not subject to the same strict rules as those contained in ss. 99, 102 and 103 of the Act for public companies.
  (*d*) Statutory pre-emption rights are mandatory in the case of new issues of shares in public companies; in the case of private companies, pre-emption rights can be excluded by the memorandum or articles.
  (*e*) The strict rules prohibiting the giving of financial assistance by a public company for the purpose of the acquisition of its own shares are not fully applicable to financial assistance given by private companies for that purpose.
  (*f*) A private company may, subject to certain safeguards, purchase its own shares out of capital; a public company is prohibited from such a purchase.

(iii) Dividends
  (*a*) There is no need for a private company to file interim accounts before distribution of profits; in the case of public companies interim accounts can in certain cases be required to support the distribution.
  (*b*) A public company may make a distribution only if (1) at the time its net assets are not less than the aggregate of the company's called-up share capital and its undistributable reserves and (2) if, and to the extent that, the distribution does not reduce the amount of those assets to less than that aggregate. This rule does not apply to private companies.

SUMMARY

1   The case of *Salomon* v. *Salomon & Co. Ltd* (1897) shows clearly the principle of separate corporate personality.

2   A company may be limited by shares or by guarantee or it may be unlimited. In the case of a company limited by shares, a shareholder cannot be called upon to contribute more to the company than the amount, if any, still unpaid on his shares.

3   Companies may be public, as defined in s. 1(3) of the Act, or they may be private. A private company is one which does not comply with the statutory definition of a public company.

4   Section 2 states the required contents of the memorandum of association.

5   The memorandum may be regarded as the constitution of a company: the articles of association are the internal regulations for the management of a company.

6   Memorandum and articles must be registered.

7   The statutory books are those documents which must be kept at the company's registered office. There are eight statutory books.

8   There are three methods of raising share capital from the public.

9   The Act gives pre-emption rights to present shareholders.

10   A company may issue shares of different classes.

11   The three kinds of shares are preference shares, ordinary shares and deferred shares.

12   The general rule is that dividends are payable only out of profits.

13   A debenture is a document by which a company undertakes to repay money which has been lent to it.

14   Every public company must have at least two directors and every private company must have at least one.

15   There are three kinds of meetings of shareholders, namely, (1) annual general meetings, (2) extraordinary general meetings and (3) class meetings.

16   Every company limited by shares must make an annual return to the registrar.

17   The appointment of auditors is governed by s. 384 of the Act.

18   The Act contains provisions against unfair prejudice and insider dealing.

19   There are three methods of winding up, namely, (1) compulsory winding up, (2) members' or creditors' voluntary winding up and (3) winding up subject to the supervision of the court.

20   In exceptional circumstances the law may provide for the lifting of the so-called veil of incorporation.

21   The points of difference between public companies and private companies have been much increased by recent legislation. The main points of difference concern (1) directors, (2) capital and (3) dividends.

EXERCISES

1 State the facts of any case which illustrates the principle of separate corporate personality. Explain the decision of the court in the case you mention.

2 Explain what is meant by 'limited liability'.

3 Give the statutory definition of a public company.

4 Explain in detail the process of formation of a company. Give the detailed contents of the main documents involved.

5 What are the statutory books?

6 What is share capital and how is it raised?

7 What are pre-emption rights?

8 Explain what is meant by 'class rights'.

9 Distinguish three kinds of share and explain in detail the main features of each.

10 What are dividends and how are they paid?

11 Write an explanatory note on debentures.

12 May a company purchase its own shares?

13 Explain the rules governing the appointment of directors.

14 What are the duties of directors?

15 What is the difference between the annual general meeting and an extraordinary general meeting?

16 Distinguish three kinds of resolution and explain each.

17 What must be included in a company's annual return?

18 Outline the rules governing company accounts. Mention the role of auditors.

19 What provisions govern unfair prejudice and insider dealing?

20 What is the difference between compulsory and voluntary winding up? Your answer should include the detailed procedure in each case.

21 What is the 'veil of incorporation' and when may it be lifted?

22 Define a private company.

23 List as many points of difference between public companies and private companies as you can.

PART III
CONTRACTS

CONTRACTUAL RIGHTS AND OBLIGATIONS

When a plaintiff sues a defendant for breach of contract he must allege that the defendant entered into a contract with him. If the defendant is able to prove that there was, in fact, no contract, then the plaintiff will fail. There is a set of legal rules governing the essential ingredients of a contract. These will be applied in order to resolve the question whether there was a contract. These rules are concerned with the concept of agreement, of consideration and of intention to create legal relations. It is well to remember, when reading the paragraphs dealing with agreement, consideration and intention, that these concepts have their great significance when the question is raised: *Is there a contract?*

The plaintiff will also be required to state which detail of the contract is alleged to have been breached. In order to succeed in this, he will have to show the terms of the contract. He will have to show the specific term which the defendant has allegedly broken. If the defendant succeeds in denying that the alleged term is a part of the contract, the plaintiff will have failed. In such cases, the argument will be on the question: *What are the terms of this contract?* When reading the paragraphs below about terms of contract, it should be remembered that these are the rules to be applied to resolve this question.

10.1 WHAT IS A CONTRACT?

A contract is an agreement: but not all agreements are contracts.

A contract is sometimes defined as a legally enforceable agreement. This means that a contract is enforceable in the sense that there is a legal remedy available in case one party should fail to comply with his promise under the agreement. The usual remedy is money compensation known as damages. The practical effect is that a contracting party has two commercial alternatives: he can either carry out the contract or pay compensation.

(a) Simple contracts and specialties

An agreement is made when a firm offer is unconditionally accepted by the offeree. The offeror and offeree then become parties to the agreement. If the agreement is to be binding it must be either a simple contract or a specialty. In the case of a simple contract, the parties must have intended to create legal relations and there must be consideration, i.e. each party must have contributed something to the bargain. In the case of a specialty, the agreement must be contained in a deed which has been formally executed by the parties. A further requirement in both cases is that the agreement must not be vitiated by misrepresentation, mistake, or undue influence.

A simple contract generally requires no formalities. If there is *agreement* supported by *consideration* and made with the *intention of creating legal relations,* there is a simple contract. There is no need for the contract to be in writing unless this is required by statute. The most important examples of contracts which are not enforceable unless in writing or evidenced in writing are those affected by the Statute of Frauds 1677 and s. 40 of the Law of Property Act 1925.

Only in special circumstances is it necessary or advisable to express the terms of a contract in the form of a deed. There are three acts in the execution of a deed, namely, signing, sealing and delivery. The common law did not require a signature before 1926, although this was required by the Statute of Frauds 1677 for certain types of contract. By the Law of Property Act 1925, s. 73, all deeds executed after 1925 must be signed. Signing is thus a relatively new requirement in a deed compared with sealing, which is a requirement going back to Norman times. It is the usage of sealing which makes the contract a specialty. In former times, the seal was imprinted on wax and a person executing a deed would put his finger on the sealed wax and say, 'This I deliver as my act and deed'. Nowadays, although coloured paper wafer seals are often stuck on the document, it is not absolutely necessary to have any kind of seal: it is sufficient if the language of the document expresses it to be a deed. There are special rules for sealing by corporations contained in s. 74 of the Law of Property Act 1925. The third act is delivery, which completes the deed. If the document is not dated it will be effective from the date of delivery.

A specialty differs from a simple contract in two respects. First, there is no need for consideration and, secondly, there is a longer limitation period, namely, twelve years as compared with six. The limitation period is the statutory period during which the plaintiff may bring his action. It is now governed by the Limitation Act 1980.

This book is mainly concerned with simple contracts, but there will be an occasional reference to specialty contracts.

It should now be clear that there are three elements essential to the formation of a simple contract: (1) agreement, (2) consideration and (3) intention to create legal relations. If any one of these elements should be missing, there is no contract. Indeed, it is not unusual for the defendant in a breach of contract action to raise the defence that there is no contract. In such cases the defendant will argue either that there was no agreement, or no consideration, or no intention to create legal relations, as the case may be.

(b) The terms of a contract

Where agreement is reached, the acceptance of the offer must be totally unconditional. It follows that the legal effect of the acceptance is to transform the contents of the offer (or counter-offer) into the contents of the agreement. The contents of the agreement should be called the terms of the agreement. Most terms of agreement are expressed by the parties in writing or by word of mouth, but there are other terms which may arise by necessary implication or by statute. In contract, we are thus concerned with express terms and implied terms and both are equally binding on the parties to a contract.

The great importance of the terms of contract is that (1) they define the rights and obligations of the parties and (2) the question whether a party is in breach of contract is tested by reference to them .

Where A and B enter into a contract, the rights of A are defined in the same terms as the obligations of B - and vice versa. For example, if A agrees to build a house for B for the sum of £150,000, A's right to receive £150,000 corresponds with B's obligation to pay that sum. Again, suppose X has agreed to sell his piano to Y but the agreement did not mention the price. In this case, the contract will not fail because of the omission to mention the price. If the sale has been clearly agreed, there is an implied term that a reasonable price is payable. In this example, X is under an express obligation to deliver the piano to Y in return for an implied right to be paid a reasonable price; or, to put it another way, Y is under an implied obligation to pay a reasonable price to X.

10.2 AGREEMENT

Agreement is reached when a firm offer is unconditionally accepted by the offeree. The rules governing offer and acceptance form an important part of the case-law of contract.

(a) The offer

An offer is a statement of the terms of a contract which the offeror is prepared to enter into with the offeree. An offer must be clear and complete so as to become the express terms in case a contract is formed.

An offer is to be distinguished from an invitation to treat, i.e. an invitation to make an offer. Invitations to treat are common in commercial dealings. For example, when a local authority wishes to have a school built, offers will be invited from building contractors. The invitation to tender will contain all the information needed by the builder to calculate his price for which he may offer to do the work. In such cases, the invitation will contain a technical description of the proposed building and a reference to the standard form conditions which are to govern the work. Each contractor who puts in a tender thereby makes an offer to carry out and complete the building for the price stated. He is, in effect, saying, 'I am prepared to become obliged to build a school of the description required and subject to the standard-form conditions for £x.' Should the offer be accepted, he will become contractually bound.

Goods with price labels attached constitute in themselves an invitation to treat when displayed in a shop window: *Fisher* v. *Bell* (1961). It is the same when goods are displayed on the shelves of a supermarket where customers help themselves: *Pharmaceutical Society* v. *Boots* (1953).* Where an auctioneer's advertisement listed goods to be sold by auction, it was held to be a mere statement of intention to sell, i.e. that it was an invitation to treat: *Harris* v. *Nickerson* (1873).

(b) Acceptance

A valid acceptance operates to create a contract between offeror and offeree. An acceptance must satisfy two requirements. First, it must be unqualified; secondly, it must be communicated to the offeror.

(i) Unqualified assent to the offer.

An acceptance demonstrates an intention to make a contract in terms identical to the terms of the offer. Where a purported acceptance alters the terms of the offer in any way, it will operate as a counter-offer. This will have the effect of rejecting the original offer which cannot thereafter be accepted. Thus, in *Hyde* v. *Wrench* (1840), a farm was offered for sale at £1,000. The offeree counter-offered to buy at £950 and this was rejected. The offeree then made a purported acceptance of the original offer for sale at £1,000. On the question whether there was a contract for sale at £1,000, it was held that there was no contract. The counter-offer had operated to reject the original offer.

Where, however, the counter-offer is accepted unconditionally, a contract is made in terms of the counter-offer: *Butler Machine Tool Co. v. Ex-Cell-O Corporation* (1979)*: *Davies & Co.* v. *Wm. Old* (1969)*.

(ii) Communication of acceptance.
The general rule is that the contract is made when acceptance is actually communicated to the offeror by the offeree. Where there is no communication there is no contract. This principle is illustrated by the case of *Felthouse* v. *Bindley* (1863). In this case the plaintiff offered by letter to buy his nephew's horse for £30.15s. In the letter, he wrote, 'If I hear no more about him, I consider the horse mine at £30.15s.' The nephew did not reply although he intended to let the uncle have the horse at that price. Six weeks later, when the nephew was instructing an auctioneer to sell some of his farm animals, he said that the horse in question was already sold and, therefore, should not be auctioned. Contrary to these instructions, the auctioneer sold the horse. The uncle, thus deprived of the horse, sued the auctioneer in the tort of conversion. He failed in his action because he could not show that there was a contract by which he became owner of the horse. He had made a valid offer but there had been no acceptance of it communicated back to him. It was not sufficient that the nephew had intended to accept, for mere mental acceptance does not operate to make a contract. Acceptance must be communicated to the offeror.

(c) Acceptance by post

Where there is an instantaneous communication of acceptance, such as orally, or by telephone or by telex, the offeree and the offeror both know immediately that a binding contract has been made between them. Where, however, the post is used for sending the acceptance, there is a time lag between the despatch of the acceptance and its receipt by the offeror. There is a problem here which must be resolved by every modern system of law. The question is: when is the contract made? It is a matter of common sense that the least inconvenient point for the making of the contract is the moment of posting. On the basis of commercial convenience, then, the rule is that where the post is the proper manner of communication of the acceptance, the contract is made at the moment when the acceptance is posted: *Henthorn* v. *Fraser* (1892).* It must follow that where the acceptance is lost in the post, the contract is made nevertheless: *Household Fire Insurance Co.* v. *Grant* (1879). The so-called postal rule should be seen as an exception to the general rule that acceptance must be communicated to the offeror.

(d) Acceptance by compliance with the requirements of the offer

The second exception to the rule that acceptance must be communicated occurs where the offeror defines in his offer the· performance required from the offeree. Offers of this kind, in effect, invite the offeree to perform his acceptance rather than to communicate it. Such offers are recognisable from the language used and the nature of the transaction involved. The most common example is the offer to pay a reward, e.g. for the return of lost or stolen property. The return of the offeror's property constitutes the performance which amounts to acceptance of the offer. A contract made in this way is known as a *unilateral* contract. The celebrated example is to be found in *Carlill* v. *Carbolic Smoke Ball Co.* (1893). In this case, the manufacturers of a medical preparation called a smoke ball published a newspaper advertisement in which they said that they would pay £100 reward to any person who caught influenza after using a smoke ball in the specified manner. The plaintiff caught influenza after using a smoke ball. She claimed the £100 reward. It was held that the advertisement was an offer to pay £100 to anybody who would perform the conditions set out in it. Performance constituted acceptance of the offer and, therefore, the plaintiff was entitled to the reward of £100.

(e) Method of communication of acceptance

Apart from the two exceptional cases where communication is not required, the acceptance must be actually communicated to the offeror. If it is not so communicated there is no contract. The question to be considered now is whether it matters *how* communication is achieved. Problems arise where the offer stipulates for some particular method of communication; or where the circumstances raise the implication that a particular method should be used. The basic question then arises: does acceptance which is communicated in any other manner operate to make a binding contract? In *Tinn* v. *Hoffman & Co.* (1873), where the offer required acceptance by return of post, it was held that there could be an acceptance by any means arriving not later than a letter sent by return, e.g. by telegram or by verbal message. In *Manchester Diocesan Council for Education* v. *Commercial and General Investments Ltd.* (1969), the *Tinn* v. *Hoffman* principle was applied and it was said that where the offeror has prescribed a particular method of acceptance, but not in terms insisting that only acceptance in that mode shall be binding, an acceptance communicated by any other mode which is no less advantageous to the offeror will conclude the contract. See also *Holwell Securities* v. *Hughes* (1973)*.

(f) Termination of an offer

The legal characteristic of an offer is that acceptance transforms the terms of the offer into the terms of an agreement. The next question to be considered is: for how long does the offer retain this characteristic? The answer is that an offer continues to retain its legal characteristic until one of the following events has occurred: rejection, revocation or lapse. Another way of saying the same thing is that an offer may be terminated by rejection, revocation or lapse.

(i) Rejection.

An offer may be terminated by the express rejection of the offeree. Where the offeree makes a counter-offer there is an implied rejection of the original offer.

(ii) Revocation.

An offer may be revoked by the offeror at any time before acceptance has taken place, i.e. until the contract has been made. Upon acceptance, the offeror is bound by the terms of the offer and he may not revoke it. The offeror's revocation is not effective until actually communicated to the offeree. Where the parties are in immediate communication with each other, no problem arises as to the validity of a revocation; but where there is a time lag in communication, e.g. where the post is used, then the rule that revocation must be communicated needs careful application. Where the so-called postal rule governs the acceptance, it should be applied first. This will decide two matters: first, whether there was any acceptance at all and, second, when acceptance (if any) took place. Next, the rule of communication of revocation must be applied to see which happened first, i.e. which is valid – the revocation or the acceptance. In *Payne* v. *Cave* (1789), the offeror made a bid at an auction sale which he withdrew before acceptance by the fall of the hammer. It was held that the revocation was effective. See also *Byrne* v. *Van Tienhoven* (1880)* and *Dickinson* v. *Dodds* (1876).*

The offeror is not precluded from withdrawing his offer before acceptance simply because he has said that he will keep his offer open for a stated period: *Routledge* v. *Grant* (1828). However, if the offeror has taken consideration in return for his undertaking to keep the offer open, he has contracted to keep it open. His position then is that he may still withdraw the offer before acceptance, but he will thereby break his binding undertaking to keep the offer open. In this case he will be liable to pay compensation to the offeree. The offeree's right to have the offer kept open is sometimes called an option.

(iii) Lapse.

Where the offeror stipulates that his offer is to remain open for a specified period of time, the offer will lapse if not accepted within that period. If no period is specified, then the offer will remain open for a reasonable time, after which it will lapse. What is reasonable is a question of fact which will depend upon the circumstances of each case. In *Ramsgate Victoria Hotel Co. Ltd.* v. *Montefiore* (1866) a hotel company purported to accept an offer to buy its shares. The purported acceptance was made five months after the offer was made. It was held that the offer had lapsed through passage of time before the acceptance was made. Therefore, there was no contract to buy the shares.

An offer may sometimes lapse on the death of either party, depending on the nature of the transaction in question, but the difficulties of this area of law fall outside the scope of an introductory book.

10.3 CONSIDERATION

(a) What is consideration?

In English law, an agreement is not binding unless each party, by the agreement, confers a benefit upon, or suffers a detriment in favour of, the other. By this requirement, a simple contract is a bargain to which each party contributes and from which each party obtains some benefit or advantage. Thus, in *Currie* v. *Misa* (1875), it was said that consideration 'may consist either in some right, interest, profit, or benefit accruing to one party, or some forbearance, detriment, loss, or responsibility given, suffered, or undertaken by the other'. The characteristic of this Victorian 'definition' is that it places in juxtaposition the benefit etc., on the one hand, and the detriment etc., on the other.

The concept of consideration usually becomes more easily understood in terms of a legal action for breach of contract where the defence is that there is no contract because the plaintiff gave no consideration to support the defendant's promise. The defendant is under no obligation to comply with his promise unless the plaintiff can show that he gave consideration in return for it. The plaintiff must be able to show that he performed some act or that he made some promise in return for the defendant's promise. If the plaintiff can show this, he will have shown that he gave consideration to support the defendant's promise which is, accordingly, binding on the defendant. Pollock used the terminology of the promise in his definition, which was adopted by the House of Lords in *Dunlop* v. *Selfridge* (1915). He said that: 'An act or forbearance of one party, or the promise thereof, is the price for which the promise of the other is bought, and the promise thus given for value is enforceable.' In this definition, the word 'value' may be equated with consideration.

Where the plaintiff's contribution to the bargain is a promise to be carried out later, the consideration is said to be executory. Where the act has been performed, the consideration is said to be executed. Executory consideration is no less effective than executed consideration.

(b) Consideration must be of some value to the defendant

If there is some clear value to the defendant, no matter how trivial, there is sufficient consideration. Even where there is no apparent value to the defendant, the fact that the plaintiff has complied with the request of the defendant will be sufficient consideration. Thus, in *Bainbridge* v. *Firmstone* (1838), the defendant had requested the plaintiff to allow him to take away his two boilers to weigh them. The plaintiff agreed to this on the undertaking of the defendant to return the boilers in good condition. When the plaintiff sued the defendant on this undertaking, it was held that consideration had moved from the plaintiff to the defendant. The consideration was that the plaintiff, at the defendant's request, had consented to allow the defendant to weigh the boilers. It was held not to be necessary to enquire what benefit the defendant expected to derive. Where consideration has no value at all to the defendant, it is said to be insufficient. The rule, as usually stated, is that consideration must be sufficient (or real).

Where the plaintiff's consideration comprises something which he is already bound to do, then it will not amount to a sufficient consideration. For example, in *Stilk* v. *Myrick* (1809), a ship's crew promised the captain that they would do the work of two seamen who had deserted the ship. They gave this promise in return for the captain's promise to share the deserters' wages among the crew. It was held that the captain's promise was not binding because the sailors had given no consideration. They were already bound by their contracts of employment to work the vessel home and this included doing the work of any deserter. This decision should be compared with that in *Hartley* v. *Ponsonby* (1858). In that case, the desertions were so numerous that the vessel was undermanned to a degree which rendered it unseaworthy. The seamen were, accordingly, released from their previous contractual obligations and free to enter into a new contract for higher wages.

In *Hartley* v. *Ponsonby* and *Stilk* v. *Myrick,* the question was whether the plaintiff owed an existing contractual obligation to the defendant. In *Ward* v. *Byham* (1956)* and *Glasbrook Bros. Ltd* v. *Glamorgan C.C.* (1925)*, the question was whether the plaintiff owed a previously existing public duty to the defendant. In *Shadwell* v. *Shadwell* (1860), *Scotson* v.

Pegg (1861) and *N.Z. Shipping Co. Ltd.* v. *A.M. Satterthwaite & Co. Ltd.* (1975) the question was whether the discharge of a contractual obligation to a third party constituted consideration. In the last-mentioned case, it was said by the Privy Council that: 'An agreement to do an act which the promisor is under an existing obligation to a third party to do, may quite well amount to valid consideration . . .'

(c) The court will not enquire into the adequacy of consideration

It is the function of the court to uphold contracts freely entered into. It is not their function to rescue a party from a bad bargain. In the absence of fraud, the validity of a contract is not affected by the inadequacy of the consideration given by one of the parties. In other words, where the plaintiff is suing for breach of contract, it is no defence that the plaintiff's consideration is worth less than the defendant's promise.

(d) Consideration must not be past

The rule of past consideration is just another way of saying that the plaintiff's consideration must be given in return for the defendant's promise. Any act done, or promise made, earlier than the defendant's promise, will constitute past consideration; and past consideration is no consideration. In *Re McArdle* (1951), as a result of the plaintiff's efforts, certain work was done to decorate and improve a house. The defendant's promise to the plaintiff was expressed to be made 'in consideration of your carrying out' the work in question. It was held that the defendant's promise was not binding because the consideration was past and, accordingly, invalid. There are three points which are usually made in connection with the rule of past consideration.

(i) Where there is an agreement to sell goods or to provide services with no provision for payment, there is an implied term that reasonable payment will be made. Any subsequent promise (by the party to benefit from the goods or services) to pay any specific amount will usually be binding. If that party is sued for the amount promised he cannot plead in his defence that the consideration for the promise is past. His promise to pay a specific amount will relate back to the implied obligation to pay a reasonable sum: *Re Casey's Patents* (1892).

(ii) Where the limitation period has run out and the right of action is statute-barred, the defendant may revive the right of action against him by a fresh acknowledgement in writing of the past debt or obligation (Chapter 13.1(f)). This is not an exception to the rule of past consideration. It is apparent only. The fresh accrual of the

plaintiff's right of action is a procedural matter, having nothing to do with the substantive contractual rights in question.

(iii) The only real exception to the rule of past consideration is contained in the Bills of Exchange Act 1882, s. 27(1) (b), which provides that 'an antecedent debt or liability' is good consideration for a bill of exchange.

(e) Consideration must move from the promisee

The plaintiff must be able to show that his consideration was given in return for the defendant's promise. Under the doctrine of privity of contract, the plaintiff must also be able to show that he is a party to the contract with the defendant. In other words, a plaintiff suing for breach of contract must show two things: first, that the consideration moved from him to the defendant and secondly, that the defendant's promise was made to him.

10.4 INTENTION TO CREATE LEGAL RELATIONS

A strong Court of Appeal made it clear in *Rose and Frank Co.* v. *Crompton & Bros Ltd.* (1923) that the intention to create legal relations is an essential and distinct element in the formation of a contract. In that case, Bankes L.J. said:

'There is, I think, no doubt that it is essential to the creation of a contract, using that word in its legal sense, that the parties to an agreement shall not only be *ad idem* as to the terms of their agreement, but that they shall have intended that it shall have legal consequences and be legally enforceable.'

In the same case, an illuminating explanation of the principle was given by Scrutton L.J. as follows:

'It is quite possible for parties to come to an agreement by accepting a proposal with the result that the agreement concluded does not give rise to legal relations. The reason for this is that the parties do not intend that their agreement shall give rise to legal relations. This intention may be implied from the subject matter of the agreement, but it may also be expressed by the parties. In social and family relations such an intention is readily implied, while in business matters the opposite result would ordinarily follow. But I can see no reason why, even in business matters, the parties should not intend to rely on each other's good faith and honour, and to exclude all idea of settling disputes by any outside intervention with the accompanying necessity of expressing themselves so precisely that outsiders may have no difficulty in understanding what they mean. If they clearly express such an intention I can see no reason in public policy why effect should not be given to their intention.'

These views were confirmed by the House of Lords. For present purposes, then, most agreements fall into one or other of the two broad classes: (*a*) business agreements and (*b*) social and domestic agreements. Each class should be considered separately.

(a) Business agreements

The judgement of Scrutton L.J. in *Rose and Frank Co.* v. *Crompton Bros. Ltd.* explains that, in the case of any business transaction. there is an implication that the parties intended to create legal relations. This can be seen to accord with ordinary common sense. It follows that any party wishing to show that an agreement is not binding will have to rebut this implication with evidence. This rebuttal normally involves the use of an express term to the effect that the agreement is 'not subject to the legal jurisdiction of the law courts': *Rose and Frank* v. *Crompton;* or that the agreement 'shall not be attended by or give rise to any legal relationship, rights, duties, consequences': *Appleson* v. *Littlewood Ltd.* (1939); or, more usually, that the agreement is 'subject to contract': *Eccles* v. *Bryant* (1948).

An agreement subject to contract is made where an offer is accepted subject to contract, or where the agreement itself is expressed to be subject to contract. This is a normal preliminary step to be taken in the course of negotiations to buy and sell land.

(b) Social and domestic agreements

In agreements of this class there is an implication that the parties did not intend to create legal relations. In *Balfour* v. *Balfour* (1919), a husband promised to pay a monthly allowance to his wife during what he thought would be a temporary separation while he was working in Ceylon. The wife did not accompany him for medical reasons. It was held by the Court of Appeal that there was no contract because the parties did not intend their arrangement to carry legal consequences. The implication that the parties did not intend to create legal relations will usually be rebutted where the husband and wife are not living amicably together. In *Merritt* v. *Merritt* (1970), Lord Denning M.R., said that:

'It is altogether different when the parties are not living in amity but are separated, or about to separate. They then bargain keenly. They do not rely on honourable understandings. They want everything cut and dried. It may safely be presumed that they intend to create legal relations.'

For a further case in which this question was considered see *Jones* v. *Padavatton* (1969).

(c) Collective agreements

At common law, agreements between trade unions, on the one hand, and employers or their associations on the other, are not binding unless there is an express provision to that effect. They are to be regarded as in the same category as agreements binding in honour only unless expressed to be binding: *Ford Motor Co. Ltd.* v. *Amalgamated Union of Engineering and Foundry Workers* (1969). The common law rule as to the nature of collective agreements is now replaced by s. 18 of the Trade Union and Labour Relations Act 1974, which provides that a collective agreement must be conclusively presumed *not* to have been intended to be a legally enforceable contract unless the agreement is in writing and contains a provision which states that the parties intend that the agreement will be a legally enforceable contract.

10.5 TERMS OF CONTRACT

The parties to a contract may not have expressed all the terms which they intend shall bind them. Further, certain terms may be implied by statute. The terms of a contract will, accordingly, fall into two classes, namely, express terms and implied terms.

(a) Expressed intention of the parties

The purpose of a contract is to create mutually enforceable rights and obligations between the parties. During the offer and acceptance process the parties, as a matter of common sense, will stipulate for their own best interests in the bargain. The express contents of the agreement will comprise the offer or counter-offer which was accepted. The express contents of the agreement are called the express terms of contract. They are statements made by the parties during the bargaining process with the intention that they will become binding upon acceptance. Material statements which are lacking in this intention are called representations. The intention of the parties is established objectively. The test question is: what would a reasonable person, knowing the facts, say was the intention of the parties?

Lord Denning has explained this matter as follows: 'The question whether a warranty was intended depends on the conduct of the parties, on their words and their behaviour, rather than on their thoughts. If an intelligent bystander would reasonably infer that a warranty was intended, that will suffice': *Dick Bentley Productions Ltd.* v. *Harold Smith Ltd.* (1965).

The express terms of a contract may be oral or in writing; or they may be partly oral and partly in writing. Written terms are usually made up entirely of words but, where it is necessary to include a technical description, drawings must be regarded as a proper method by which intention may be expressed. For example, the terms of a contract to manufacture a generator or to build a bridge would, of necessity, include drawings.

Where the terms of contract are contained in a set of documents, these are usually described as the contract documents. They will often be listed in a master document called the Articles of Agreement. Where the entire agreement appears in documentary form, the so-called parol evidence rule applies. By this rule, the court will allow extrinsic evidence to be adduced to vary the terms of a document only in very exceptional circumstances. The parties are generally taken to have expressed their entire agreement in the documents.

(b) Implied intention of the parties

Terms will be implied by the court to give effect to the presumed intentions of the parties; but a term will not be implied contrary to an express term: *Trollope & Colls, Ltd.* v. *North West Regional Hospital Board* (1973).

Terms will be implied to give effect to a local custom, to the custom of a particular market or to trade usage. A term will be implied to give what the courts call 'business efficacy' to the contract; but the implication of such a term must be a matter of necessity to save the contract. It will not be implied as a matter of reasonableness: *Trollope & Colls, Ltd.* v. *North West Regional Hospital Board* (1973). In *Luxor* v. *Cooper* (1941), it was said in the House of Lords that the implication must be 'necessary to give the transaction such business efficacy as the parties must have intended'. In other cases, the courts have applied the so-called 'officious bystander' test which was put forward in *Shirlaw* v. *Southern Foundries Ltd.* (1926) as follows:

'*Prima facie* that which in any contract is left to be implied and need not be expressed is something so obvious that it goes without saying; so that if, while the parties were making their bargain, an officious bystander were to suggest some express provisions for it in the agreement, they would testily suppress him with a common 'Oh, of course'.'

In *The Moorcock* (1889), there was an implied term, in a contract by which a ship was brought alongside a Thames wharf, that there would be no dangerous obstructions on the river-bed. In that case a ship had been damaged at low tide as it rested on some obstruction. Lord Esher M.R. said that:

'. . .when business requires a ship to be brought alongside their wharf, in my opinion honesty of business requires, and we are bound to imply it, that the defendants have undertaken to see that the bottom of the river is reasonably fit for the purpose, or that they ought, at all events, to take reasonable care to find out whether the bottom of the river is reasonably fit for the purpose for which they agreed that their jetty should be used, and then, if not, either procure it to be made reasonably fit for the purpose, or inform the persons with whom they have con-tracted that it is not so.'

In a building contract there is an implied term that the materials used by the builder are of reasonably good quality: *Young & Marten Ltd.* v. *McManus Childs Ltd.* (1968).

Where the defendant entered into a binding agreement to give the plain-tiff 'first refusal' of the fee simple of certain property, it was held that there was an implied term that he could not give the property away to a third party without first offering it to the plaintiff: *Gardner* v. *Coutts & Co.* (1968).

(c) Terms implied by statute

Examples of statutory implied terms are to be found in the Sale of Goods Act 1979 and the Supply of Goods and Services Act 1982. Taken together, these Acts provide for implied terms relating to a number of matters concerning goods sold, otherwise supplied or bailed. These implied terms are intended to protect the interests of the buyer, transferee or bailee, as the case may be, with regard to the transfer of title, correspondence of goods with description, quality and fitness for purpose, and correspondence of bulk with sample. These matters are dealt with in some detail in Chapter 16.5 below.

The Supply of Goods and Services Act 1982 provides further for implied terms in contracts for the supply of services as follows.

(i) Care and skill.

In a contract for the supply of a service where the supplier is acting in the course of a business, there is an implied term that the supplier will carry out the service with *reasonable* care and skill: 1982 Act, s. 13.

150

(ii) Time.
Where, under a contract for the supply of a service by a supplier acting in the course of a business, the time for the service to be carried out is not fixed by the contract, left to be fixed in a manner agreed by the contract or determined by the course of dealing between the parties, there is an implied term that the supplier will carry out the service within a *reasonable* time: 1982 Act, s. 14.

(iii) Consideration.
Where, under a contract for the supply of a service, the consideration for the service is not determined by the contract, left to be determined in a manner agreed by the contract or determined by the course of dealing between the parties, there is an implied term that the party contracting with the supplier will pay a *reasonable* charge: 1982 Act, s. 15.

(d) Conditions and warranties

Terms of contract are divided, according to importance, into two classes, namely, conditions and warranties. The significance of the distinction between the two classes appears only when the contract is broken. All the while a contract is being performed, it matters not whether any particular term is a condition or a warranty. Where, however, a condition is broken, the aggrieved party may elect to treat the contract as repudiated. This means that he can treat himself as discharged from any future obligation under the contract and also sue for damages. A condition is thus a term which goes to the root of the contract. Where, on the other hand, a warranty is broken, the plaintiff's remedy is in damages only. In an action for damages for breach of contract the issue between the parties is often whether the defendant has broken a condition or a warranty. The parties sometimes describe the terms of their contract as conditions or warranties, but such descriptions do not bind the court. The distinction will always rest on the relative importance of the term in question: *Schuler* v. *Wickman Tool Sales Ltd.* (1973).

(e) Certainty of terms

There are two strands of principle to follow in connection with the need for certainty with regard to the terms of a contract. The first is where there is a meaningless term in an otherwise complete contract and the second is where there is a general uncertainty as to the intention of the parties which cannot be resolved by the implication of terms.

(i) Meaningless terms.
A meaningless term contained in an otherwise certain contract will be rejected leaving the remaining terms valid and binding. In *Nicolene* v.

Simmonds (1953), an order for goods was accepted by a letter which included the following statement, 'I assume that we are in agreement that the usual conditions of acceptance apply'. It was held by the Court of Appeal that, since there were no 'usual conditions', the term was meaningless and could be rejected without impairing the contract as a whole, which remained binding on the parties.

(ii) Incomplete negotiation.
An agreement to agree in the future, or an agreement to negotiate further, will not be binding. In *Courtney & Fairburn* v. *Tolaini Bros.* (1975), it was held that, with regard to three proposed building projects, an agreement to negotiate fair and reasonable contract sums did not result in a binding contract. Where an essential term is not expressed and yet cannot be implied, the agreement will be void for uncertainty. For example, in *Bushwall Properties Ltd.* v. *Vortex Properties Ltd.* (1976), there was an agreement for the sale and conveyance of 51½ acres of land for £500,000. The agreement provided for payment of this price in three instalments. It was provided further that on the payment of each instalment, 'a proportionate part of the land shall be released forthwith' to the purchaser. The agreement did not define the parts of the land to be released as each 'proportionate part'. It was therefore void for uncertainty. The simplest example of the failure of an agreement for uncertainty is, perhaps, *Scammell & Nephew Ltd.* v. *Ouston* (1941). In this case it was agreed that the balance of the purchase price of a lorry would be had on hire-purchase terms over a period of two years. It was held by the House of Lords that, since no details of the terms had been agreed, there was no concluded agreement: the expression 'on hire-purchase terms' was too vague to be given any definite meaning.

(f) Exclusion clauses

An exclusion clause is a clause designed to limit or exclude liability which would otherwise be incurred by the party who puts forward such a clause, namely, the *proferens*. Most exclusion clauses seek to protect the *proferens* from liability in contract or tort – particularly negligence. The *proferens* will enjoy the effective protection of an exclusion clause only if the clause is able to pass three tests. First, the clause must be shown to be part of the contract. Secondly, on its true construction, it must give the protection sought by the *proferens;* and, thirdly, the clause must not be rendered ineffective by the Unfair Contract Terms Act 1977.

(i) Part of the contract.
The first test of an exclusion clause is whether it is part of the contract. For this purpose the ordinary rules of offer and acceptance are applied.

The most important requirement is that the clause should be communicated by the *proferens* to the other party before, or at the time when, the contract is made: *Olley* v. *Marlborough Court Hotel* (1949). There will be no effective communication unless it can be shown that the clause was sufficiently drawn to the attention of the other party: *Parker* v. *S.E. Rly Co.* (1877); *Thornton* v. *Shoe Lane Parking* (1971). The clause will not be part of the contract unless it is written or printed on a document of a kind which is intended to bear contractual terms. The clause will not be binding, for instance, if it is printed on the back of a receipt for money or on the cover of a cheque book: *Chapelton* v. *Barry UDC* (1940); *Burnett* v. *Westminster Bank* (1966). A clause may, nevertheless, be regarded as part of the contract if it can be shown that it appeared on a non-contractual document consistently during the course of previous dealings over a period of time. In *Spurling* v. *Bradshaw* (1956), a clause which was communicated consistently on the back of the invoice in each of a series of transactions was held to be part of the contract. In *McCutcheon* v. *MacBrayne* (1964) the clause was printed on a so-called 'risk note' in several, but not all, of the previous transactions between the parties: the dealings were thus inconsistent and the clause was not regarded by the court as communicated and was, therefore, not part of the contract.

(ii) Construction.

The principle was laid down by the House of Lords in the *Suisse Atlantique* case (1967) and has been confirmed and restated by the House in a number of subsequent cases that *the question whether, and to what extent, an exclusion clause is to be applied to any breach of contract (or negligence) is a matter of construction of the contract.* Previously, if the *proferens* was guilty of a fundamental breach of contract, he was regarded as having repudiated the entire contract, including the exclusion clause, from which he could no longer derive any advantage, for the court would not construe it. This was the doctrine of fundamental breach which has been thoroughly rejected by the House of Lords in *Photo Productions* v. *Securicor Transport* (1980) and *Ailsa Craig* v. *Malvern Fishing Co.* (1983).

If an exclusion clause is effective, it is part of the contract as a whole. Therefore, the contract has to be construed as a whole to discover whether the clause is part of it. Where the language is vague or ambiguous, the court will construe it in a manner which is most likely to give effect to what must have been the common intention of the parties when they entered into the contract. This will result in the clause itself being construed *contra proferentem*, i.e., in case of vagueness or ambiguity, against the interest of the *proferens*.

(iii) The Unfair Contract Terms Act 1977.

If an exclusion clause is held to be part of the contract and is also, on its true construction, effective at common law to give to the *proferens* the protection he seeks, the clause will be ultimately effective only if it is not rendered of no effect, or of reduced effect, by the Unfair Contract Terms Act 1977. This Act is of great importance in modern contract and commercial law and its main provisions are set out in the Appendix to this book. The effect of the 1977 Act is that certain kinds of exclusion clause have no effect at all, e.g. clauses which purport to exclude or restrict liability for death or personal injury resulting from negligence: 1977 Act, s. 2(1). See also ss. 6(1), 6(2), 7(2) and s. 5. A further effect of the 1977 Act is that certain other kinds of exclusion clause are effective only in so far as they satisfy the requirements of reasonableness. By s. 11 of the 1977 Act, the requirement of reasonableness is satisfied if the clause in question is fair and reasonable, having regard to circumstances which were, or ought reasonably to have been, known to or in the contemplation of the parties when the contract was made. Schedule 2 contains guidelines for the assistance of the court in determining the question of reasonableness. For the effect of the 1977 Act on sale of goods law see Chapter 16.6.

In *Mitchell* v. *Finney Lock Seeds* (1983), the House of Lords took the view that the majority in the Court of Appeal had adopted too hostile an approach to the common law construction of an exclusion clause; but on the question whether the clause satisfied the requirements of reasonableness, the House of Lords decided that the Court of Appeal were right in their decision that it had failed. In deciding the reasonableness question, the court has a wide discretion as to which factors to take into account. In this case a farmer had bought and sown worthless seeds and the exclusion clause purported to limit the sellers' liability to the price of the seed. The clause was held not to satisfy the requirements of reasonableness because: (1) the clause was imposed by the sellers - it was not negotiated; (2) the fault in the case was entirely on the part of the sellers; (3) the fault could not have been discovered by the buyers at the time of delivery (the seed was not cabbage seed and the buyers had no way of knowing this); (4) there was no insurance cover available to the buyers to protect them from this kind of risk, but there was a measure of insurance protection available to the sellers; and (5) there was a greatly disproportionate allocation of risk between the parties, the sellers' risk being no more than the price of the seed while the buyer risked the value of the season's crop on the acreage sown.

10.6 ENFORCEMENT OF CONTRACTS

A contract is legally enforceable in the sense that a breach of contract by one party gives rise to a remedy in favour of the other. The usual remedy is monetary compensation which is called damages. In most cases, this compensation is paid after discussion and voluntary settlement by the parties. Failing such a settlement, the aggrieved party must decide whether to sue for damages. Where a breach is proved or admitted, it is the duty of the court to assess the amount of *damages* payable according to the rules in *Hadley* v. *Baxendale* (1854). By these rules, any loss caused by the breach is recoverable if it is of a kind which can be regarded as within the reasonable contemplation of the parties as likely to result from such a breach. If the loss is not of a kind which would have been foreseeable at the time of contracting, then it is too remote to be recoverable.

(a) Primary and secondary obligations

In *Photo Productions Ltd.* v. *Securicor Transport Ltd.* (1980), Lord Diplock explained the relationship between the obligation to honour the contract, on the one hand, and the obligation to compensate for breach, on the other. The explanation introduces the concept of primary and secondary obligations in contract law. Lord Diplock said:

> 'Every failure to perform a primary obligation is a breach of contract. The secondary obligation on the part of the contract breaker to which it gives rise by implication of the common law is to pay monetary compensation to the other party for the loss sustained by him in consequence of the breach.'

(b) Specific performance

In equity, the court has a jurisdiction to order the specific performance of an obligation under a contract. This jurisdiction is discretionary, and will not be exercised where damages would be an adequate remedy. A decree of specific performance is generally regarded as an appropriate remedy in cases of breach of contract to make or take a conveyance of an interest in land.

SUMMARY

1   A contract is a legally enforceable agreement in the sense that the law provides a remedy in case of breach by one of the parties.

2   A simple contract is an agreement supported by consideration and entered into with the intention of creating legal relations.

3   A contract in the form of a deed is known as a specialty. A specialty differs from a simple contract in two main respects. First, there is no need for consideration. Secondly, the limitation period is twelve years as opposed to six.

4   Agreement is reached when an offer is unconditionally accepted. The terms of the offer are thereby transformed into the express terms of the agreement.

5   An offer is a statement of the terms to which the offeror is prepared to bind himself in the event of acceptance by an offeree. An invitation to make an offer is called an invitation to treat.

6   Acceptance does not operate unless and until it has been communicated to the offeror.

7   There are two exceptions to the rule of communication of acceptance. First, where an acceptance is properly made by post. Secondly, where acceptance is made by compliance with the requirements of the offer, thus leading to the formation of a unilateral contract.

8   An offer may be terminated by rejection, revocation or lapse.

9   The definition of consideration in *Curry* v. *Misa* (1875) places in juxtaposition the concepts of benefit and detriment enjoyed or suffered by the parties. The definition given by Pollock and adopted by the House of Lords in *Dunlop* v. *Selfridge* (1915) regards consideration as the price by which the defendant's promise is bought.

10   The rules governing consideration are: Consideration must be of some value to the defendant. The courts will not enquire into the adequacy of consideration. Consideration must not be past.

11   The intention to create legal relations is an essential and distinct element in the formation of a contract. In business matters, there is a rebuttable presumption that the parties intended to create legal relations. In social relations there is a rebuttable presumption that the parties did *not* intend to create legal relations.

12   The terms of a contract may be express and implied. A term will not be implied contrary to an express term. Terms will be implied to give effect to a custom, or to give effect to a necessary implication, or to give effect to the requirements of a statute.

13   Terms of contract may be divided into conditions and warranties. Breach of condition gives rise to a right to treat the contract as repudiated and at an end, coupled with the right to sue for damages. Breach of warranty gives rise to a right to recover compensation (damages) only.

14   The terms of a contract must be certain. Meaningless terms will be rejected from an otherwise certain contract. An agreement which is incompletely negotiated will be void for uncertainty.

CASE NOTES

Butler Machine Tool Co. v. *Ex-Cell-O Ltd.* (1979) C.A.
A seller offered to sell certain tools on his own terms and conditions which included a variation of price clause. The buyer 'accepted' the offer on his own terms and conditions which were different from those of the seller. In particular, the buyer's terms did not include a variation of price clause. The seller accepted the buyer's order by filling in a tear-off slip to that effect and sending it to the buyer.

HELD: The buyer had effectively rejected the seller's offer by his order (which was a counter-offer). A contract was formed when the seller accepted the counter-offer by sending the tear-off slip back to the buyer.

Byrne v. *Van Tienhoven* (1880)
The defendants wrote from Cardiff to the plaintiffs in New York on 1 October 1879 offering to sell 1000 boxes of Hensol brand tinplates at 15s. 6d. per box. This was received in New York on 11 October and on the same day the plaintiffs sent a telegram accepting the offer. A letter confirming the acceptance was sent on 15 October. On 20 October the plaintiffs received a letter from the defendants stating that the offer was withdrawn owing to the rise in the market price of tinplates. This letter was posted on 8 October. The defendants refused to deliver the tinplates and the plaintiffs sued for breach of contract. The defence was that no contract had been made since the offer had been withdrawn.

HELD: The withdrawal was not effective because it did not reach the plaintiffs until after the contract was made on 11 October by their valid acceptance by telegram.

Davies & Co. Ltd. v. *William Old Ltd.* (1969)
Shop-fitting sub-contractors offered to do certain work on terms that they would be paid for the work as and when it was included in a formal valuation and certified by the architect, regardless of whether the main contractor had been paid. The main contractor responded by sending his standard form of order to the sub-contractors. The form of order included a clause which stated that the main contractor should pay the sub-contractors only when he himself had been paid by the employer. The sub-contractors accepted the order.

HELD: The 'pay when paid' clause was part of the counter-offer which was accepted by the sub-contractors and was, accordingly, binding.

Dickinson v. *Dodds* (1876) C.A.
The defendant delivered to the plaintiff on Wednesday 10 June 1874 a signed offer to sell a house for £800. The offer was expressed to be left over until 9 a.m. on Friday, 12 June. On the following day the plaintiff was informed by a Mr Berry that the defendant had been offering or agreeing to sell the house to another person. On Friday morning, Berry, as the plaintiff's agent, delivered the plaintiff's acceptance of the defendant's offer. The defendant told Berry that he had already sold the house. The plaintiff, contending that there was a contract, brought this action for specific performance.

HELD: The defendant's offer was no longer effective when the plaintiff knew that Dodds was no longer minded to sell the house to him. It followed that the purported acceptance did not result in the making of a contract.

Glasbrook Bros. Ltd. v. *Glamorgan County Council* (1924) H.L.
During a miners' strike, the local police authority took the view that mobile patrols were sufficient to protect the colliery property. It was agreed, however, between the colliery owners and the authority that the police would garrison the colliery on payment at specified rates. After the strike, the colliery owners refused to pay as agreed, contending that the police had done no more than they were bound to do under their public duty. It was thus argued that the police authority had given no consideration and that the promise to pay was, accordingly not binding.

HELD: The measures taken by the police under the agreement were more than the police authority considered necessary for the protection of the property. The colliery owners were, therefore, bound by their promise to pay.

Henthorn v. *Fraser* (1892) C.A.
The plaintiff wished to buy certain property from the defendant building society. On 7 July the secretary of the building society gave the plaintiff a letter which stated: 'I hereby give you the refusal of the Flamank Street property at £750 for fourteen days'. On 8 July a letter from the plaintiff's solicitor accepting the offer was posted at 3.50 p.m. The letter was received at the defendant's office after working hours on that day. Earlier on 8 July, a letter was sent by the secretary of the building society stating: 'Please take notice that my letter to you of the 7th inst. giving you the option of purchasing the property, Flamank Street, Birkenhead, for £750, in fourteen days, is withdrawn and the offer cancelled'. This letter was posted about midday and was received by the plaintiff at 5.30 p.m. on the 8 July. The plaintiff brought this action for specific performance, contending that a contract was made on 8 July.

HELD: A contract was made when the letter written on behalf of the plaintiff by his solicitor was posted on 8 July. Lord Herschell said: 'Where the circumstances are such that it must have been within the contemplation of the parties that, according to the ordinary usages of mankind, the post might be used as a means of communicating the acceptance of an offer, the acceptance is complete as soon as it is posted'.

Holwell Securities v. *Hughes* (1974) C.A.
An option was granted as part of an agreement. By this agreement, the option was to be exercised by notice in writing within six months. Notice of the exercise of the option was posted within the six-month period but it was lost in the post. The question was whether the exercise was valid as for a postal acceptance or whether actual communication of the notice was necessary.

HELD: The mere posting did not constitute a valid exercise of the option which required actual notice.

Pharmaceutical Society v. *Boots* (1953) C.A.
Boots operated a self-service chemist shop. By statute it is not lawful to sell certain poisons unless the sale is effected by or under the supervision of a registered pharmacist. The Society contended that the sale of poisons took place when a customer removed the goods from the open shelf in the store and that, accordingly, the sales were contrary to the requirements of the statute. This argument failed before the Court of Appeal.

HELD: The goods on the open shelves constituted an invitation to treat; the contract was made when the cashier accepted the customer's offer to buy the goods presented at the cash desk; the cashiers being under the supervision of a registered pharmacist, the sales were not contrary to the requirements of the statute.

Ward v *Byham* (1956) C.A.
The father of an illegitimate girl offered to the mother an allowance of £1 per week for the child 'providing you can prove that she will be well looked after and happy'. The mother agreed. When sued for arrears of payment, the father of the child contended that his promise was not binding because the mother had given no consideration to support it. He argued that the mother of an illegitimate child was under a duty to maintain it.

HELD: The mother's promise that the child would be well looked after and happy was more than the duty to maintain the child. The mother had given consideration, therefore, to support the father's promise to pay.

EXERCISES

1 'Not all agreements are contracts.' Explain this statement.
2 What is the difference between an offer and an invitation to treat?
3 What is the connection between the details of the offer and the terms of the contract subsequently made?
4 There are three essential elements to the formation of a simple contract. What are they? Describe each element in detail.
5 In what circumstances may a defendant successfully argue that no contract was made?
6 Define consideration. Your definition should distinguish between executed consideration and executory consideration. Mention relevant authorities.
7 State the rules governing consideration, mentioning as many relevant cases as you can.
8 State and explain the three ways in which an offer may be terminated.
9 Need the parties express their intention to create legal relations? Explain your answer in full detail.
10 What is the 'officious bystander' test? When is it appropriate?
11 Give examples of contract terms which are implied by statute.
12 To be valid and effective, an exclusion clause must (1) be part of the contract; (2) on its true construction, be applicable to the default of the *proferens;* and (3) not be rendered ineffective by the Unfair Contract Terms Act 1977. Develop.
13 What is the difference between a condition and a warranty?
14 'The terms of a contract must be certain.' Explain and illustrate this statement.

WORKSHOP

1 Read the case notes at the end of this chapter. State briefly the principle on which the court reached its decision in each case. Suggest factual situations to which these principles might apply.
2 Consider the following factual situations and say whether or not a contract has been formed. In each case state the principle which you used to arrive at your answer. State also the authority for each principle mentioned.

(a) Fred sees a gold watch in a shop window with the price marked £20. He goes into the shop and offers £20 to the shopkeeper and asks for the watch. The shopkeeper says that he can have the watch for £120. He explains that the price label was a mistake.

(*b*) Rudolph offers to sell his horse to Harry for £450. Harry replies that he will not pay more than £350 unless the saddle and harness is included in the price. Rudolph then says that Harry can have the horse for £350.

(*c*) Jane offers to buy John's car for £500. John says, 'I'll let you have the car for £560'. Jane replies, 'Agreed, so long as I can pay by ten monthly instalments of £56'.

(*d*) Ted placed a notice in a newspaper as follows: 'Lost – a gold fountain pen engraved with the initials E.D. A reward of ten pounds will be paid to any person who returns the pen to the owner.' The notice set out Ted's address. Bert, one of Ted's friends, found the pen and returned it to Ted. Bert did not know about the notice in the newspaper.

(*e*) Douglas makes an offer by post to Maggie. Maggie replies by return of post to say that she accepts unconditionally. Maggie's reply is lost in the post and never reaches Douglas.

(*f*) Judd, a house painter, writes to Peter offering to paint the outside of Peter's house for £634, the offer to remain open for seven days. A fortnight later, Peter telephones Judd to say that he accepts the offer.

(*g*) Julie has long wanted a painting owned by Myrtle. She writes to Myrtle offering to buy the painting for £320, saying that if she does not hear from Myrtle to the contrary within a week, she will consider the picture hers at the price. Myrtle does not reply and a week later Julie sends her a cheque for £320 asking her to send the picture.

(*h*) Milo asks Fred for permission to use her holiday cottage in the lake district. Freda replies, 'Yes, of course'.

(*i*) Jim, feeling grateful towards Monty, who gave him a long lift in his car, says, 'I will give you £7 towards the cost of the petrol you have used'.

3 What principle was applied in *Stilk* v. *Myrick* (1809)? Name and state the facts of another case in which the same principle was applied.

4 Explain carefully the decision in *Re McArdle* (1951).

5 Consider the case of *Bainbridge* v. *Firmstone* (1838). Why was it unnecessary to enquire what benefit the defendant expected to derive from weighing the boilers?

6 Compare and contrast the following two cases: *Nicolene* v. *Simmonds* (1953) and *Scammell & Nephew Ltd.* v. *Ouston*.

7 How would you have advised the parties in *Bushwall Properties Ltd.* v. *Vortex Properties Ltd.* when they were negotiating the contract?

8 From the Unfair Contract Terms Act 1977 make a list of the kinds of exclusion clause which are without effect. Make another list of those

which are effective in so far as they satisfy the requirements of reasonableness.

9   In what circumstances will terms be implied in contracts for the supply of services on the basis of reasonableness?

THE AUTHENTICITY
OF AGREEMENT

In the previous chapter it was explained that agreement is one of the vital elements in the formation of a contract. The contract may, however, be vitiated if the element of agreement is affected by mistake, by misrepresentation or by coercion. Agreement must be a true consensus – it must be authentic.

11.1 MISTAKE

It sometimes happens that, at the time of contracting, there is some misapprehension or mistake in the mind of one of the parties, or perhaps in the minds of both parties. Mistake may affect the validity of the contract by rendering it void or voidable, according to the circumstances, or the mistake may not affect the contract at all.

Mistake may be initially classified as follows:

(*a*) Common mistake, i.e. both parties have suffered from the same misapprehension. In terms of offer and acceptance this means that a consensus was reached when acceptance took place. In other words, common mistake does not prevent the formation of an agreement.
(*b*) Mutual mistake, i.e. the parties are at cross-purposes; the acceptance does not correspond with the offer although the parties, at the time of contracting, think that it does.
(*c*) Unilateral mistake, i.e. only one party is mistaken.

This section deals with mistake at law, which may render a contract void, and mistake in equity, which may render a contract voidable and, finally, mistake of identity caused by fraud.

(a) Mistake at law

(i) Common mistake as to a fundamental fact.

Where both parties have suffered in common from the same mistake of fact, the validity of the contract is unlikely to be affected. Only if it can be shown that the mistake was such as to prevent the formation of the contract will it be operative, i.e. will the mistake render the contract void. In *Bell* v. *Lever Brothers* (1932) the House of Lords made it clear that this kind of mistake will not be operative unless the common mistake of the parties is as to the existence of a fact or quality which makes the subject-matter of the contract essentially different from what the parties believed it to be. In that case the common mistake was as to the validity of a contract of employment. Both parties thought (mistakenly) that it was valid when, in fact, it was voidable at the option of one of the parties. The House of Lords decided that this mistake was not sufficiently fundamental to render void an agreement between the same parties to determine the contract of employment. An example of operative common mistake may be found in *Galloway* v. *Galloway* (1914) in which a marriage separation agreement was declared void because the parties had entered into it in the belief that they were lawfully married; in fact they were not. The fact that the parties were not married was considered to be fundamental to the separation agreement.

(ii) Res extincta.

A special aspect of this kind of mistake is where, unknown to the parties to a sale of goods contract, the goods are not in existence (*res extincta*). This is now covered by the Sale of Goods Act 1979, s. 6 which provides that: 'Where there is a contract for the sale of specific goods, and the goods without the knowledge of the seller have perished at the time when the contract was made, the contract is void'.

(iii) Mistake as to the identity of the subject-matter.

Where the sense of the offer is different from the sense in which it was accepted there can be no real agreement. The parties are at cross-purposes and the mistake is thus mutual. The court will declare the apparent contract void. Mutual mistake is illustrated by the case of *Raffles* v. *Wichelhaus* (1864) in which there was a contract for the sale of a consignment of cotton 'to arrive ex Peerless from Bombay'. There were at the time two ships called Peerless in Bombay; the buyer meant one and the seller the other. It was held that the contract was void.

(iv) Mistake in expressing the offer.

Where an offer is accepted by an offeree who knows (or is deemed to know) of a material mistake in the expression of the offeror's intention, the contract may be void. In *Hartog* v. *Colin & Shields* (1939) an offer to sell hare skins was accepted by an offeree who knew that the offeror had mistakenly stated his price as being price per pound weight when he meant a price per piece. It was held that the contract was void.

(v) Non est factum.
The ancient defence of *non est factum* (it is not his deed) is now regarded as part of the law of unilateral mistake at common law. This defence allows an exception to the general rule that persons are bound by the terms of any document which they execute. The cases show that a person who is mistaken as to the nature of a document which he has signed or sealed as a result of blindness, illiteracy or fraudulent misrepresentation, may be excused liability if he can show that he took all reasonable precautions before signing. The modern law on this matter was discussed and explained by the House of Lords in *Saunders* v. *Anglia Building Society* (1971). In this case, an elderly lady who was unable to read because her spectacles were broken, and who was fraudulently induced to sign a form of agreement of sale of a house, was held to be bound by her signature in spite of her mistake because she had not made the clear and satisfactory case which is required of those raising the defence of *non est factum.*

(b) Mistake in equity

The application of the common law principles governing mistake can sometimes unfairly cause hardship to one or other of the parties. For example, in cases of common mistake of fact, the contract will in most cases be upheld notwithstanding the mistake. Further, where the parties have reduced their agreement to writing, the common law regards the written terms as binding regardless of whether there was a mistake in composing them. Many cases of these kinds are suitable for the intervention of equity to eliminate unnecessary unfairness or hardship. Finally, equity may take the defendant's mistake into account in an action for specific performance. Thus, there are three matters to consider in connection with mistake in equity.

(i) Rescission for common mistake.
The court has an equitable jurisdiction to set aside a contract even though it is valid at common law regardless of the mistake. Mere rescission of such a contract will seldom produce a fair result and so the usual remedy sought in this connection is rescission on terms. This means that the court will, in suitable cases, order the original contract to be rescinded on condition that the parties will have the opportunity to enter into a fresh contract with the common mistake removed from it. In *Solle* v. *Butcher* (1950), both parties to a lease of a recently improved flat mistakenly believed it

to be no longer subject to rent control under the Rent Restriction Acts. The agreed rent was £250 per annum. The controlled rent had been £140 per annum but the landlord could have taken formal steps to have the controlled rent increased to £250 after the improvements had been carried out; he could not, however, do this while the new lease at £250 was in force. When the tenant sought a declaration that the flat was subject to a controlled rent of £140 per annum, the Court of Appeal held that the statutory controlled rent was £140 per annum but that the landlord was entitled to rescission of the lease on terms that he allow the tenant to enter into a new lease at £250 per annum. In *Grist* v. *Bailey* (1966) the common mistake in a contract for the sale of a house for £950 was that there was an existing statutory tenant in occupation. There was, in fact, no existing tenant and, accordingly, the house was worth £2,250. It was held that, because the vendor was not at fault in not knowing of the death of the statutory tenant, he was entitled to rescission of the contract on terms that he should enter into a contract of sale at a proper vacant possession price should the purchaser so wish.

(ii) Rectification.

Where parties have reached agreement and then seek to reduce it to writing (whether or not in a deed) and a mistake is made so that the written terms do not accord with the original oral terms, the court has an equitable jurisdiction to order that the written terms be rectified. The remedy of rectification enables either party to insist on the terms of the original agreement, i.e. to avoid the effect of this kind of mistake. The party seeking rectification must be able to prove the original oral agreement. In *Craddock* v. *Hunt* (1923) a vendor agreed orally to sell a house without the adjoining yard. By a mistake in both the contract and the conveyance the yard was included. When the vendor discovered the mistake he sought rectification of contract and conveyance. It was held by the Court of Appeal that he was entitled to have both documents rectified so as to accord with the original agreement to exclude the yard.

(iii) Withholding specific performance.

Specific performance is an equitable remedy and, accordingly, is granted or withheld at the discretion of the court. It is not awarded as of right as in the case of a common law remedy such as damages for breach of contract. On general equitable principles, specific performance will not be ordered if it would cause undue hardship to the defendant. Thus, the court is not likely to order specific performance against a defendant who entered into the contract under some material misapprehension which was not his fault. Where the mistake is due to the defendant's own fault, as in *Tamplin* v. *James* (1880), the court is likely to award specific performance against him. In that case, the purchaser of property at an auction sale had not bothered to look at the plans on display and, in consequence, mistakenly thought that some gardens were included in the sale of an inn. As there was no excuse for the defendant's mistake, specific performance was ordered against him.

(c) Mistake as to the identity of a party

The identity of the parties to a contract is not normally a problem. In negotiations, each party usually knows with whom he is dealing. Problems may arise, however, in two ways. First, where there is a question as to whether the person accepting an offer was indeed an offeree, for only those to whom an offer has been addressed are able to make a valid acceptance: *Boulton* v. *Jones* (1857). Secondly, in a contract for the sale of goods, the seller may have been induced to sell to a fraudulent buyer who concealed his true identity and pretended to be someone else. In this second case, problems may arise concerning the title of third parties with whom the fraudulent person has dealt. It is only with this second case that this section is concerned.

In essence, the rule is that if a fraudulent person obtains goods from a seller by using a false identity, any third party who obtains those goods will get good title if he is a *bona fide* purchaser. If the original seller is able to retrieve the goods before the purchase by the *bona fide* third party he will recover his former title. Another way of saying this is that the fraudulent person gets a voidable title to the goods, which he can pass on as a valid title to a *bona fide* purchaser.

In the cases, the question always is: Who has good title – the original seller or the ultimate third party? English law has no compromise to offer. Title will be in one or other of the parties, and will be decided by the rule mentioned above. In *Lewis* v. *Averay* (1972) a plausible rogue pretending to be a well known actor induced the plaintiff to sell and give possession of a motor-car. The cheque given for the car turned out to be worthless. The rogue sold the car to the defendant who bought it in good faith for £200. The rogue then vanished. The question of title was decided by the Court of Appeal in favour of the defendant – the innocent third party to whom the rogue sold the car. The difficulty in such cases (see also *Phillips* v. *Brooks* (1919) is that the court has to decide between two innocent parties. In *Lewis* v. *Averay* considerable weight was given to the fact that it was the original seller who let the rogue have the goods, thus enabling him to commit the fraud, whereas the innocent purchaser had acted with complete circumspection.

11.2 MISREPRESENTATION

Not all material statements made in the course of contract negotiations are intended to be included in the contract. A statement of fact which is made without this intention will become a 'representation' if it is relied upon by the other party and thus helped to induce the contract. Misrepresentation occurs where a representation proves to be false. Misrepresentation spans contract and tort, for a misrepresentation may constitute deceit or negligence. (Chapter 6.6(c) and Chapter 7).

(a) Remedies for misrepresentation

The law of misrepresentation can, perhaps, be best understood through the various remedies which are available according to the circumstances.

(i) No damages in contract.
By definition, a representation is not a term of contract. It follows that misrepresentation is not to be equated with breach of contract. Consequently, damages (i.e. money compensation) is not available at common law to a contracting party who has suffered a loss through entering into a contract under the inducement of a misrepresentation.

(ii) Rescission.
The circumstances of the misrepresentation may be such that the court will, in its equitable jurisdiction, order rescission of the contract. However, this remedy may be regarded as available only in exceptional circumstances because of the effect of the several bars to rescission (see (b) below).

(iii) Position in contract law.
Taking (i) and (ii) above together, it will be seen that there is often no remedy in the common law of contract available for misrepresentation. It follows that a plaintiff may have to look to the law of torts or to statute law for a remedy.

(iv) Damages in tort.
Where the plaintiff is able to bring his action in deceit or negligence he may, if successful, recover damages. Such actions in tort, however, constitute a burdensome, risky and expensive remedy to a party who simply wishes to get compensation for his contract losses resulting from a misrepresentation.

(v) Statutory damages.
Under the Misrepresentation Act 1967, s. 2, damages may be awarded for misrepresentation between parties negotiating a contract. The defendant will be liable for misrepresentation unless he is able to show the

grounds on which he believed his statement to be true (see (d) below). Bearing in mind the inadequacies of the common law and equity in connection with misrepresentation, the 1967 Act will be seen as a substantial reform.

(b) Rescission

A person who has been misled by a misrepresentation may seek rescission in equity. In deciding whether to order rescission, the court will consider all relevant circumstances, particularly whether there is one of the known bars to rescission. Any of the following matters may have a relevance in any case:

(i) Restitution.
The court will not order rescission unless it is possible to restore the parties to their original position (*restitutio in integrum*). This means that the misrepresentee must be prepared to restore to the other party any benefits of the contract, e.g. goods or money must be returned. In some cases rescission has been awarded even where the misrepresentee is unable to make precise restitution, e.g. where he is able to account for profits or to make an allowance for deterioration of property. Similarly, a seller claiming back his property must be prepared to restore the price. In *Lagunas Nitrate Co* v. *Lagunas Syndicate* (1899) rescission of a contract to sell nitrate grounds was refused because the purchaser had vigorously worked out the property immediately after the contract.

(ii) Third party rights.
No rescission will be ordered where a third party has obtained an interest in the subject-matter of the contract.

(iii) Affirmation.
If the misrepresentee affirms the contract, expressly or by implication, after discovering the truth of the misrepresentation he will be disentitled to rescission. For example, the buyer of goods cannot rescind if he uses the goods after becoming aware of the misrepresentation.

(iv) Lapse of time.
Claims for equitable relief must be pursued promptly. The maxim is: delay defeats the equities. In *Leaf* v. *International Galleries* (1950), it was held that a contract for the sale of an oil painting could not be rescinded after a lapse of five years.

(c) Damages in tort

In connection with misrepresentation by contracting parties the possibility of an action for damages in tort may arise. The action may be for deceit or for negligence (see Chapter 6.6(c) and Chapter 7).

(i) Deceit.
A plaintiff seeking to recover damages for deceit must be able to show that the misrepresentation was made by the defendant (1) knowing it to be false, (2) without belief in its truth, or (3) recklessly, not caring whether it is true or false: *Derry* v. *Peek* (1889). This requirement places a heavy burden on the plaintiff and accordingly this remedy is seldom available to a party who has been misled by a false statement during contract negotiations.

(ii) Negligence.
A misrepresentation may constitute the tort of negligence if it involves a breach of the duty of care: *Hedley Byrne* v. *Heller* (1963). Again, this remedy in tort is not always appropriate in the case of negligent statements made in contract negotiations.

(d) Damages under the Misrepresentation Act 1967

By s. 2(1) of this Act:

> Where a person has entered into a contract after a misrepresentation has been made to him by another party thereto and as a result thereof he has suffered loss, then, if the person making the misrepresentation would be liable to damages in respect thereof had the misrepresentation been made fraudulently, that person shall be so liable notwithstanding that the misrepresentation was not made fraudulently, unless he proves that he had reasonable ground to believe and did believe up to the time the contract was made that the facts represented were true.

This provision should be analysed to disclose the elements in the cases for the plaintiff and defendant respectively.

(i) Case for the plaintiff.
The plaintiff must be able to show that (1) he entered into a contract with the defendant; (2) after the defendant had made a misrepresentation; (3) as a result of which he has suffered a loss; and (4) the defendant would be liable in damages had the misrepresentation been made fraudulently. (This is altogether less onerous than the case to be made out by the plaintiff in deceit or negligence.)

(ii) Case for the defendant.
If the plaintiff is able to prove the four elements of his case as outlined in (i) above, the defendant will be liable in damages unless he can prove all

of the elements of the defence allowed by the 1967 Act. He must prove (1) that he had reasonable ground to believe that the facts represented were true and (2) that he did believe up to the time the contract was made that the facts represented were true.

For an example of the application of the Misrepresentation Act 1967, s. 2(1), see *Howard Marine & Dredging Co.* v. *Ogden* (1978).*

(e) Exclusion of liability

Where contracting parties expressly agree that liability for misrepresentation is to be restricted or excluded altogether, the restriction or exclusion will be of no effect except in so far as it satisfies the requirement of reasonableness as stated in the Unfair Contract Terms Act 1977: Misrepresentation Act 1967, s. 3 as set out in the Unfair Contract Terms Act, s. 8. See Appendix.

11.3 DURESS AND UNDUE INFLUENCE

Coercion to enter into a contract may take the form of violence or threatened violence or it may, at the other end of the scale, take the form of a very subtle influence of one mind over another. Where coercion is recognised by the common law it is called 'duress'. Where coercion is recognised in equity it is called 'undue influence'.

(a) Duress

Until recent times the common law concept of duress was restricted to cases where a party had been coerced into contracting by violence or threat of violence to his person. In such cases the contract was voidable at the suit of the party who had been coerced. The case of *The Sibeon and the Sibotre* (1976) illustrates the much wider concept of duress obtaining currently. In that case it was explained that duress would occur if, for example, the violence or threat of violence was to real or personal property as opposed to the actual person of the coerced party. The test now applied by the courts is whether there has been 'a coercion of the will, which vitiates consent'. This recent development of common law duress has led to the establishment of what has become known as 'economic duress' in English law. In *Pao On* v. *Lau Yiu Long* (1980) the defendant shareholders of a company were forced to give a guarantee against loss which might occur in the performance of a contract. The plaintiffs forced the defendants to give the guarantee by threatening to break that contract. It was held by the Privy Council that there was no duress because there had been no coercion of the will which vitiates consent and that the guarantee was therefore valid. In *The Atlantic Baron* (1979) shipbuilders had contracted to build a supertanker for an agreed price payable by instalments. Under threat of failing to complete the ship, the builder forced the purchaser to pay an extra 10 per cent on all instalments after the first. It was recognised by the court that this constituted duress, but it was held that the contract could not be set aside because it had been affirmed by the purchaser who had failed to protest until six months after delivery.

(b) Undue influence

Equity has long granted rescission of contracts where there was no relief at common law because of its early narrowness of approach, i.e its restriction to violence and threats to the person. There are two situations to consider: first, where the plaintiff is required to prove that undue influence was exercised and, secondly, where there is a presumption of undue influence arising from the special relationship of the parties.

(i) Proving undue influence.
Equitable rescission is available to a contracting party who can prove that the other party exercised such a dominant influence over his mind that he was unable to exercise a free and independent will when entering into the contract. For example, in *Williams* v. *Bayley* (1866), the father of a person who had defrauded a bank settled property on the bank for fear that the bank might prosecute. It was held that, even though the bank had not expressly threatened to prosecute, the settlor was not a free agent at the time of the settlement, which could therefore be set aside for undue influence.

(ii) The presumption of influence.
Certain relationships of confidence are recognised in equity as giving rise to a presumption of influence in case of contract or gift. The cases show that the following relationships give rise to the presumption: parent and child, guardian and ward, religious adviser and person advised, solicitor and client, doctor and patient, trustee and beneficiary. There is no special relationship for this purpose in the case of husband and wife, employer and employee, agent and principal. Undue influence is also presumed in any relationship where one party reposes confidence in the other enabling that other to take an unfair advantage. For example, in *Lloyds Bank* v. *Bundy* (1975) a father mortgaged his house to a bank as security in order to give the bank a guarantee of his son's business debts. Although the presumption does not normally arise as between banker and customer, it did so in this case because the father had placed himself entirely in the hands of the bank manager and had been given no opportunity to obtain independent advice. The mortgage could not therefore be enforced.

(iii) Rebutting the presumption.

Where a contract is made between parties who are in one or other of the special relationships the contract may be challenged by the party who has reposed confidence in the other. Where this occurs, that other party must prove that no undue influence occurred and that the contract (or gift, as the case may be) was made by the exercise of independent will. The most effective way to rebut the presumption is to show that there was available independent and competent advice and that the adviser had knowledge of all the relevant facts. An example of presumed influence is *Lancashire Loans* v. *Black* (1934) in which a mother persuaded her daughter (then unmarried and living at home) to enter into an agreement in the mother's interest with a money lender. The mother was also a party to the agreement. The daughter, who did not understand the transaction and who was not independently advised, was able to have the agreement set aside for undue influence even though she brought her action after marrying and leaving her mother's home.

SUMMARY

1 At law, the validity of a contract will be affected by mistake only if the mistake was such as to prevent the formation of true consensus. Where mistake has this effect it is called operative mistake and it renders the contract void.

2 Common mistake will not be operative unless it is mistake as to the existence of a fact or quality which makes the subject-matter of the contract essentially different from what the parties believed it to be.

3 Where the sense of the offer is different from the sense in which it was accepted the parties are at cross-purposes and there is no real agreement. This usually takes the form of a mutual mistake as to the identity of the subject-matter of the contract.

4 The defence of *non est factum* is available to a person who is mistaken as to the nature of a document which he has signed as a result of blindness, illiteracy or fraud, provided he can show that he took all reasonable precautions before signing.

5 In cases of common mistake, the court has an equitable jurisdiction to order the original contract to be rescinded on condition that the parties are given the opportunity to enter into a fresh contract with the common mistake removed from it.

6 Rectification may be available in equity where the parties have reached an agreement and then have made a mistake in reducing its terms to writing.

7 Specific performance is not likely to be awarded against a defendant who entered into the contract under some material misapprehension which was not due to his own fault.

8   If a fraudulent person obtains goods from a seller by using a false identity, any third party who obtains those goods will get good title provided that he is a *bona fide* purchaser without notice of the fraud. Until title passes to a *bona fide* purchaser, the fraudulent person's title is voidable so that the original seller may recover his title to the goods.

9   There is no common law remedy in contract for misrepresentation. In tort, damages may be available for deceit or negligent mis-statement.

10   Damages are now available under the Misrepresentation Act 1967, s. 2, unless the defendant is able to show that he had reasonable ground to believe and did believe that the facts represented were true.

11   In equity, a party who has entered into a contract after a misrepresentation may be entitled to rescission provided that there is no bar.

12   Common law duress occurs where a contract has been entered into as a result of a coercion of will which has vitiated consent. This is a wider test than formerly obtained and it includes what has become known as economic duress.

13   Unless there is a presumption of undue influence arising out of a special relationship of confidence, it must be proved that one party exercised such a dominant influence over the mind of the other that he was unable to exercise a free and independent will when entering into the contract.

14   Where there is a presumption of undue influence, it must be shown that no undue influence occurred. This is usually proved by showing that there was available independent and competent advice.

CASE NOTE

Howard Marine & Dredging Co. v. *Ogden & Sons Ltd.* (1978) C.A.
The plaintiffs were negotiating with the defendants for the hiring of two of the plaintiffs' barges. The plaintiffs' marine manager stated to the defendants that the payload of each barge was, in effect, 1600 tonnes. In fact, the payload was only 1055 tonnes each. This statement was based on an honest recollection of the entry in Lloyd's Register. The true figure in the documents of each barge had not registered in the marine manager's mind. As a result of this false statement, the barges were useless to the defendants and they refused to pay the hire charges. The defendants counter-claimed for damages under s. 2(1) of the Misrepresentation Act 1967 and for negligence.

HELD: The defendants could succeed on their counter-claim because the plaintiff's marine manager did not have the reasonable grounds required by s.2(1); further, the defendants were liable for breach of the duty of care, i.e. for negligence.

EXERCISES

1   'Agreement must be authentic, i.e. it must be reached without mistake, without misrepresentation and without coercion.' Discuss this statement.

2   Explain and illustrate with cases the difference between common mistake, mutual mistake and unilateral mistake.

3   Outline the difference between mistake at law and mistake in equity. Mention some cases to illustrate your answer.

4   When will common mistake be operative?

5   When is mutual mistake operative?

6   Explain the defence of *non est factum*. When is it available?

7   When might the court award rescission on terms?

8   When is rectification an appropriate remedy?

9   In what circumstances will mistaken identity affect the validity of a contract?

10   What do you understand by the word 'misrepresentation'?

11   What are the remedies for misrepresentation at common law, in equity and by statute?

12   What are the bars to rescission?

13   What is economic duress?

14   In what circumstances will undue influence be presumed? Explain how the presumption may be rebutted.

15   Compare duress and undue influence.

WORKSHOP

1   Read the case note at the end of this chapter. State briefly the principle involved in the case and suggest factual situations to which it might apply.

2   Joe has just bought a brief-case from Albert. The brief-case is made of plastic material but Joe and Albert both believe it to be leather. What would your advice to Joe be when he discovers the mistake? Would your advice have been any different if Albert had described the case as leather when he offered it for sale?

3   Harry has signed a form guaranteeing John's bank overdraft. When he

signed this document, a bank official had purposely covered up the heading 'GUARANTEE' saying: 'this is just for information only'.

4 Charles says to Maudie, 'You can have my motor-car for £345.' Maudie accepts. It transpires that Charles intended to sell his Mini whereas Maudie thought he was offering his Ford Escort. Advise Maudie.

5 Bert entered into a contract for the purchase of a house from Tracy. The price was £11,000. Both parties mistakenly thought that the house was occupied by a statutory tenant. In fact the statutory tenant has died and the house with vacant possession is worth £15,000. Advise Tracy.

6 Robert, a plausible rogue, has stolen a cheque-book from Jinko, a well known pop singer. He uses a cheque from the stolen book to pay for a motor-cycle which James has sold to him for £900. James would not have parted with the motor-cycle had Robert not pretended so well to be Jinko. Robert sells the motor-cycle to Annie who takes it in good faith for the price of £750. James now seeks to recover the motor-cycle from Annie. Advise him.

7 Paul is claiming damages under s. 2 of the Misrepresentation Act against Peter with regard to a statement made by him in connection with a house he has recently sold to Paul. The statement was: 'There are more than a dozen fast trains to London from the local British Rail station.' There were, at the time of the contract, only three such trains per day. Advise Peter as to the requirements of the Act for his defence.

CHAPTER 12

CONTRACTUAL VALIDITY

The validity of a contract may be affected by lack of written evidence, by public policy or by lack of capacity in one of the parties.

12.1 CONTRACTS WHICH MUST BE EVIDENCED IN WRITING

There are two kinds of contract which are not enforceable in the courts unless there is written evidence adduced. First, in the case of contracts of guarantee, section 4 of the Statute of Frauds 1677 requires written evidence of the contract and, secondly, in the case of contracts for the sale or other disposition of land, the Law of Property Act 1925, similarly requires written evidence.

(a) Contracts of guarantee

Section 4 of the Statute of Frauds provides that:

> No action shall be brought whereby to charge the defendant upon any special promise to answer for the debt, default or miscarriage of another person unless the agreement upon which such action is brought, or some memorandum or note thereof, shall be in writing and signed by the party to be charged therewith or some other person thereunto by him lawfully authorised.

This section applies to guarantees but not to indemnities. It is, therefore, important to know how guarantee differs from indemnity. A contract debtor and the party who guarantees that, in the event of default by the debtor he, the guarantor, will pay the creditor. The guarantor's promise is made to the creditor – not to the debtor. The guarantor does not become liable to pay the creditor unless and until the principal debtor is in default in payment. The word 'surety' means the same as guarantor.

Section 4 does not apply to indemnity. A person giving an indemnity makes himself primarily liable to pay the creditor whereas a person giving a guarantee makes himself secondarily liable, i.e. only after default of the primary debtor.

(b) Contracts for the sale or other disposition of an interest in land

Section 40(1) of the Law of Property Act 1925 provides that,

> No action may be brought upon any contract for the sale or other disposition of land or any interest in land, unless the agreement upon which such action is brought, or some memorandum or note thereof, is in writing and signed by the party to be charged or by some other person thereunto by him lawfully authorised.

This provision applies to almost all contracts to do with land, e.g. sale, lease, right of entry, the sale of gravel taken from the land, or the con-ferring of a right to enter and cut and take away a growing crop. As in the case of the Statute of Frauds, the Law of Property Act does not specify exactly what evidence in writing is required to make a contract actionable. If the contract itself is in writing and is signed by the defendant or his lawful agent, then the statute is satisfied. It is, however, not quite so simple where the plaintiff relies upon a 'note or memorandum in writing'. The question sometimes arises as to whether the note or memorr-andum submitted by the plaintiff is sufficient to satisfy the statute. The decided cases show that the statute will be satisfied if the note contains the following matters:

   (i) the name or description of the parties;
  (ii) a description of the whole subject-matter to be transferred;
 (iii) the consideration to be given for the subject-matter (this is not required in the case of a guarantee);
  (iv) the material terms agreed upon; and
   (v) the signature of the defendant or his agent.

Where a plaintiff is unable to put such written evidence before the court, the contract, which might have been clearly agreed orally, will not be enforceable. In the words of the statute, an action may not be brought. However, a contract which is thus unenforceable at law may sometimes be enforceable in equity under the doctrine of part performance.

(c) The equitable doctrine of part performance

Where a plaintiff has entered into an oral contract within the ambit of s. 40(1) of the Law of Property Act 1925 and has actually partly performed his side of the bargain, the acts of part performance may, in equity, constitute sufficient evidence to render the contract specifically enforceable. To satisfy the test of sufficiency, the plaintiff must show that his acts of part performance prove (i) that there must have been *some* contract between him and the defendant and (ii) that the acts in question are consistent with the contract alleged. Further, the plaintiff must be able to show that the circumstances are such that it would be fraudulent on the part of the defendant to take advantage of the contract not being in writing. In this regard, the courts apply the maxim that equity will not allow a statute to be used as an instrument of fraud. Finally, the plaintiff must also show proper parol evidence of the oral contract. For examples of the doctrine of part performance, see *Dickinson* v. *Barrow* (1904) and *Wakeham* v. *Mackenzie* (1968).

12.2 ILLEGAL CONTRACTS

The general rule is that no action will be allowed upon a contract which contains an illegal element. The applicable maxim is *ex turpi causa non oritur actio* (no action arises from a base cause). It is against the policy of the common law to allow such an action and, in this regard, the policy of the common law must be regarded as part of the wider public policy. The principle applies equally to contracts which are illegal in their very inception and to those which are lawful in their formation but which are performed unlawfully, e.g. contrary to the provisions of a statute. In *Holman* v. *Johnson* (1775) Lord Mansfield stated the law as follows:

'No court will lend its aid to a man who founds his cause of action upon an immoral or an illegal act. If from the plaintiff's own stating or otherwise, the cause of action appears to arise *ex turpi causa*, or the transgression of a positive law of this country, then the court says he has no right to be assisted.'

(a) Illegal contracts identified

The decided cases show that a wide range of wrongdoing will be treated as illegal so as to incur the application of this principle of public policy. From the cases it is possible to classify illegal contracts into various types. The scheme adopted by Cheshire and Fifoot recognises six types as follows:

(i) Contracts to commit a crime, a tort or a fraud on a third party.
It is self-evident that the courts will not enforce a contract to commit a crime or a tort, for example, the obtaining of goods by false pretences or the publication of a libel. In *Bigos* v. *Boustead* (1951) it was held that a contract of a kind prohibited by UK currency regulations was illegal. There is also a wider rule of public policy which precludes a person from taking legal action to recover the fruits of his crime: *Beresford* v. *Royal Insurance Co. Ltd.* (1937).

(ii) Sexually immoral contracts.
No precise statements can be made about this kind of illegality because public policy will reflect the changing moral standards from generation to generation. As an illustration, however, in *Pearce* v. *Brooks* (1866) it was held that a coachbuilder who had hired out a vehicle to a young woman, knowing that she would use it in the furtherance of her profession as a prostitute, could not sue to recover arrears of hire charges.

(iii) Contracts prejudicial to the public safety.
Contracts which either benefit an enemy country or disturb the good relations of the UK with a friendly country are prohibited by the common law. Usually, in time of war, dealings with enemy aliens are prohibited by statute. With regard to dealings affecting friendly countries, the following have been held illegal: an agreement to raise funds to support a revolt in a friendly country and an agreement to export goods into a country contrary to its laws of prohibition.

(iv) Contracts prejudicial to the administration of justice.
An agreement which interferes in any way with the proper administration of justice will be held to be illegal. There are many instances of this kind of illegality but the most obvious examples are an agreement to stifle a prosecution or to give false evidence in a criminal trial or an agreement by which an accused person gives an indemnity to cover bail put up for him: *Herman* v. *Jeuchner* (1885).

(v) Contracts liable to corrupt public life.
Any contract to buy or procure public office or a public honour is illegal. In *Parkinson* v. *The College of Ambulance* (1925) the plaintiff agreed to donate £3,000 to the College of Ambulance in return for the procurement of a knighthood. In an action to recover the money, it was held that the agreement was illegal and that the plaintiff could not pursue his action.

(vi) Contracts to defraud the revenue.
Any contract which directly or indirectly attempts to defraud a national or local taxing authority will be illegal. In *Alexander* v. *Rayson* (1936)

the terms of a contract of employment allowed the employee to recover excessive amounts of money as tax-free expenses. In an action to recover arrears of salary and expenses it was held that the employee could not recover under either head because the contract was illegal.

(b) The general consequences of illegality

If during the course of an action the judge becomes aware of some illegality he will stop proceedings and will make no order of any kind. It follows that the plaintiff will be unable to recover damages for breach of contract, nor will he be able to recover money paid or property transferred under the contract. The plaintiff will not be able to sever the illegal element and claim on the remaining part of his contract for the illegality will taint the entire contract: *Alexander* v. *Rayson* (1936).

(c) Exceptions to the rule

Where the plaintiff is not equally at fault with the defendant, the court may allow him to proceed since it is not against public policy to assist an innocent plaintiff. Thus:

(i) Where the contract is lawful in its inception but is performed in an unlawful manner by one of the parties without the knowledge of the other, then that other party will not be denied his right of action on the contract: *Archbolds* v. *Spanglett* (1961). However, where that other party knows of the illegal performance and has not objected to it he will not be allowed an action: *Ashmore* v. *Dawson* (1973).

(ii) Where a contract is prohibited by statute in order to protect a particular class of persons, the plaintiff will be allowed his action if he belongs to that class: *Nash* v. *Halifax Building Society* (1979).

(iii) A plaintiff will be allowed to sue on an illegal contract if he can show that he was induced to enter into it by the fraud, duress, oppression or breach of trust on the part of the defendant. For example, in *Hughes* v. *Liverpool Victoria Legal Friendly Society* (1916) the plaintiff, who had been fraudulently induced to enter into an illegal contract of insurance by an agent, was allowed to recover the premiums he had paid.

(iv) Where no part of the illegality has been performed and the plaintiff is able to show that he genuinely repents of entering into the contract, he will be allowed his action, for the law encourages repentance. The repentance must, however, be genuine: see *Bigos* v. *Boustead* (1951).

12.3 CONTRACTS IN RESTRAINT OF TRADE

Certain kinds of contract are void, wholly or in part, as being against the public interest. It should be noticed that the legal effect is quite different from the effect of those contracts which incur the full stigma of illegality. For present purposes the most important category of void contract is the contract in restraint of trade. Also included, however, are two further categories, namely, contracts to oust the jurisdiction of the courts and contracts striking at marriage and parenthood, the latter being outside the scope of this book.

Any contract clause which seeks to oust the jurisdiction will be declared void and severed from the contract. Arbitration clauses are not regarded as attempts to oust the jurisdiction unless there is a provision purporting to restrain a party from submitting questions of law to the courts: *Lee* v. *Showmens' Guild* (1952) and *Baker* v. *Jones* (1954). In the important case of *Scott* v. *Avery* (1856) it was decided that it was not an ouster of jurisdiction for a clause to provide that the award of an arbitrator is a condition precedent to litigation.

(a) Contracts in restraint of trade

A contract in restraint of trade is one in which a party agrees to some restriction on his freedom to carry on his occupation, trade, business or profession. Such contracts fall into three categories, as follows:

(i) Contracts of employment.
It is not unusual for an employee to accept some restraint on the future exercise of his right to carry on his trade or profession, particularly after leaving his employment under the contract containing the restraint.

(ii) Contracts for the sale of a business.
Where a business is sold, the vendor usually accepts a restraint so as to protect the purchaser of the business. This element in the sale of a business is called the 'goodwill', i.e. the probability that old customers and clients will continue to deal with the business even under new ownership. This probability would reduce in the event of the vendor failing to undertake not to open a competing business.

(iii) Contracts for the regulation of trading relations.
Into this category fall a number of kinds of agreement, e.g. to regulate the manufacturing output of some commodity, to control prices or to control the trading connections of a particular business or a particular piece of land. The last-mentioned is called a 'solus' agreement.

(b) The 'reasonableness' rule

The rule governing the validity of restraint clauses was laid down by the House of Lords in the two cases *Nordenfelt* v. *Maxim Nordenfelt* (1894) and *Mason* v. *Provident Clothing and Supply Co. Ltd.* (1913). Taking these two cases together, the position is as follows:

(i) The general rule is that all restraints of trade are contrary to public policy and therefore void.

(ii) Exceptionally a restraint may be justified and upheld if it is reasonable – reasonable, that is, in reference (1) to the parties concerned and (2) to the interests of the public. The restraint must be so framed and so guarded as to afford adequate protection to the party in whose favour it is imposed, while at the same time it is in no way injurious to the public.

(iii) Partial restraints as well as general restraints are subject to the reasonableness rule.

(iv) A restraint upon an employee in favour of his employer will be upheld less readily than a restraint upon the vendor of a business in favour of the purchaser.

For examples of the application of the reasonableness test with regard to restraints on employees see *Mason* v. *Provident Clothing and Supply Co. Ltd.* (1913), *Morris* v. *Saxelby* (1916)* and *Fitch* v. *Dewes* (1921).* For examples of restraints upon vendors of businesses see *Nordenfelt* v. *Maxim Nordenfelt* (1894) and *British Reinforced Concrete Co.* v. *Schelff* (1921).* For an example of a restraint in a contract for the regulation of trade see *English Hop Growers* v. *Dering* (1928).*

(c) Severance

Contract clauses in restraint of trade are *prima facie* void and therefore, unless upheld by the court on the basis of the reasonableness test, will be regarded as severed from the rest of the contract. In other words, only the restraint is affected and the remainder of the contract provisions are valid and binding. Thus, a plaintiff may sue on such a contract for damages for breach, for the recovery of money due – all according to the general rules of contract. A comparison should now be made with the effects of illegality as explained above (Chapter 12.2(b) and (c)).

Where a contract clause, taken as a whole, is regarded by the court as against public policy, the entire clause will be declared void and severed: see, in particular, *Attwood* v. *Lamont* (1920).* However, where a clause contains several undertakings, only those undertakings which offend public policy will be severed, leaving the remaining undertakings as valid and binding: *Goldsoll* v. *Goldman* (1915).

(d) Statutory control of restrictive practices

The common law rules governing commercial restraint agreements are clearly not sufficient to protect the interests of the public in a modern industrial country. In the first place, restrictive trade practices are not likely to be brought before the court unless the matter is challenged by one of the parties. Even then the court will usually place more emphasis on the question of reasonableness between the contracting parties than on the question of reasonableness as regards the public interest. Moreover, those restrictive agreements which would, if brought before the court, be regarded as damaging to the public are not likely to be challenged by the parties. In the best public interest a system of mandatory disclosure and registration of restrictive agreements should be available.

The Restrictive Trade Practices Act 1976 and the Fair Trading Act 1973 provide for the registration of agreements or arrangements which are likely to restrict competition. Any such restriction will be void if found to be 'contrary to the public interest' by the Restrictive Practices Court.

12.4 CAPACITY

Capacity is an incident of personality. Capacity can attach only to natural persons (i.e. human beings) or corporations. The general rule is that natural persons have full contractual capacity, the exceptions being minors (infants), drunken and insane persons and, in time of war, enemy aliens. With regard to a corporation, the capacity to contract depends upon the manner in which that corporation was created. Contracts entered into by minors, by insane or drunken persons and by corporations are considered below.

(a) Contracts entered into by minors

A minor is a person who has not yet reached the age of capacity, which is defined in The Family Law Reform Act 1969, s. 1, as eighteen years. Minors' contracts may be divided into three categories, namely, void contracts, voidable contracts and valid contracts.

(b) Minors' Void Contracts

By the Infants' Relief Act 1874, s. 1, three kinds of minors' contract are declared to be 'absolutely void', namely, for the repayment of money lent or to be lent, for goods supplied or to be supplied (other than necessaries) and accounts stated. With regard to loans contracted during infancy, it is further provided by the Betting and Loans (Infants) Act 1892 that any agreement made after full age to repay such loan is void.

(i) Loans to Minors.
The Act of 1874 precludes action to recover any loan made to a minor. Even where the minor has induced the loan by fraudulently stating that he is of full age the lender cannot recover in tort, for to allow the action would be an indirect enforcement of a contract absolutely void by statute: *Leslie* v. *Sheill* (1914). It has been held that, since a minor's debt is void, any guarantee of the debt is also void and not enforceable: *Coutts* v. *Brown-Lecky* (1946).

(ii) Goods supplied or to be supplied (other than necessaries).
The expression 'supplied' indicates that the 1874 Act applies to contracts of any kind under which there is a supply of goods, e.g. sale, loan, barter or hire-purchase. In *Pearce* v. *Brain* (1929) a contract by which a minor exchanged his motor-cycle for a motor-car was held to be void under the Infants' Relief Act 1874, although he could not recover his motor-cycle after using the car for a few days as there had thus not been a total failure of consideration to him. Contracts for the supply of necessaries are specifically excluded by the Act and are therefore binding on minors.

(iii) Accounts stated.
The 1874 Act provides that all accounts stated with minors are void. An account stated with a minor is an agreed balance payable by the minor after a series of transactions with the other party.

(c) Minors' voidable contracts

Certain kinds of contract are voidable at the option of the minor although binding on the other contracting party. These contracts, sometimes described as being of 'continuing obligation' are: sale or lease of land, subscription for shares not fully paid up, partnership agreements and marriage settlements. To be effective, the repudiation must take place before, or within a reasonable time of, the minor's reaching full age. After repudiation the minor escapes all contractual liabilities which would otherwise have accrued after the date of repudiation. The minor cannot recover money paid under a voidable contract unless there has been a total failure of consideration: *Valentini* v. *Canali* (1889).

(d) Minors' valid contracts

A minor is bound by contracts for 'necessaries' and by contracts for his education, training or beneficial service.

(i) Necessaries.

In *Peters* v. *Fleming* (1840) it was explained that necessaries are not simply those articles which are necessary to support life, but include such articles 'fit to maintain the particular minor in the state, station and degree in which he is'. In this case it was held that rings and a watch chain were necessaries in the case of the son of a wealthy man. At common law, necessaries might be goods or services. Examples of necessaries would be food, clothing and lodgings for the minor and his dependants, if any. In all cases the test against the background of the minor's station in life would have to be satisfied. The Sale of Goods Act 1979 provides in s. 3(2) that, 'Where necessaries are sold and delivered to a minor ... he must pay a reasonable price for them.' Section 3(3) defines 'necessaries' as 'goods suitable to the condition in life of the minor concerned and to his actual requirements at the time of sale and delivery'. In *Nash* v. *Inman* (1908) a minor, a Cambridge undergraduate, was sued for £145 – the price of clothing supplied to him. The clothing included eleven fancy waistcoats. There was evidence that the minor's father had amply supplied him with clothes to suit his condition in life. It was held therefore that the clothes were not necessaries and that the contract was void under the Infants Relief Act 1874.

(ii) Beneficial service.

A minor is bound by a contract of apprenticeship or a contract of beneficial service provided, in either case, that the terms of contract are reasonable and, on the whole, substantially to the benefit and advantage of the minor. In *De Francesco* v. *Barnum* (1889) it was held that an apprentice dancer was not bound by an agreement whose terms were, on balance, far more onerous on the apprentice than on the master. The rule has been extended to contracts analogous to contracts of beneficial service: for example, in *Doyle* v. *White City Stadium* (1935) a professional boxer was held to be bound by the terms of a contract to fight in a boxing match, even though the terms incorporated the rules of the British Boxing Board of Control by which he was disqualified from winning the match as a result of a foul blow. In this case the court took the view that the rules included in the contract encouraged fair boxing and were, therefore, on the whole for the minor's benefit, even though in the particular circumstances they caused his disqualification. A further example is to be found in *Chaplin* v. *Frewin* (1966). In this case the minor was the son of a famous film star. He sought to exploit his position by entering into a contract with a publisher for the publication of his memoirs which were to be written by professional journalists, based on information provided by the minor. The minor was held to be bound by this contract which was, on the whole, for his benefit as he intended to take up the profession of journalist after completing the memoirs.

(e) Contracts by insane or drunken persons

A contract made by a person of unsound mind is voidable at that person's option only if it can be shown that the other party knew of the unsoundness of mind. The classic statement of the law in this connection was made in *Imperial Loan* v. *Stone* (1892) as follows:

'A contract made by a person of unsound mind is not voidable at that person's option if the other party to the contract believed at the time he made the contract that the person with whom he was dealing was of sound mind. In order to avoid a fair contract on the ground of insanity the mental incapacity of the one must be known to the other party.'

(f) Contracts with corporations

There are three kinds of corporation aggregate which must each be taken separately when discussing contractual capacity.

(i) Chartered corporations.
At common law, a corporation may be created by Royal Charter. The generally accepted view is that such corporations have full contractual capacity. In other words, where a chartered corporation enters into a contract which is not authorised by the terms of its Royal Charter, the contract is, nevertheless, valid.

(ii) Statutory corporations.
A statutory corporation is one which is created by statute. Such a corporation must be distinguished from a registered company, i.e. a corporation created by the process of registration under the Companies Act. The contractual capacity of a statutory corporation is determined by the powers and duties conferred on the corporation by its particular incorporating statute. Any contract within the statute is *intra vires* and binding; any contract outside the powers given by the statute is *ultra vires* and void. The most important examples of modern statutory corporations are those which have been set up to control nationalised industries such as railways, airlines and energy. All are subject to the *ultra vires* doctrine.

(iii) Registered companies.
When a company is created by registration according to the requirements of the Companies Act 1985, a number of documents must be lodged with an official known as the Registrar of Companies. One of these essential documents is the company's memorandum of association, which must always contain an 'objects clause' setting out the objects of the company.

Contractual capacity is determined by the application of the doctrine of *ultra vires* to the objects clause. This general rule is now subject to s. 9(1) of the European Communities Act 1972 which provides that an *ultra vires* contract is enforceable by the other party provided that he entered into the contract in good faith.

SUMMARY

1 Section 4 of the Statute of Frauds 1677 provides that contracts of guarantee are not enforceable unless evidenced in writing and signed by the defendant.

2 Section 40(1) of the Law of Property Act 1925 provides that contracts for the sale or other disposition of land or any interest in land are not enforceable unless evidenced in writing and signed by the defendant.

3 Both section 40(1) and section 4 require that the contract must be in writing or evidenced by a written note or memorandum and signed by the defendant.

4 Where a contract is unenforceable because of a failure to satisfy the evidential requirements of s. 40(1) of the Law of Property Act 1925, and the plaintiff has partly performed his side of the contract, equity may come to his aid. If his acts of part performance are sufficient in the eyes of equity, the doctrine of part performance will apply with the result that he will be allowed an action for specific performance of the contract notwithstanding that the statute is not satisfied.

5 To show sufficient acts of part performance, the plaintiff must prove (a) that there must have been *some* contract between him and the defendant and (b) that the acts in question are consistent with the contract which the plaintiff alleges.

6 It is against public policy to allow an action on a contract containing an illegal element. The plaintiff cannot recover damages for breach of contract nor can he recover money or property transferred under the contract.

7 As an exception to the general rule, where the plaintiff is not equally at fault with the defendant, it is not against public policy to assist the innocent plaintiff.

8 Restraints of trade are against the public interest and are consequently void. Exceptionally, a restraint may be upheld on the grounds that it is reasonable. Reasonableness is tested as between the parties and as regards the public.

9 Restraint clauses which are not upheld on grounds of reasonableness are severed from the contract, the rest of which holds good.

10 By the Infants' Relief Act 1874, s. 1, the following kinds of contracts with minors are declared to be 'absolutely void': (1) money lent or to be lent, (2) goods supplied or to be supplied other than necessaries and (3) accounts stated.

11 Contracts of continuing obligation are voidable at the option of the minor.

12 A minor is bound by a contract for necessaries and is bound to pay a reasonable price for them. Similarly, a minor is bound by a contract of beneficial service.

13 The rules governing the contractual capacity of corporations vary according to whether the corporation is a chartered, statutory or registered company.

14 The rule that the contractual capacity of a registered company is determined by the application of the doctrine of *ultra vires* to the objects clause in the Memorandum of Association is now subject to s.9(1) of the European Communites Act 1972. By this section, a company's *ultra vires* contract is enforceable by the other party provided that he entered into the contract in good faith.

CASE NOTES

Attwood v. *Lamont* (1920) C.A.

A tailor's cutter was employed as head of the tailoring department in a store with a number of departments. He undertook in his contract of employment not to engage in the trade of tailor, dressmaker, draper, milliner, hatter, haberdasher, gentlemen's outfitter or ladies' or children's outfitter at any place within a radius of ten miles of the store.

HELD: The clause merely listed the departments in the store and thus constituted a single covenant for the protection of the business. The clause could not be severed and must stand or fall unaltered. The clause was void as it was wider than necessary in the circumstances.

British Reinforced Concrete Co. v. *Schelff* (1921)

The partners in a small business of supplying steel for road reinforcement contracted to sell their patent and goodwill to a large company involved in many aspects of reinforced concrete work. The partners undertook not to engage in any similar business for three years. In breach of this undertaking, one of the partners took employment as manager of the reinforced materials department of a company in competition with B.R.C.

HELD: The restraint clause was invalid as it was wider than necessary to protect the actual small business which had been transferred by the partners.

English Hopgrowers v. *Dering* (1928) C.A.

Each member of a hopgrowers' association had agreed to deliver his entire crop to the association for onward sale. By this system, price-fixing was done by the association and competition between members was eliminated.

HELD: Each member was bound by the restraint involved in delivering only to the association. The restraint was reasonable.

Fitch v. *Dewes* (1921) H.L.

A solicitor's managing clerk in Tamworth agreed as part of a three-year contract of employment never to be engaged as a solicitor within seven miles of Tamworth Town Hall. The question to be decided was whether the unlimited restriction as to time was binding.

HELD: The unlimited restriction as to time was not against the public interest and it was reasonable for the managing clerk to give such an undertaking.

Morris v. *Saxelby* (1916) H.L.

An employee undertook not to compete with his employer for a period of seven years after leaving the employment. The employment was the sale and manufacture of pulley blocks, overhead runways and travelling cranes.

HELD: The restraint was not reasonable in reference to the interests of the parties and was prejudicial to the interests of the public. The restraint clause was, therefore, void.

EXERCISES

1   State the provisions of s. 4 of the Statute of Frauds 1677 and those of s. 40(1) of the Law of Property Act 1925.
2   What kinds of contract are affected by s. 40(1) of the Law of Property Act?
3   What details would constitute a note or memorandum sufficient to satisfy the statute?
4   What is the equitable doctrine of part performance? In what circumstances will it apply? Illustrate your answer with decided cases.
5   'No court will lend its aid to a man who founds his cause of action upon an immoral or an illegal act': *Holman* v. *Johnson* (1775), per Lord Mansfield. Explain and give examples from decided cases.
6   Where the parties are not equally at fault in entering into an illegal

contract, the innocent plaintiff may have an action on that contract. Illustrate this proposition with examples.

7   What kinds of contracts are categorised as void as being against the public interest? What is a contract in restraint of trade?

8   What rule governs the validity of restraint clauses? Give some examples of the application of the rule.

9   What is meant by the 'severance' of restraint clauses?

10   Contracts entered into by minors may be divided into three categories. Describe each category and comment on the validity of the contracts in each issue.

11   What rules govern the capacity of corporations to enter into contracts?

WORKSHOP

1 Monty, a builder, has agreed to sell a house in the course of construction to Susan. The agreement is entirely oral and the agreed price is £65,000. As the house nears completion, Susan makes a number of requests with regard to fittings and decorations in the house. On completion, Susan tells Monty that she no longer wants the house. Advise Monty.

Would your advice be different if Susan had not made any of the requests to Monty?

2 Henry, an influential business man with high political connections promises Arthur that he will arrange for a knighthood to be awarded to him in return for the payment of £10,000. Arthur pays the amount to Henry, but no knighthood is forthcoming. Arthur asks you whether he can recover the money paid to Henry. Advise him.

3 ABC p.l.c. manufacture heavy machinery. XYZ p.l.c. have entered into a contract for the purchase of certain machinery from ABC p.l.c. By statute, this machinery must not be carried on the road except on a 'low loader'. XYZ send their own carrier to take delivery of the machinery at the premises of ABC p.l.c. The loading is supervised by the manufacturer's production manager. Due to the negligence of the carrier, the machinery is damaged in transit and XYZ have refused any payment to ABC p.l.c. Advise ABC p.l.c.

4 In a contract for the export of tee shirts to the USA, the arbitration clause provides (a) that the contract is governed by English law and (b) that, in the event of a dispute, questions of law will not be submitted by the arbitrator to the court. Comment on the validity of this provision.

5 Herman was employed as a junior clerk in the London office of a chartered accountant. His contract of employment contains a clause which provides that on leaving this employment he will not, for a period

of twenty years, enter the employment of any other accountant within the area of Greater London.

Herman has just left this employment and wishes to know whether he may take up a very good offer of employment in London. Advise him.

6 Michael has lent £300 to Percy, aged 15 years. On the due date for repayment, Percy tells Michael that he has no intention of paying back the £300.

Can Michael sue Percy for the money? Would it make any difference if Percy had fraudulently told Michael that he was 18 years of age at the time of the loan?

7 Frank, aged 17 years, has recently bought an overcoat from Alice's expensive boutique for £130. Frank has paid £30 deposit and has promised to pay the balance within four weeks. The next day, Frank discovered that he could have bought an identical coat for £63 at the local department store. Frank now refuses to pay any further money to Alice. Advise Alice whether she has a claim against Frank.

8 Adwise Limited is empowered by its objects clause to deal in any way in the advertising industry but is expressly precluded from engaging in the manufacture of goods of any kind. Contrary to this restriction, Adwise Limited has bought a furniture factory and is engaged in manufacturing. Rufus, a timber merchant has sold large quantities of timber to Adwise Limited and is now owed a total sum of £15,980. Adwise have now told Rufus that they are not bound to pay him because the contracts were *ultra vires*. Advise Rufus.

BREACH OF CONTRACT AND DISCHARGE

13.1 BREACH OF CONTRACT

A breach of contract occurs where a party does not comply with one or more of the terms of contract, express or implied. In such cases there may be a remedy available to the other party. At common law, damages (liquidated or unliquidated) may be claimed or, in a proper case, a *quantum meruit*. In equity the courts have power to award the decree of specific performance, that is to say, the court may order a defaulter to comply with his contractual promise. This remedy will never be available where damages would be regarded as a satisfactory remedy in the circumstances.

Where the parties have agreed on a genuine pre-estimate of the loss which would occur in the event of a particular breach, that pre-estimated amount is called liquidated damages; otherwise all damages are unliquidated, i.e. not settled in amount until the court's decision.

The word 'damage' must not be confused with 'damages'. 'Damage' is the loss or injury caused by the breach of contract and 'damages' is the amount of compensation awarded by the court.

(a) Unliquidated damages

The purpose of damages is to restore a party to the position he would have been in if the breach had not occurred, i.e. if there had been no damage. Unliquidated damages is compensation calculated according to the common law rules governing the matter. Where, by these rules, the damage is not too remote, the amount of damages will be ascertained by the court to give effect to the principle of restitution in full. Where, however, the damage is regarded as too remote, no damages will be recoverable.

Two of the leading cases on remoteness of damage and measure of damages are *Hadley* v. *Baxendale* (1854) and *Victoria Laundry* v. *Newman Industries Ltd.* (1949). In the first-mentioned case it was said that:

> 'Where two parties have made a contract which one of them has broken, the damages which the other party ought to receive in respect of such breach of contract should be such as may fairly and reasonably be considered either arising naturally, i.e. according to the usual course of things, from such breach of contract itself, or such as may reasonably be supposed to have been in the contemplation of both parties, at the time they made the contract, as the probable result of the breach of it.'

This is the classic statement of the law of damages.

The two alternative rules were restated by the Court of Appeal in the *Victoria Laundry* case as follows:

> 'In cases of breach of contract, the aggrieved party is only entitled to recover such part of the loss actually resulting as was at the time of the contract reasonably foreseeable as liable to result from the breach. What was at that time reasonably foreseeable depends upon the knowledge then possessed by the parties or, at all events, by the party who commits the breach. For this purpose knowledge 'possessed' is of two kinds: one imputed, the other actual. Everyone, as a reasonable person, is taken to know the 'ordinary course of things' and consequently what loss is liable to result from a breach of contract in that ordinary course. This is the subject-matter of the 'first rule' in *Hadley* v. *Baxendale*. But to this knowledge, which a contract-breaker is assumed to possess whether he actually possesses it or not, there may have to be added in a particular case knowledge which he actually possesses of special circumstances outside the 'ordinary course of things', of such a kind that a breach in those special circumstances would be liable to cause more loss. Such a case attracts the operation of the 'second rule' as to make additional loss also recoverable.'

In *The Heron II* (1969) the House of Lords preferred the earlier concept of the 'reasonable supposition of what had been in the contemplation of both parties' to the concept of 'foreseeability' which was introduced in the *Victoria Laundry* case. In this regard the rules of contract differ from those of the law of torts. In either case, the assessment of damages is not an exact science. For further examples of the application of the test of remoteness see *W. L. Thompson Ltd.* v. *Robinson (Gunmakers) Ltd.* (1955)* and *Anglia T.V.* v. *Reed* (1972).*

The rules of remoteness enable the court to determine the kind or category of loss which is to be recoverable. These categories are sometimes referred to as heads of claim or heads of loss. Once the heads are determined, the principle of restitution in full is applied to measure the damages recoverable. Where, however, the claimant has failed to take any reasonable steps which were available to him to reduce or mitigate the damage caused by the breach, his claim will be defeated to that extent.

(b) Liquidated damages

There are some kinds of breach of contract for which damages can be pre-assessed by the parties and included in the express terms of contract. For example, most building contracts provide for the payment of a stated sum of money by the contractor for each week of delay beyond the agreed date for completion. Where such amounts of money are genuinely pre-estimated as the likely loss to flow from the delay, i.e. the breach, it becomes a binding and enforceable part of the contract. If, on the other hand, the parties stipulate for an amount which is not a genuine pre-estimate but rather a sum introduced merely to deter a breach of contract, that amount will not be regarded as liquidated damages. Such an amount will be a penalty and the penalty clause will be void.

The principles were authoritatively stated in the House of Lords in *Dunlop* v. *New Garage* (1915) as follows:

'(i) Though the parties to a contract who use the word penalty or liquidated damages may *prima facie* be supposed to mean what they say, yet the expression used is not conclusive. The court must find out whether the payment stipulated is in truth a penalty or liquidated damages. This doctrine may be said to be found *passim* in nearly every case. (ii) The essence of a penalty is a payment of money stipulated as *in terrorem* of the offending party; the essence of liquidated damages is a genuine covenanted pre-estimate of damage; (iii) The question whether a sum stipulated is a penalty or liquidated damages is a question of construction to be decided upon the terms and inherent circumstances of each particular contract, judged of as at the time of making the contract, not as at the time of the breach. (iv) To assist this task of construction various tests have been suggested, which, if applicable to the case under consideration, may prove helpful or even conclusive. Such are: (a) It will be held to be a penalty if the sum stipulated for is extravagant and unconscionable in amount in comparison with the greatest loss which could conceivably be proved to have followed from the breach. (b) It will be held to be a penalty if the breach consists only in not paying a sum of money, and the sum stipulated is a sum greater than the sum which ought to have been paid. (c) There is a presumption (but no more) that it is a penalty when a single lump sum is made payable by way of compensation, on the occurrence of one or more or all of several events, some of which may occasion serious and others but trifling damage.'

(c) Quantum meruit

A *quantum meruit* claim is a claim for reasonable remuneration for work done or services supplied.

An entitlement to *quantum meruit* may be contractual or quasi-contractual.

(i) Contractual quantum meruit.
This is a convenient remedy in two cases. First, it may found a claim where there is a contract for the supply of services but no express agreement for payment; in such cases there is an implication that reasonable remuneration will be paid. In the event of non-payment, the plaintiff may sue on the *quantum meruit: Powell* v. *Braun* (1954). Secondly, a *quantum meruit* claim will lie where an original contract containing terms for payment is discharged and replaced by a new contract. A simple illustration was given by Lord Atkin in *Steven* v. *Bromley* (1919): 'If I order from a wine merchant twelve bottles of whisky at so much a bottle, and he sends me ten bottles of whisky and two of brandy, and I accept them, I must pay a reasonable price for the brandy.'

In the case of sale of goods contracts which do not contain a stipulation as to price, the Sale of Goods Act 1979 provides for the payment of a reasonable price.

(ii) Quasi-contractual quantum meruit.
There are two main instances of *quantum meruit* as a quasi-contractual remedy. First, where a contract has been discharged as a result of the default of one of the parties, the other party may claim on a *quantum meruit* for any work done under that contract. Such a claim may be made as a convenient alternative to a claim for damages for breach of contract: *De Bernady* v. *Harding* (1853). The second case of a *quantum meruit* entitlement arising *quasi ex contractu* occurs where work is done by one person for another but without a valid contract. This state of affairs usually arises where the parties were under the erroneous impression that they had entered into a contract: *Craven-Ellis* v. *Canons Ltd.* (1936). It is important to understand that *quantum meruit* arises independently as a rule of common law: it does not arise as a result of the acceptance of services proffered.

(d) Specific performance

The common law courts never had the power to order a defendant to comply with his contractual obligation: but in the courts of equity this power had long been exercised as the decree of specific performance. Since the Judicature Acts the jurisdiction has been exercised by the present courts. The decree is awarded or withheld at the discretion of the court and not as of right. Specific performance originated because common law damages proved, in some cases, to be an inadequate remedy. It follows that the remedy is never available in the vast majority of cases, for damages is usually an adequate remedy. The essential characteristic of specific performance is its equitable nature: it will be granted only if, in all the circumstances of the case, it would be just and equitable to do so. Thus, for example, specific performance will not be decreed if it would cause undue hardship on the defendant or if the plaintiff has unduly delayed his action or if the plaintiff has not come with 'clean hands'. For examples of specific performance see *Tamplin* v. *James* (1880)* and *Webster* v. *Cecil* (1861)*. Specific performance will never be awarded (1) for breach of a contract for personal services, (2) where it would require the constant supervision of the court or (3) where the contract is wanting in mutuality.

(e) Injunction

Where a defendant has broken a negative promise, i.e. a promise not to do something, the equitable remedy which may be available is an injunction. This is an order to restrain the defendant from breaking a negative term of contract. An injunction will never be awarded if the result would be to coerce the defendant into complying with the positive part of his contract which itself would not have been specifically enforceable: *Lumley* v. *Wagner* (1852) and *Warner Bros* v. *Nelson* (1937).*

(f) Limitation of actions

The Limitation Act 1980 provides time limits within which an action founded on contract or tort must be brought. The Act also makes provision to cover those cases where the defendant has fraudulently concealed the plaintiff's right of action and also for the extension of the limitation period in case of the plaintiff's disability.

(i) Action on a simple contract.
An action founded on simple contract cannot be brought after the expiration of six years from the date on which that cause of action accrued: s. 5.

(ii) Action on a specialty.

An action upon a specialty cannot be brought after the expiration of twelve years from the date on which the cause of action accrued: s. 8.

(iii) Fraudulent concealment of right of action.

Where any fact relevant to the plaintiff's right of action has been deliberately concealed from him by the defendant the period of limitation will not begin to run until the plaintiff has discovered the concealment or could with reasonable diligence have discovered it: s. 32.

(iv) Effect of disability (e.g. minors).

If on the date when any right of action accrued the person to whom it accrued was under a disability, the action may be brought at any time before the expiration of six years from the date when he ceased to be under a disability or died (whichever first occurred) notwithstanding that the period of limitation has expired: s. 28.

(v) Acknowledgement or part payment of a debt.

Where any right of action has accrued to recover any debt or other liquidated pecuniary claim and the person liable for the claim acknowledges the claim or makes any payment in respect of it the right will be treated as having accrued on and not before the date of the acknowledgement or payment: s. 29. In other words, the section provides that a statute-barred right of action will be revived by a fresh acknowledgement or part payment of the debt. Where this occurs, the period of limitation starts over again.

(vi) Limitation of equitable claims.

The above-mentioned provisions of the Limitation Act 1980 do not apply to claims for equitable relief. However, s. 36(1) provides for an exception to be made in cases where these provisions might be applied by way of analogy. Hence any equitable claim which is the same in nature as a common law claim will attract the rules in the Act. Otherwise there is no hard and fast rule governing delays in bringing an action on an equitable claim. The maxim 'delay defeats the equities' will apply: a plaintiff who is guilty of unreasonable delay will be barred from relief. See *Leaf* v. *International Galleries* (1950),* where a claim for rescission of a contract for the sale of a painting was held to be barred after the lapse of five years.

13.2 DISCHARGE OF CONTRACT

When the rights and obligations created by a contract cease to exist the contract, thus exhausted, is said to be discharged. Discharge can occur in any of four ways, i.e. by acceptance of breach, by performance, by agreement or by frustration.

(a) Acceptance of breach

Where there is a serious breach of contract the aggrieved party may be able to escape further liability to perform the contract by giving the other party notice that his breach of contract is accepted as a repudiation. In a proper case this will result in the discharge of the aggrieved party from all obligations which would otherwise have accrued under the contract. The aggrieved party may, in addition, sue for damages. Whether the notice has this effect depends always on the nature of the breach complained of. It must be either a fundamental breach or a breach of condition (Chapter 10(5)(d)).

(i) Fundamental breach.

Where a breach is such as to deprive the other party of substantially the whole benefit of the contract, or otherwise where the contract is rendered useless for the purpose for which it had been entered into, the breach gives rise to the aggrieved party's option. He may either do nothing, in which case the contract remains undischarged notwithstanding the breach, or he may give notice to the other party that he accepts the breach as a repudiation of the contract. In the latter case, he will be discharged from further obligations under the contract and can immediately claim damages. He does not have to wait for the original time for performance to arrive: this is called 'repudiatory breach': *Hochster* v. *De la Tour* (1853).

In *Federal Commerce and Navigation* v. *Molena Alpha* (1979) it was held by the House of Lords that a threat to commit a repudiatory breach can have the same effect as an actual repudiatory breach even where the threat is accompanied by a subjective desire to maintain the contract. The reason is that the subjective desire of the one party does not prevent the other party from drawing the consequences of the threat of anticipatory breach.

(ii) Breach of condition.

Where there is a breach of condition (see Chapter 10.5(d)) the aggrieved party has the right to elect to treat himself as discharged from further obligations under the contract and to claim damages from the contract-breaker. Where, on the other hand, the breach does not amount to a breach of condition, the remedy will be in damages only; there will then be no right to treat the contract as repudiated.

(iii) The right of election.

From the paragraph above it should be clear that it is not the breach, however serious, which causes the discharge; it is rather the acceptance of breach by the giving of notice to the contract-breaker. Where a fundamental breach or a breach of condition remains unaccepted, the contract remains valid and binding on both parties: *White and Carter* v. *McGregor* (1962).*

(b) Discharge by performance

The general rule is that a party is not discharged unless and until he has entirely performed his contractual obligations. In cases where a party has promised entire performance in return for payment on completion, the other party is not bound to make any payment until such completion has been achieved. Such contracts are sometimes called 'entire' contracts. In *Cutter* v. *Powell* (1795) a seaman who had undertaken to complete a voyage in return for a stipulated sum died before completing the voyage. It was held that a claim on behalf of his estate to recover on a *quantum meruit* should fail. The seaman was not entitled to any payment at all until completion of his contractual obligations, i.e. completion of the entire voyage. A recent example of the rule will be found in *Bolton* v. *Mahadeva* (1972).* The apparent harshness of the requirement of complete performance is mitigated by the doctrine of substantial performance. By this doctrine, a party who has undertaken entire performance may recover payment if he can show that he has substantially performed his side of the bargain. He will be able to recover the original contract price less an amount representing his deficient performance: *Dakin* v. *Lee* (1916).

(c) Discharge by agreement

It is open to contracting parties to enter into a subsequent agreement to bring about the discharge of the original contract. It is also open to contracting parties to provide within their original contract for its discharge on the occurrence of any specified event. In either case the question to be asked is whether the agreement as to discharge is binding.

The parties may intend to bring their contractual relations to an end *simpliciter* or they may combine the discharge agreement with a further agreement on fresh terms. This latter course is called 'novation'. The question to be asked always is whether the subsequent agreement was binding. Whether the discharge has been effected will depend on this question. In this connection, the rule of consideration is vital. The actual consideration in question will vary according to whether the original contract remains executory – that is to say, where each party remains under some obligation to the other – or whether one of the parties has totally performed his side of the bargain.

(i) Original contract remains executory.

In this case, since each party is under an obligation to the other, a mutual waiver of rights will constitute a binding subsequent agreement to discharge the original contract. Each party by his waiver gives consideration to the other. The agreement of waiver may be coupled with an entirely new binding contract, i.e. novation.

(ii) Original contract performed by one party only: the common law position.

In this case, mutual waiver is not possible for lack of consideration passing from the party who remains under obligation. He must, therefore, give consideration to the other party to make the subsequent agreement binding. This is sometimes called 'accord and satisfaction' – the accord being the agreement to discharge the old agreement and the satisfaction being the new consideration introduced. The consideration may be some new element introduced at the creditor's request, such as payment on a different date, or at a different place, or for the debtor to perform in some entirely different manner. Under this rule, the new element introduced by the creditor may involve the payment of a lesser sum than that under the original contract. In *Pinnel's* case (1602) it was said that payment of a lesser sum on the day in satisfaction of a greater, cannot be any satisfaction for the whole; but the gift of a horse, hawk or robe in satisfaction is good; for it must have been intended that the horse, hawk or robe might be more beneficial to the creditor or otherwise he would not have accepted it in satisfaction. For a modern instance of this rule see *D & C Builders* v. *Rees* (1965).

(iii) Original contract performed by one party only: position in equity.

If no fresh element is introduced to constitute consideration moving from the debtor to the creditor, any purported waiver by the creditor will not be binding. At common law, the original agreement remains binding on the debtor and can be sued on by the creditor even though he has purportedly waived his strict rights. In such cases, equity may come to the aid of the debtor in the form of the doctrine of promissory estoppel.

Suppose the creditor says to the debtor, 'I will waive my right against you. You need not pay what you owe me'. If the debtor agrees to accept the waiver, it can be said that, subsequent to the original agreement, there was another agreement made between the same parties by which the original debt was waived. Suppose now that the creditor changes his mind. Suppose he claims to recover the amount of the debt from the debtor. The question whether he will succeed depends upon whether the subsequent agreement was binding. If the debtor gave no consideration to support the waiver, then it will not be binding and the creditor can sue on the original contract for the debt outstanding. At law, he will not be bound by the promise to waive the debt. If the debtor has ordered his affairs in reliance on the waiver, it is clearly unfair towards him; but that is the position at common law.

In equity, however, the matter is seen in a different light. If the debtor is able to show that, in the circumstances, it would be inequitable to allow the creditor to renegue on his promise, then equity will not allow the creditor to say that he did not intend his promise to be binding. In *Central London Property Trust Ltd.* v.*High Trees House Ltd.* (1947), Denning J. (as he then was) said that he preferred to apply the principle that a promise intended to be binding, intended to be acted on and in fact acted on, is binding in so far as its terms properly apply. In *Combe* v. *Combe* (1951), Denning L.J. (as he then was), explained the principle as follows:

'Where one party has, by his words or conduct, made to the other a promise or assurance which was intended to affect the legal relations between them and to be acted on accordingly, then, once the other party has taken him at his word and acted on it, the one who gave the promise or assurance cannot afterwards be allowed to revert to the previous legal relations subject to such qualifications which he himself introduced, even though it is not supported in point of law by any consideration but only by his word.'

By the doctrine of promissory estoppel, the strict legal rights of the creditor are suspended so long as the waiver lasts. If, due to a change in circumstances, it ceases to be inequitable for the creditor to pursue his legal rights, then he may give notice that he intends to revert to his strict legal rights: *W. L. Alan & Co. Ltd.* v. *El Nasr Export and Import Co.* (1972).

Finally, in connection with the doctrine of promissory estoppel, it must be understood that the doctrine operates as a defence. It does not give rise to a cause of action. To use the striking words of counsel in *Combe* v. *Combe*, it is a shield and not a sword.

(d) Discharge by frustration

The question to be considered is: where, due to some unforeseen event, performance by one of the parties becomes impossible, is that party liable in contract for his non-performance or is he excused performance? The general rule is that a contracting party is not excused by supervening impossibility; he is absolutely bound by the terms of the agreement. The common law judges took the view that parties could consider all eventualities and stipulate accordingly in their contract.

(i) The rule of absolute liability.
The general rule that a party is not excused his contractual obligations

on grounds of supervening impossibility was established in *Paradine* v. *Jane* (1647). In that case the defendant was sued for rent of a farm due under a lease. He argued that he ought to be excused because, due to the invasion of a hostile army, he had been expelled from the farm and could not earn profits to pay the rent. On the application of the rule of absolute liability the defence failed. The rule was then applied rigorously by the courts for more than two centuries after which the cases show that, in some circumstances, the general rule of absolute liability may be relaxed by the occurrence of an event which will discharge both parties from further liability. Where this occurs, the so-called doctrine of frustration is being applied.

The first case of relaxation of the general rule of absolute liability was *Taylor* v. *Caldwell* (1863). In this case there was a contract for the hire of a music hall for the purpose of giving four concerts. Before the due date of the first concert the music hall was destroyed by fire without fault of either party. The court took the view that the parties had contracted on the basis of the continued existence of the music hall at the time when the concerts were to be given, that being essential to their performance. It was held that, the music hall having ceased to exist without fault of either party, both parties were excused, the plaintiffs from taking the gardens and paying the money, and the defendants from performing their promise to give the use of the hall.

(ii) The frustrating event.

To bring about the discharge of both parties, the frustrating event must satisfy the following conditions. (1) It must render performance impossible or futile and not merely more onerous: *Davis Contractors* v. *Fareham U.D.C.* (1956): *National Carriers* v. *Panalpina* (1981). (2) The event must not have been due to the fault of one of the parties: *Taylor* v. *Caldwell* (1863): *Robinson* v. *Davison* (1871). (3) The event must not be embraced in an express term of the contract nor be covered by an absolute undertaking to perform. (4) The event must not be such as would be considered by the parties as a risk normally inherent in the contract: *Amalgamated Investment and Property Co.* v. *John Walker & Sons* (1976).

(iii) The consequences of frustration.

The frustrating event brings the contract to an end forthwith automatically. Both parties are, from that moment, discharged from any future obligations to perform. Contractual obligations which accrued before the occurrence of the frustrating event, however, are not affected and remain binding. In *Krell* v. *Henry* (1903) there was a contract to hire a third-floor flat in Pall Mall for the two days to view the coronation processions of King Edward VII. The King fell ill and the coronation processions were cancelled before the time for payment of rent. In that case it was held that the owner of the flat could not recover the agreed rent. This case should be compared with *Chandler* v. *Webster* (1904) where the facts were much the same as those in *Krell* v. *Henry*, except that the rent of £141 was payable immediately after the contract was made. In fact only £100 was paid in advance with the balance remaining due. This was the position between the parties when the processions were cancelled causing the contract to be frustrated. It was held that the balance of £41 remained payable and that the £100 could not be recovered.

With regard to the £100, the plaintiff had argued that he was entitled to its recovery in quasi-contract on the ground that there had been a total failure of consideration. The Court of Appeal, however, took the view that since the contract was not void *ab initio,* but had been discharged only on the cancellation of the procession, there had not been a total failure of consideration. In the *Fibrosa* case (1942) the House of Lords held that money paid in advance could be recovered in quasi-contract where there had been a total failure of consideration and that there could be such a total failure even though the contract was not void *ab initio.* The unfair result of this case was due to the fact that the party having to return the advance payment was not compensated for money spent on the contract preparations, i.e. preparing his factory and machinery to meet the contract order.

(iv) The Law Reform (Frustrated Contracts) Act 1943.
This Act was passed to remove some of the injustice which could be caused by frustration. It gives the court a power to order the payment or withholding of money as between the parties to a frustrated contract as the court considers to be just, taking into account expenses incurred for the purpose of performance of the contract.

SUMMARY

1   The rule in *Hadley* v. *Baxendale* (1854) is as follows:

'Where two parties have made a contract which one of them has broken, the damages which the other party ought to receive in respect of such a breach of contract should be such as may fairly and reasonably be considered either arising naturally, i.e. according to the usual course of things, from such breach of contract itself, or such as may reasonably be supposed to have been in the contemplation of both parties, at the time they made the contract, as the probable result of the breach of it.'

2   In *Victoria Laundry* v. *Newman Industries* (1949) it was said that:

'In cases of breach of contract, the aggrieved party is only entitled to recover such part of the loss actually resulting as was at the time of the contract reasonably foreseeable as liable to result from the breach.'

3   The essence of a penalty is a payment of money stipulated as *in terrorem* of the offending party; the essence of liquidated damages is a genuine covenanted pre-estimate of damage. Penalty clauses are void; liquidated damages clauses are binding.

4   A *quantum meruit* claim is a claim for reasonable remuneration which may arise either out of contract or out of quasi-contract.

5   Specific performance is an equitable remedy awarded or withheld at the discretion of the court. It will never be awarded where damages are an adequate remedy.

6   The Limitation Act 1980, s.5, provides that an action founded on simple contract cannot be brought after the expiration of six years from the date on which the cause of action accrued. Section 8 of the 1980 Act provides that an action upon a specialty cannot be brought after the expiration of twelve years from the date on which the cause of action accrued.

7   A contract may be discharged in any one of four ways, i.e. by acceptance of breach, by performance, by agreement or by frustration.

8   Where there has been a fundamental breach or a breach of condition the aggrieved party may elect to treat the contract as repudiated and consider himself discharged from further performance and may sue immediately for damages.

9   Where a party has promised entire performance in return for payment on completion, the other party is not bound to make any payment until such completion has been achieved. This rule is, however, subject to the doctrine of substantial performance.

10   A contract may be discharged by a subsequent binding agreement to that effect. Where the original contract has been performed by one party only, the debtor must give fresh consideration to bind the creditor to the subsequent agreement to discharge the original contract. The subsequent agreement is sometimes called 'accord and satisfaction'.

11   Where there is no accord and satisfaction, and the creditor sues on the original contract after promising to waive his rights under it, the debtor may be able to raise promissory estoppel in his defence.

12   The doctrine of frustration of contract operates as an exception to the rule of absolute liability. By this doctrine, both parties are excused further performance where an unforeseen event makes further performance by one of the parties impossible or futile. The frustrating event must not have arisen by the fault of either party.

13   At common law, the effect of frustration was to discharge parties from future obligations. Obligations which have accrued at the time of

the frustrating event remain unaffected. Money can be recovered on a frustrated contract if the plaintiff can show a total failure of consideration: the basis of such a claim is quasi-contractual.

14 As the common law often produced an unfair result on frustration of a contract, the Law Reform (Frustrated Contracts) Act 1943 was passed to give powers to the court to order the payment or the withholding of money as the court considers to be just.

CASE NOTES

Anglia Television v. *Reed* (1971) C.A.
The television company contracted with R, an actor, for making a television film. Before this contract was made, the company had incurred preliminary expenses of £2750 with regard to the proposed film. R repudiated the contract and the company accepted the repudiation. In their claim for damages for breach of contract, the company included the wasted preliminary expenditure which was incurred *before* the contract.

HELD: Expenditure incurred before the contract is recoverable as damages provided it is such as would reasonably be in the contemplation of the parties as likely to be wasted if the contract were broken.

Bolton v. *Mahadeva* (1972) C.A.
The plaintiff agreed to install a central heating system in the defendant's house for £800. The system did not work and the defendant refused to pay anything. The plaintiff sued for payment.

HELD: By the general rule that no payment is due under a lump-sum contract until complete performance, the plaintiff was not entitled to any money.

Leaf v. *International Galleries* (1950) C.A.
One Leaf bought a painting of Salisbury Cathedral which was described by the sellers as a genuine Constable. After five years, Leaf discovered that it was not a genuine Constable. He brought this action for rescission of the contract of sale for innocent misrepresentation.

HELD: The claim for rescission must fail because it was not brought within a reasonable time.

Tamplin v. *James* (1880)
An inn and an adjoining shop were put up for auction. Accurate plans of the property to be sold were displayed in the auction room. The purchaser

wrongly believed that the property knocked down to him included the garden at the rear of the inn. As a result of his mistake he refused to complete. The vendors brought this action for specific performance of the contract of sale.

HELD: There was no excuse for the mistake and the plaintiff was entitled to specific performance.

Thompson (W.L.) Ltd. v. Robinson (Gunmakers) Ltd. (1955)

On the day after contracting to buy a Standard Vanguard motor car, the buyers told the sellers that they would not accept delivery of the car. At the time, the local demand for that type of car was not great enough to absorb all the cars available to the sellers for sale. The sellers brought this action for damages for breach of contract.

HELD: The proper measure of damages was the profit which the sellers would have made on the sale.

Warner Bros. v. Nelson (1936)

A well-known film actress undertook as a term of her employment with the plaintiff company not to engage in any other stage or motion picture production or engage in any other occupation without the written consent of the plaintiff.

HELD: Where the enforcement of negative covenants does not amount to a decree of specific performance of the positive covenants or to obliging the employee to remain idle or perform the positive covenants, they can be enforced by injunction. The granting of such an injunction is discretionary. In this case an injunction to enforce the negative covenants would be granted limited to the duration of the contract or three years, whichever should be the shorter.

Webster v. Cecil (1861)

The defendant was the owner of certain real property which the plaintiff wished to purchase. The plaintiff offered to buy this property for £2000 but the defendant rejected the offer. Then the defendant offered the property to the plaintiff by letter for £1250. This was clearly an error, but the plaintiff accepted by return of post. The defendant promptly gave notice to the plaintiff that the figure of £1250 was in error and that the intended figure was £2250. The plaintiff now sued for specific performance.

HELD: The plaintiff was not entitled to specific performance because he must have known of the mistake when he accepted the defendant's written offer.

White and Carter Ltd. v. *McGregor* (1962) H.L.

The appellant company carried on the business of advertising on plates attached to litter bins which they supplied to local authorities. The respondent, who carried on a garage business, entered into a contract for advertising on litter bins. On the day following, he purported to cancel the contract. The appellants refused to accept the cancellation and went ahead with the advertising.

HELD: The cancellation was a repudiation of contract. The contract was not discharged because the repudiation was not accepted. Since the contract remained alive, the respondent was liable to pay the sum due under the contract.

EXERCISES

1 State in general terms the difference between liquidated and un-liquidated damages.

2 Explain carefully and in detail what is meant by 'remoteness' of loss. By what test is it decided whether any part of loss following a breach of contract is too remote to be recovered?

3 In *Dunlop* v. *New Garage* (1915) the principles governing penalties and liquidated damages were enunciated. State them accurately.

4 Explain with examples the difference between contractual and quasi-contractual *quantum meruit.*

5 In what circumstances will a decree of specific performance not be awarded?

6 State the statutory rules governing the limitation of actions in contract.

7 What rule governs delay in bringing an action for an equitable remedy?

8 A contract may be discharged by acceptance of breach. What kind of breach must have been committed? How does 'acceptance' take place. Illustrate your answer with decided cases.

9 Explain the so-called rule in *Cutter* v. *Powell.*

10 Explain carefully how a contract may be discharged by agreement between the parties. Distinguish in your answer between the case where the original contract remains executory on both sides and that where one party has performed completely.

11 What is the equitable doctrine of promissory estoppel?

12 How does a contract become discharged upon the occurrence of an event which makes further performance by one of the parties impossible or futile? Mention some decided cases in your answer.

WORKSHOP

1 Read the case notes at the end of this chapter, referring back to the relevant parts of the text. State the principle applied by the court in each of the decided cases.

2 Tamsin, a clothing manufacturer, delayed the delivery of an export consignment bought by Ahmed. As a result of this delay, Ahmed had to rearrange the shipment schedule of the consignment of clothing. As a result, the consignment was despatched on a ship which sailed three weeks after the ship which was originally to be used by Ahmed. In a violent storm, this ship was lost together with its cargo, including the consignment of clothing which Ahmed had bought from Tamsin. Ahmed now seeks damages from Tamsin to include his costs and losses consequent on the sinking. Advise Tamsin.

3 By reason of breach of a contract of carriage of goods by sea, a consignment of fruit was delayed. During this period of delay, the prices on the fruit market at the port of destination had fallen abruptly. The consignor now seeks damages to include the market price difference between the contracted date of arrival of the ship and the actual date of arrival. Explain with reasons whether he will succeed.

4 Olive is negotiating with Albert, a building contractor, for the building of a house to meet Olive's requirements. Olive has an unemployed husband and four children. The lease on the flat in which she lives is due to end at the date agreed for completion of the house by Albert. Olive wishes to include in her contract with Albert a liquidated damages clause. She asks you to advise on the amount to be stipulated. Advise her in detail.

PART IV
COMMERCIAL LAW

AGENCY

Agency is an essential feature of commercial life. Its rules may be found to govern almost any kind of transaction for the basic maxim is *qui facit per alium facit per se*. He who does anything by another does it by himself.

14.1 PRINCIPAL AND AGENT

An agency is created where a person, having the capacity to do an act for his own benefit on his own account, employs another person to do it. The person who employs the other is called the principal and the person employed is called the agent. The power to act which is thus delegated is called the agent's authority. This authority is the essential characteristic of agency. The general rule is that whatever a person can do in his own right he may authorise an agent to do for him. The principal is thus bound by the agent's dealings with third parties as if he had dealt with them himself. *Qui facit per alium facit per se* is the general maxim. The other maxim is *delegatus non potest delegare* - an agent cannot delegate his authority to another unless authorised expressly to do so.

The usual purpose of an agency agreement is to authorise the agent to enter into contracts on behalf of the principal.

Where an agent deals with a third party on behalf of the principal and within his authority, a legal relationship is created between the principal and the third party. The agent drops out having fulfilled his purpose. In other words, an agent acting within his authority binds his principal and does not himself assume personal liability. It follows that, if a right of action accrues to the third party in connection with the transaction, it is the principal whom he will sue - not the agent.

14.2 THE CREATION OF AGENCY

The agency relationship arises in a number of ways, namely, by agreement, by apparent authority, by authority of necessity and by ratification.

(a) Agency by agreement

The usual manner of conferring authority is by agreement between principal and agent. The agent may be an employee under a contract of employment, e.g. a salesman or contracts manager; or he may be an independent contractor, e.g. an estate agent, travel agent or solicitor. An agency agreement requires no particular form unless the agent is required to enter into a contract under seal, in which case the authority must be conferred on him under seal, i.e. by power of attorney.

Agencies are sometimes classified into special agencies, general agencies and universal agencies. A special agent is given authority to perform a particular act or service on behalf of his principal. A general agent is one who is authorised to deal with all of his principal's business of a particular kind. A universal agent has authority to act for his principal in all matters.

An agent engaged for the sale of goods is called a mercantile agent. He may be either a broker or a factor, i.e. a commission agent. The main difference between a broker and a factor is that a factor has more extensive authority. In particular, (1) a factor has possession of the goods, while a broker has not; (2) a factor can sue and act in his own name, unlike a broker; and (3) a factor may buy and sell in his own name, whereas a broker normally cannot do so. A factor may act under a *del credere* authority, in which case he guarantees payment for the goods in return for an extra (*del credere*) commission.

The terms of an agency agreement may be express or implied. The authority arising from the agreement may thus also be express or implied. The implied authority of an agent may be regarded as an instance of implied contract to give effect to the presumed intentions of the principal and agent. An agent has implied authority to perform any act which is necessarily incidental to the execution of his express authority. For example, where an agent is authorised to sell his principal's land, he has implied authority to sign the contract of sale or any note or memorandum. Similarly, where an agent is authorised to make all arrangements for building, say, a new office block, he has implied authority to sign contracts to engage an architect and a consulting engineer; he has implied authority to sign (but not to seal) the building contract with the contractor.

Another kind of implied authority is that which is sometimes called customary authority. For example, where an agent has authority to act in a particular market he must act in accordance with the custom of that market.

(b) Apparent authority

Where a person has, by words or conduct, represented to a third party that he has given authority to an agent, he may subsequently be estopped from denying the existence of an agency if the third party sues him as principal. The apparent principal will be bound by the apparent agent's act as if authority had actually been conferred. In any claim against the apparent principal, the third party must be able to show that, as a result of the representation, the person with whom he dealt appeared to have actual authority and that he relied on that appearance. Apparent authority may arise where an actual agency has been terminated and a third party, accustomed to dealing with the agent, continues to deal with him in the mistaken belief that he still has authority: *Trueman* v. *Loder* (1840) and *Summers* v. *Solomon* (1857). This type of apparent authority is sometimes called agency by estoppel: the principal is estopped (prevented) from denying that the agency continues to exist.

The doctrine of apparent authority has been extended by the rule in *Watteau* v. *Fenwick* (1893) to cases where the principal has not held a person out as his agent. By this rule, once it is established that the agent has been given authority, the principal is liable for all acts of the agent which are within the authority usually conferred upon an agent of that character, notwithstanding any purported restriction of that authority as between principal and agent. The test question is: what is the usual authority of an agent of this class?

In *Watteau* v. *Fenwick* (1893), the defendant was owner of a public house. By the terms of the contract between the defendant and the manager of the public house, the manager had no authority to buy any goods for the business except beer and minerals. By the agreement, all other goods were to be supplied by the defendants. In breach of this agreement, the manager bought certain goods, including cigars, from the plaintiff. Credit was given to the manager in his own name. The action was brought to recover the price of the goods. It was held by the Divisional Court that the claim should succeed because authority to purchase such goods is usually conferred on a public house manager.

(c) Agency of necessity

The master of a ship may, in case of emergency, enter into contracts concerning the cargo or the ship and bind the cargo owners and the shipowner respectively. The master's authority arises out of the necessity of the case and where it is impossible to obtain instructions from the cargo owners or the shipowner. A master will enjoy the authority of necessity only where he acts *bona fide* in the interests of all concerned.

Agency of necessity can also arise with regard to perishable goods in the hands of a land carrier. Agency of necessity is a rare occurrence in modern times and is likely to remain so, for the courts have shown a disinclination to extend the ambit of the doctrine: *Munro* v. *Wilmot* (1949).

(d) Ratification

Where a person acts in the name of another but without authority, the act may be ratified by the person in whose name it was done. The act in question may be one which is outside the authority of an agent or it may be an act performed by a person with no authority at all. Ratification is valid only if made within a reasonable time and with full knowledge of all material facts or where the principal was prepared to ratify in any event. Where a person contracts in his own name, making no mention of a principal, there can be no subsequent ratification of the contract: *Keighly, Maxted & Co.* v. *Durant* (1901). It was said by Lord Macnaghton in that case:

'. . .by a wholesome and convenient fiction, a person ratifying the act of another, who, without authority, has made a contract openly and avowedly on his behalf, is deemed to be, though in fact he was not, a party to the contract. Does the fiction cover the case of a person who makes no avowal at all, but assumes to act for himself and for no one else? . . . Ought the doctrine of ratification to be extended to such a case? On principle I should say certainly not.'

14.3 THE AGENCY AGREEMENT

Many of the rights and duties of principal and agent will be defined by the express terms of the agency agreement. It is usual, for example, to find a description of the service to be performed by the agent and the remuneration to which he is entitled all set out in the agency agreement. There are additional terms which are usually implied in agency agreements giving implied rights and duties to both parties. These implied terms are usually grouped, first, into those which impose duties on the agent and, secondly, those which impose duties on the principal. It is obvious that the duties of the agent constitute the rights of the principal, and *vice versa*.

(a) Implied duties of the agent

These are as follows:

(i) Obedience.
An agent must obey the instructions of his principal.

(ii) Skill and care.
Where an agent holds himself out as following any particular trade or profession, there is an implication that he has the knowledge and skill ordinarily to be found in members of that trade or profession and that he will act with reasonable care. For example, a surveyor engaged to buy property must buy at the lowest price reasonably obtainable.

(iii) No delegation.
An agent has no power to delegate unless expressly authorised. If the principal suffers a loss due to wrongful delegation, he may claim damages from the agent.

(iv) Good faith.
Agency is a relationship of confidence. The agent must not allow his own interests to come into conflict with those of his principal. For example, if he is authorised to buy goods, he must not sell his own goods to the principal without full disclosure. Another aspect of the principle of good faith is that the agent must not use confidential information obtained during the agency for his own advantage. A contract made by the agent in breach of the duty of good faith may be voidable at the option of the principal if he acts before third parties have obtained rights as *bona fide* purchasers for value without notice of the agent's breach of duty.

(v) Accounts.
An agent must render proper accounts and must keep his principal's money separate from his own. Generally, the agent is under a fiduciary duty with regard to the principal's money or property in his possession, but there are statutory controls governing certain professional agents, e.g. the Solicitors' Deposit Interest Rules (1975) made under s. 33(3) of the Solicitors Act 1974, and ss. 12 to 17 of the Estate Agents Act 1979.

(b) Implied duties of the principal

Subject to the express terms of the agency agreement the agent can enforce the following rights arising by implication against the principal:

(i) Remuneration.
The agent's remuneration, usually a commission, is payable according to the terms, express and implied, of the agency agreement. The implied terms

governing the nature and amount of remuneration will depend on what is usual in the trade or business undertaken by the agent.

(ii) Indemnity.

An agent is entitled to an indemnity from his principal against all liabilities properly incurred or discharged by him under the agency.

(iii) Lien.

There are two kinds of lien available to an agent on all of the principal's property properly in the possession of the agent. First, a particular lien is available until all claims arising under the agency have been satisfied. Secondly, a general lien is available until all his claims against the principal have been satisfied, whether arising out of the agency or not.

14.4 POSITION OF THIRD PARTIES

The question now to be considered in more detail is whether the agent has brought about a legal relationship between the principal and a third party. The important question often is whether the principal can sue or be sued by the third party. Broadly, there are three possibilities according to how the agent goes about his business.

(a) The disclosed principal

Where an agent discloses the existence of his principal, any subsequent contract is effected between principal and third party. Assuming that the agent acts within his authority, the rights and obligations are between principal and third party; none accrues to the agent. The principal and the third party may sue or be sued on the contract in the event of breach, according to the ordinary rules of contract.

(b) The undisclosed principal

Where an agent, acting within his authority and intending to deal on behalf of his principal, does not disclose the fact of the agency, the principal is said to be undisclosed. Where this occurs, the agent appears to any third party to be dealing in his own right, and the so-called doctrine of the undisclosed principal will apply. This means that in the event of breach by the principal, the third party may sue either the agent or the principal as he chooses. In the event of breach by the third party, the principal may sue him unless the agent contracted in terms which were inconsistent with an agency, e.g. by describing himself as owner of goods belonging to the principal.

(c) Pretended agency

Where a person enters into a contract, falsely telling the other party that he does so as agent for another, he is clearly bound by that contract and can sue or be sued on it. He may also be liable for breach of warranty of authority.

14.5 BREACH OF WARRANTY OF AUTHORITY

In *Yonge* v. *Toynbee* (1910) Buckley L.J. summarised the law governing the liability of a person who falsely holds himself out as having the authority to act as agent. The liability is to third parties. He said that:

'. . .the liability of the person who professes to act as an agent arises (a) if he has been fraudulent; (b) if he has without fraud untruly represented that he had authority when he had not, and (c) also where he innocently represents that he has authority where the fact is either (i) that he never had authority, or (ii) that his original authority has ceased by reason of facts of which he has not knowledge or means of knowledge. Such last-mentioned liability arises from the fact that by professing to act as agent he impliedly contracts that he has authority, and it is immaterial whether he knew of the defect in his authority or not.'

It is clear from this statement that the action for damages for breach of warranty of authority is available on the footing of breach of express or implied contract and that it is no defence for the agent to say that he did not know that his agency had ceased. As Buckley L.J. pointed out in the above passage, liability for fraud is different from and must be distinguished from liability for breach of warranty of authority. If a person professing to act as agent has fraudulently misrepresented the scope of his authority he will be liable in tort for deceit.

14.6 TERMINATION OF AGENCY

The authority of an agent may be brought to an end by discharge according to the rules of general contract law or by a valid revocation by the principal.

(a) Discharge

Where the agency was created by contract, the agent's authority may be discharged by performance, frustration, agreement or acceptance of breach, i.e. as for contracts generally.

Where the agency was created for a particular task or for a defined period, it comes to an end on completion of that task or that period, i.e. when the agent has done what he promised to do. This is known as discharge by performance.

Where some supervening event makes further performance by the agent impossible or futile, then the agent is discharged from liability for further performance by the doctrine of frustration, e.g. by death of either party, or liquidation in the case of a company.

Principal and agent may agree to bring the agency to an end. Such an agreement may be a separate and subsequent agreement or it may be provided for in the original agency agreement. If the original agreement makes no express provision for a period of notice to terminate the agency, then a reasonable period will be implied.

An agency contract may be brought to an end if one of the parties has broken the contract in a manner which amounts to a repudiation and the other party gives notice that he accepts the repudiation.

(b) Revocation

Where the agent's authority is coupled with an interest it is irrevocable and any purported revocation by the principal will be ineffective. An example of an agency coupled with an interest is where the principal has agreed with the agent that the agent may hold the proceeds of a transaction as security for a debt owed to him by the principal.

Where the agent has no interest coupled with his authority, the principal may revoke the authority at any time. The question may then arise whether the revocation was in breach of contract or not. This will depend on whether the revocation was in accordance with the notice (if any) required by the contract.

Section 5 of the Powers of Attorney Act 1971 gives a measure of protection to the donee of the power of attorney and to third persons where the power of attorney is revoked. A donee who acts in pursuance of the power at a time when it has been revoked will not, by reason of the revocation, incur any liability if at the time he did not know that the power had been revoked. Further, where a power has been revoked and a person, without knowledge of the revocation, deals with the donee, the transaction between them will, in favour of that person, be as valid as if the power had then been in existence.

SUMMARY

1 An agency is created where a person, having the capacity to do an act for his own benefit on his own account, employs another person to do it. The delegated power to act is called the agent's authority. An agent acting within his authority binds his principal and does not himself assume personal liability.

2 An agency can be created by agreement, by apparent authority, by necessity or by ratification.

3 Subject to the terms of an express agreement between principal and agent, there are a number of implied obligations binding on both agent and principal.

4 Where the principal is undisclosed, any third party may sue the principal or the agent as he chooses. The principal may sue the third party unless the agent contracted in terms inconsistent with the agency.

5 The liability to third parties for breach of warranty of authority was summarised by Buckley L.J. in *Yonge* v. *Toynbee* (1910).

6 The authority of an agent may be brought to an end by discharge of the agreement or by revocation by the principal.

EXERCISES

1 'The agent's authority is the essential characteristic of agency.' Explain carefully what is meant by the word 'authority' in this context.

2 How may a principal confer authority on his agent?

3 How may apparent authority be created and what is its effect?

4 Explain how the doctrine of apparent authority has been extended by the decision in *Watteau* v. *Fenwick?*

5 What is an agency of necessity?

6 'The limit of the doctrine of ratification is marked by the decision in *Keighly, Maxted & Co.* v. *Durant.*' Explain this statement, making reference to the view of Lord Macnaghten.

7 What terms are normally expressed in an agency agreement?

8 What terms may be implied (a) to create duties on the part of the agent and (b) to create duties on the part of the principal?

9 What is the difference between (a) a disclosed principal and (b) an undisclosed principal? Explain the legal position in each case.

10 Summarise the law governing breach of warranty of authority.

11 Distinguish between discharge and revocation as methods of terminating an agency. What is the position where the authority is coupled with an interest?

12 What is provided by s. 5 of the Powers of Attorney Act 1971?

WORKSHOP

1 Derek agrees with Dorothy to sell her horse Dobbin in consideration of a 10 per cent commission. The day after the agreement, Dorothy is killed in a motor accident. Ten days after the accident, Derek sells Dobbin for £500 to Percy. Dorothy's personal representatives have now written to Derek to say that there was no authority to sell and that Derek must return the £50 commission retained by him. Advise Derek.

2 Beryl, a practising surveyor, has agreed to sell a house for Albert. On Albert's behalf, Beryl enters into a written binding contract for the sale of the house to Richard for £87,500. Albert has now discovered that the house should have been valued at between £100,000 and £115,000. Albert has decided to claim damages of £10,000 from Beryl. Advise her.

3 Bruce is a salesman employed by the Handmade Furniture Company Limited. He sells a table and set of chairs to Ferdy without disclosing that he was acting as agent – giving the impression that he was acting on his own behalf. Ferdy has taken possession of the furniture and has refused to pay the price agreed. Advise the company (who provided the table and chairs) whether they have a valid claim against Bruce.

4 Bingo Limited have appointed Antony as manager of a bingo hall authorising him to purchase all necessary goods required for the business with the exception of electrical goods which were to be supplied only by Bingo Limited. On taking up his duties, Antony decided to improve the lighting in the hall and, to this end, ordered £876 worth of bulbs and lighting fittings from Readylite Limited. Bingo Limited have refused to pay the bill from Readylite. Advise the parties as to their legal position.

5 Henry, who owes Lillian £1,000 has agreed with her that she may act as his agent for the purpose of collecting the rent from tenants in a block of flats owned by Henry. They further agreed that Lillian was to retain £1,000 from rents collected in satisfaction of the debt owed by Henry. When Lillian had collected only £250, Henry wrote to her purporting to revoke her authority to collect any more rent.

Comment on the validity of this revocation.

6 Morgan grants an irrevocable power of attorney to Sandy authorising him to sell and convey his farm Blackacre. Before any contract is concluded, Morgan dies. Is Sandy's authority to sell Blackacre affected by Morgan's death? Or may he go ahead and sell Blackacre and keep his commission?

PARTNERSHIP

15.1 THE NATURE OF PARTNERSHIP

(a) The Partnership Act 1890

The law of partnership was codified by the Act, which expressly saves the rules of equity and common law except so far as they are inconsistent with the Act. The main features of the statutory code governing partnership are set out below. All section references are to the Partnership Act 1890.

(b) Definition

Partnership is the relation which subsists between persons carrying on a business in common with a view of profit: s. 1(1).

The word 'business' has a very wide meaning, for it includes every trade, occupation or profession: s. 45. 'Profit' is not defined in the Act, but its legal meaning implies a comparison between the state of a business at two specific dates usually separated by an interval of a year. The fundamental meaning is the amount of gain made by the business during the year. This can be ascertained only by a comparison of the assets of the business at the two dates.

The relationship between members of corporations is specifically excluded from the definition of partnership: s. 1(2).

(c) Rules for determining the existence of partnership

In case of dispute as to whether a partnership exists, section 2 provides three rules to determine the question. They are as follows:

(i) Co-ownership.
Joint tenancy, tenancy in common, joint property, common property, or part ownership does not of itself create a partnership as to anything so

held or owned, whether the tenants or owners do or do not share any profits made by the use thereof: s. 2(1).

(ii) Gross returns.
The sharing of gross returns does not of itself create a partnership, whether the persons sharing such returns have or have not a joint or common right or interest in any property from which or from the use of which the returns are derived: s. 2(2).

(iii) Profit sharing.
The receipt by a person of a share of the profits of a business is *prima facie* evidence that he is a partner in the business: s. 2(3).

(d) The firm and the firm-name

Persons who have entered into a partnership are called collectively a firm, and the name under which their business is carried on is called the firm-name: s. 4(1).

Partners may, subject to the law of passing off, use any firm name they wish to use. A firm name may end with the words 'and company' or 'company', but it is an offence under s. 34 of the Companies Act 1985 to use a name ending with the word 'limited'.

By ss. 1–5 of the Business Names Act 1985 there are controls over the use of a firm name which does not consist of the names of all partners who are individuals and the corporate names of all partners who are bodies corporate without any addition other than Christian names or initials. Section 2 provides that business must not be carried on under a name which would be likely to give the impression that the business is connected with Her Majesty's Government or with any local authority. Any contravention of this provision is an offence.

By s. 4, firms whose names are subject to s. 1 must ensure that the name of each partner (together with an address for the service of documents) is stated in legible characters on all business letters, written orders for goods or services, invoices and receipts and written demands for payment. Section 4 further provides that the partners' names and addresses must be displayed in a prominent position in any place where the business is carried on and to which customers and suppliers of goods or services have access. Any contravention of this provision is an offence and may result in the dismissal by the court of legal proceedings brought by the defaulting partners: s. 5.

(e) Number of partners

By s. 716 Companies Act 1985 the maximum number of partners is twenty. However, the section further provides that this limit does not apply to partnerships of solicitors, accountants and stockbrokers. The Secretary of State may exempt other professions by statutory instrument and has done so.

15.2 RELATIONS OF PARTNERS TO PERSONS DEALING WITH THEM

(a) Power of a partner to bind the firm

Every partner is an agent of the firm and his other partners for the purpose of the business of the partnership; and the acts of every partner who does any act for carrying on in the usual way business of the kind carried on by the firm of which he is a member bind the firm and his partners, unless the partner so acting has in fact no authority to act for the firm in the particular matter, and the person with whom he is dealing either knows that he has no authority, or does not know or believe him to be a partner: s. 5. This important provision gives the law of agency a key part to play in the law of partnership. There is a good deal of case law relating to this section, the general effect of which is that partners in trading firms have wider apparent authority than those in a professional firm. However, no partner has apparent authority to bind his firm by deed, or by giving a guarantee or by a submission to arbitration. A partner must be expressly authorised to carry out any of these acts.

(b) Liability of partners

Every partner in a firm is liable jointly with the other partners for all debts and obligations of the firm incurred while he is a partner; and after his death his estate is also severally liable for such debts and obligations, subject to the prior payment of his separate debts: s. 9. Since liability is joint, a creditor may sue all or any of the partners. By s. 3 Civil Liability Act 1978, a judgement obtained against any partner will not be a bar to an action against any of the others.

Alternatively, a creditor may sue the firm in the firm name. The latter procedure has the effect of joining all partners as co-defendants. This procedure is permitted even though the firm itself is not a legal person.

(c) Holding out

Everyone who by words spoken or written or by conduct represents himself, or who knowingly suffers himself to be represented, as a partner in a particular firm, is liable as a partner to anyone who has on the faith of any such representation given credit to the firm. This rule applies whether the representation has or has not been made or communicated to the person so giving credit by or with the knowledge of the apparent partner making the representation or suffering it to be made: s. 14(1).

(d) Incoming and outgoing partners

A person who is admitted as a partner into an existing firm does not thereby become liable to the creditors of the firm for anything done before he became a partner: s. 17(1). A partner who retires from a firm does not thereby cease to be liable for partnership debts or obligations incurred before his retirement: s. 17(2). In these cases, however, the incoming partner may assume liability, and the outgoing partner may escape it, by novation, i.e. a binding contract with a creditor of the firm. By such an agreement, the creditor agrees that the members of the firm as previously constituted should be discharged from liability and that those of the new firm should assume liability for the debt.

(e) Liability for torts

Where, by any wrongful act or omission of any partner acting in the ordinary course of the business of the firm, or with the authority of his co-partners, loss or injury is caused to any person not being a partner in the firm, or any penalty is incurred, the firm is liable to the same extent as the partner so acting or omitting to act: s. 10. The firm is also liable for the misapplication of money received by a partner or by the firm: s. 11. With regard to these provisions, every partner is liable jointly with his co-partners and also severally for everything for which the firm becomes liable: s. 12. This means that, in tort, all partners share the liability jointly and each partner is liable severally, i.e. separately. In practice, where one partner is sued separately, he will join his other partners as co-defendants if they have any means.

15.3 RELATIONS OF PARTNERS TO ONE ANOTHER

The mutual rights and duties of partners are usually set out in a formal agreement and, by section 19, whether ascertained by agreement or defined by the Act, they may be varied by the consent of all the partners. Such consent may be either express or inferred from a course of dealing. The interests of partners in the partnership property and in their rights and duties in relation to the partnership must be determined, subject to any agreement express or implied between the partners, by the rules set out in section 24 as follows:

Rule 1. All the partners are entitled to share equally in the capital and profits of the business, and must contribute equally towards the losses, whether of capital or otherwise, sustained by the firm.

Rule 2. The firm must indemnify every partner in respect of payments made and personal liabilities incurred by him:

- (*a*) in the ordinary and proper conduct of the business of the firm; or
- (*b*) in or about anything necessarily done for the preservation of the business or property of the firm.

Rule 3. A partner making, for the purpose of the partnership, any actual payment or advance beyond the amount of capital which he has agreed to subscribe, is entitled to interest at the rate of 5 per cent per annum from the date of the payment or advance.

Rule 4. A partner is not entitled, before the ascertainment of profits, to interest on the capital subscribed by him.

Rule 5. Every partner may take part in the management of the partnership business.

Rule 6. No partner shall be entitled to remuneration for acting in the partnership business.

Rule 7. No person may be introduced as a partner without the consent of all existing partners.

Rule 8. Any difference arising as to ordinary matters connected with the partnership business may be decided by a majority of the partners, but no change may be made in the nature of the partnership business without the consent of all existing partners.

Rule 9. The partnership books are to be kept at the place of business of the partnership (or the principal place, if there is more than one), and every partner may, when he thinks fit, have access to and inspect and copy any of them.

Rules 1 to 9 have sometimes been described as a code for partners, but it must be emphasised that if any of the nine rules is required to be changed for any particular partnership, then any desired change may be made by express agreement. For example, if it is desired that partners are to be remunerated for their work on behalf of the partnership, this can be effected by agreement.

No majority of the partners can expel any partner unless a power to do so has been conferred by express agreement between the partners: s. 25. However, a partner may apply to the court under section 35 for the dissolution of a partnership and, in effect, the withdrawal of another partner.

15.4 ACCOUNTABILITY OF PARTNERS: DUTY OF GOOD FAITH

The general rule is that partners are bound to render true accounts and full information of all things affecting the partnership to any partner or his legal representative: s. 28.

By section 29, every partner must account to the firm for any benefit derived by him without the consent of the other partners from any transaction concerning the partnership, or from any use by him of the partnership property, name or business connection.

If a partner, without the consent of the other partners, carries on any business of the same nature as and competing with that of the firm, he must account for and pay over to the firm all profits made by him in that business: s. 30.

Although partnership agreements are not strictly within the class *uberrimae fidei,* the partners, unlike the shareholders in a registered company, are in a fiduciary relation to each other and therefore full disclosure and good faith are required in all their mutual dealings. This is the combined effect of sections 28, 29 and 30.

15.5 DISSOLUTION OF PARTNERSHIP

A partnership contract may be avoided or rescinded according to the general rules of contract law. Further, a partnership may be dissolved in any one of four ways under the provisions of sections 32 to 35.

(a) Dissolution by expiration or notice

Subject to any agreement between the partners, a partnership is dissolved:

  (i) if entered into for a fixed term, by the expiration of that term:
 (ii) if entered into for a single adventure or undertaking, by the termination of that adventure or undertaking:
(iii) if entered into for an undefined time, by any partner giving notice to the other or others of his intention to dissolve the partnership.

In the last-mentioned case the partnership is dissolved as from the date mentioned in the notice as the date of dissolution, or, if no date is so mentioned, as from the communication of the notice: s. 32.

(b) Dissolution by bankruptcy, death or charge

Subject to any agreement between the partners, every partnership is dissolved as regards all partners by the death or bankruptcy of any partner:

s. 33(1). Any continuation by surviving partners will constitute a new partnership after this provision has taken effect.

A partnership may, at the option of the other partners, be dissolved if any partner permits his share of the partnership property to be charged under the Act for his separate debt: s. 33(2).

(c) Dissolution by illegality of partnership

A partnership is in every case dissolved by the happening of any event which makes it unlawful for the business of the firm to be carried on: s. 34.

(d) Dissolution by the court

On application by a partner the court may decree a dissolution of the partnership in any of the following cases:

(i) Insanity.
Under the Mental Health Act 1959, where a judge is satisfied on medical evidence that a partner is incapable, by reason of mental disorder, of managing his property and affairs.

(ii) Permanent incapability.
When a partner, other than the partner suing, becomes in any other way permanently incapable of performing his part of the partnership contract.

(iii) Conduct prejudicial.
When a partner, other than the partner suing, has been guilty of such conduct as, in the opinion of the court, is calculated to prejudicially affect the carrying on of the business.

(iv) Breach of partnership agreement.
When a partner, other than the partner suing, wilfully or persistently commits a breach of the partnership agreement, or otherwise so conducts himself in matters relating to the partnership business that it is not reasonably practicable for the other partner or partners to carry on the business in partnership with him.

(v) Business at a loss.
When the business of the partnership can only be carried on at a loss.

(vi) Just and equitable.
Whenever in any case circumstances have arisen which, in the opinion of the court, render it just and equitable that the partnership be dissolved: s. 35.

15.6 **THE EFFECTS OF DISSOLUTION OF PARTNERSHIP**

The Act provides for the consequences of dissolution of partnership, the most important of which are as follows:

(a) **Apparent partners**

Where a person deals with a firm after a change in its constitution he is entitled to treat all apparent members of the old firm as still being members of the firm until he has notice of the change: s. 36(1). Where such a person had dealings with the old firm, all members of the old firm remain liable on all transactions with him until he has actual notice of the change in constitution. Where such person has not dealt with the old firm, notice in the *London Gazette* of the change in constitution will be sufficient to excuse former members of the partnership from liability.

(b) **Partnership property**

On dissolution of a partnership every partner is entitled, as against the other partners in the firm, to have the property of the partnership applied in payment of the debts and liabilities of the firm, and to have the surplus assets applied in payment of what may be due to the partners respectively after deducting what may be due from them as partners to the firm: s. 39.

(c) **Distribution of assets**

In settling accounts between the partners after a dissolution of partnership, the following rules must, subject to any agreement, be observed:

(i) losses, including losses and deficiencies of capital, must be paid first out of profits, next out of capital, and lastly, if necessary, by the partners individually in the proportion in which they were entitled to share profits;

(ii) the assets of the firm including the sums, if any, contributed by the partners to make up losses or deficiencies of capital, must be applied in the following manner and order:

1. in paying the debts and liabilities of the firm to persons who are not partners in it;
2. in paying to each partner rateably what is due from the firm to him for advances as distinguished from capital;
3. in paying to each partner rateably what is due from the firm to him in respect of capital;
4. the ultimate residue, if any, must be divided among the partners in the proportion in which the profits are divisible: s. 44.

SUMMARY

1   The law of partnership was codified by the Partnership Act 1890. (All references below are to this Act unless otherwise indicated.)

2   A partnership is the relation which subsists between persons carrying on a business in common with a view of profit: s. 1(1).

3   Partners may choose any firm-name subject always to the law of passing off, the Companies Act 1985 and the Business Names Act 1985.

4   Every partner is an agent of the firm and his other partners for the purpose of the business of the partnership: s. 5.

5   Every partner is liable jointly with the other partners for all debts and obligations of the firm incurred while he is a partner: s. 9.

6   Where a tort is committed by a partner acting in the ordinary course of the firm's business, the firm is under the same liability as that partner.

7   The relations of partners to one another are governed by the nine rules set out in s. 24, subject always to any partnership agreement to the contrary.

8   Partners are in a fiduciary relation to each other and therefore full disclosure and good faith are required in all their mutual dealings.

9   A partnership may be dissolved according to the general rules of contract law or by the provisions of ss. 32, 33, 34 and 35.

10   Where a person deals with a firm after a change in its constitution he is entitled to treat all apparent members of the old firm as still being members of the firm until he has notice of any change: s. 36.

11   On dissolution every partner is entitled, as against the other partners, to have the property of the partnership applied in payment of the debts of the firm, and to have any surplus assets applied in payment of what may be due to the partners respectively: s. 39.

12   Subject to any agreement to the contrary, the rules contained in s. 44 must be applied in settling accounts between partners after dissolution.

EXERCISES

1   'The Partnership Act 1890 codifies the law of partnership.' Explain this statement.

2   Define 'partnership'.

3   What rules are applied to resolve a dispute as to whether a partnership exists?

4   'Partners may use any firm-name they wish to use.' To what extent is this statement true?

5   State the provisions of ss. 1–5 of the Business Names Act 1985.

6   Is there a permitted maximum number of partners in any firm?

7   What is the importance of s. 5 of the Partnership Act?

8   Explain the effect of the joint liability of partners to honour the firm's obligations.

9   Summarise the rules governing the relationship of partners to persons dealing with them.

10   What is the relationship between any partnership agreement and ss. 19 and 24 of the Partnership Act?

11   Set out in full the rules contained in s. 24 of the Partnership Act.

12   Explain the relation which exists between partners in their mutual dealings.

13   Partnerships may be dissolved in any of four ways. What are they?

14   What is an 'apparent' partner?

15   What are the rights of partners with regard to partnership property and the settlement of accounts on dissolution?

WORKSHOP

1 Tessa and Michael own a flat jointly. They decide to let it and to take equal shares in the profits. Is there necessarily a partnership between Tessa and Michael?

2 Henry and Peter carry on the business of manufacturers of leather goods in partnership. Arthur is also a partner but, by the partnership agreement, he is precluded from taking any part in the management of the business. Arthur has entered into an agreement with Liza for the purchase of a consignment of hides. These hides are not the kind required for the business and Henry and Peter do not wish to take delivery. Advise them.

3 Flash and Co., a firm of advertising consultants, have just incurred an obligation to pay Julia, an interior decorator, the sum of £25,000 for decorating and fitting out the firm's premises. After the due date for payment, Andrew is admitted to the partnership. The debt to Julia remains unpaid and she intends to sue Andrew whom she believes to be the only solvent partner. Advise her.

4 Bert, Fred and Charlie are partners in a firm of office cleaners. Due to Fred's negligence, the fitted carpets of an entire fifteen storey office block are ruined. The owners of the office block, who have spent £18,500 on replacement carpets, now claim that amount from Fred. Fred has no personal wealth, nor has Bert; but Charlie is a millionaire. Advise Fred.

5 Roger is in partnership with Ruth and Trevor. He wishes to introduce his son, Christopher, into the partnership but he knows that Ruth will refuse to agree. Are there any circumstances in which Christopher might, nevertheless, be made a partner?

SALE OF GOODS

(Unless otherwise indicated, all section references are to the Sale of Goods Act 1979.)

16.1 THE CONTRACT OF SALE

The Sale of Goods Act 1893 codified the law of sale, but during the course of time a few amending statutes were passed, notably the Unfair Contract Terms Act 1977. See Chapter 10.5(f) and the Appendix. The present law is now consolidated by the Sale of Goods Act 1979. The Act deals with certain specific matters such as transfer of property and implied terms, leaving the rules of common law and the law merchant to apply except to the extent that they might be inconsistent with the Act: s. 62(2).

A contract of sale of goods is a contract by which the seller transfers or agrees to transfer the property in goods to the buyer for a money consideration, called the price: s. 2(1). There are no special rules governing the formation of a contract of sale and so it follows that the general rules of offer and acceptance apply. By s. 4 a contract of sale may be made in writing (either with or without seal), or by word of mouth, or partly in writing and partly by word of mouth, or may be implied from the conduct of the parties.

16.2 PERFORMANCE OF THE CONTRACT

It is the duty of the seller to deliver the goods, and of the buyer to accept and pay for them, in accordance with the terms of the contract of sale: s. 27. Delivery means the transfer of possession of the goods. Possession must be distinguished from the property in the goods, i.e. the ownership.

Although it is the purpose of the sale of goods contract to pass ownership from the seller to the buyer, this does not necessarily occur at the same time as delivery. Whether it is for the buyer to take possession of the goods or for the seller to send them to the buyer is a question depending in each case on the contract, express or implied, between the parties: s. 29(1). Apart from any such contract, the place of delivery is the seller's place of business if he has one and, if not, his residence; except that if the contract is for the sale of specific goods, which to the knowledge of the parties when the contract is made are in some other place, then that place is the place of delivery: s. 29(2).

16.3 THE TRANSFER OF PROPERTY IN THE GOODS TO THE BUYER

(a) The intention of the parties

It is often necessary to discover who owns the goods at some particular stage in the transaction of sale. For example, where goods are destroyed, damaged or stolen, it may be necessary to ascertain at whose risk they were at the time of the event. By s. 20(1), it is provided that, *prima facie,* the risk passes with the property. It follows that the decision and the responsibility to insure passes normally with the property in the goods. In other words, the goods are at the seller's risk until the property passes, at which point the risk passes to the buyer.

The general rule is that the property passes to the buyer when the parties intend that it will pass, i.e. in accordance with the contract: s. 17. Unless a different intention appears, the following are rules for ascertaining the intention of the parties as to the time at which the property in the goods is to pass to the buyer: s. 18.

Rule 1. Where there is an unconditional contract for the sale of specific goods in a deliverable state the property in the goods passes to the buyer when the contract is made, and it is immaterial whether the time of payment or the time of delivery, or both, be postponed.

Rule 2. Where there is a contract for the sale of specific goods and the seller is bound to do something to the goods for the purpose of putting them into a deliverable state, the property does not pass until the thing is done and the buyer has notice that it has been done.

Rule 3. Where there is a contract for the sale of specific goods in a deliverable state but the seller is bound to weigh, measure, test, or do some other act or thing with reference to the goods for the purpose of ascertaining the price, the property does not pass until the act or thing is done and the buyer has notice that it has been done.

Rule 4. When goods are delivered to the buyer on approval or on sale or return or other similar terms the property in the goods passes to the buyer:

(*a*) when he signifies his approval or acceptance to the seller or does any other act adopting the transaction;

(*b*) if he does not signify his approval or acceptance to the seller but retains the goods without giving notice of rejection, then, if a time has been fixed for the return of the goods, on the expiration of that time, and, if no time has been fixed, on the expiration of a reasonable time.

Rule 5. (1) Where there is a contract for the sale of unascertained or future goods by description, and goods of that description and in a deliverable state are unconditionally appropriated to the contract, either by the seller with the assent of the buyer or by the buyer with the assent of the seller, the property in the goods then passes to the buyer; and the assent may be express or implied, and may be given either before or after the appropriation is made.

(2) Where, in pursuance of the contract, the seller delivers the goods to the buyer or to a carrier or other bailee or custodier (whether named by the buyer or not) for the purpose of transmission to the buyer, and does not reserve the right of disposal, he is to be taken to have unconditionally appropriated the goods to the contract.

(b) Retention of seller's title

Where there is a contract for the sale of specific goods or where goods are subsequently appropriated to the contract, the seller may, by the terms of the contract or appropriation, reserve the right of disposal of the goods until certain conditions are fulfilled; and in such a case, notwithstanding the delivery of the goods to the buyer, or to a carrier or other bailee for the purpose of transmission to the buyer, the property in the goods does not pass to the buyer until the conditions imposed by the seller are fulfilled: s. 19(1).

It is not unusual for a contract of sale to include a clause which provides that the property in the goods remains in the seller until payment of the price has been made in full by the buyer. Such clauses are known as 'retention of title clauses' or 'Romalpa clauses', after a case of that name. Such clauses often give the seller rights of disposition within clause 19 and, in addition, a right of entry into the buyer's premises. Some clauses allow legal title to pass to the buyer while the seller retains the beneficial interest in the goods until payment to him in full. Some clauses even provide for an interest to remain in the seller after the goods have lost their identity and are admixed with other goods. These clauses may give rise to difficult legal problems but the basic principle is simple enough.

In the original Romalpa case, *Aluminium Industrie Vaassen BV* v. *Romalpa Aluminium Ltd.* (1976), the question was whether the sellers of aluminium foil under contracts containing retention of title clauses could trace their title into money which was the proceeds of sale by the buyers of foil supplied by the sellers. It was held that the original sellers could trace their title into the proceeds of sale because title to the foil itself had been retained by the sellers and the buyers became bailees of the foil delivered to them.

Re Bond Worth Ltd. (1979) provides an example of a further refinement in the drafting of retention of title clauses. A very complex clause provided that 'equitable and beneficial ownership' should remain with the sellers until full payment had been made. It was not suggested in this case that the sellers retained the legal title to the goods. It was held by Slade J. that a charge had been created which was registrable under the Companies Act.

In *Clough Mill Ltd.* v. *Martin* (1984) it was held by the Court of Appeal that, on the basis of s. 19(1) of the Sale of Goods Act, a retention of title clause was effective to enable an unpaid seller to exercise his rights of title and disposition of goods which were still identifiable and in the possession of the buyer. It was further held in that case that, since ownership had never passed to the buyer, the question whether any charge under the Companies Act was void for non-registration did not arise. A company cannot create a charge on property which it does not own.

16.4 THE NEMO DAT RULE AND ITS EXCEPTIONS

Where the seller has a good title to the goods, the effect of the contract of sale is to transfer that title to the buyer. Where, however, the seller has some defect in his title or, indeed, if he is not the owner at all, problems will arise. The general rule is that no one can transfer a better title than that which he has: *nemo dat quod non habet.*

There are some important exceptions to this rule as follows.

(a) Estoppel

Property may pass where the owner of the goods is by his conduct estopped (precluded) from denying the seller's authority to sell: s. 21(1). The test for the operation of this provision is whether the buyer relied on the owner's conduct as indicating that the seller had a right to sell: *Eastern Distributors Ltd.* v. *Goldring* (1957).

(b) Market overt

Where goods are sold in market overt the buyer acquires a good title provided he buys in good faith and without notice of any defect or want of title on the part of the seller: s. 22(1). Market overt obtains in shops in the City of London and in markets in other parts of the country where it has been established by long usage or by an Act of Parliament.

(c) Mercantile agent without authority

By s. 2 of the Factors Act 1889, where a mercantile agent is, with the consent of the owner, in possession of goods or the documents of title to goods, any sale or other disposition of the goods made by him when acting in the ordinary course of business of a mercantile agent shall be as valid as if he were expressly authorised by the owner to make the transaction: *Folkes* v. *King* (1923).

A mercantile agent is one having, in the customary course of his business as such agent, authority either to sell goods, or to consign goods for the purpose of sale, or to buy goods, or to raise money on the security of goods.

(d) Seller remaining in possession

Where a person having sold goods continues in possession of the goods, or of the documents of title, the delivery of the goods or transfer of the documents to any person receiving them in good faith under a contract of sale will pass a good title to that person: s. 24. Under this provision if a seller sells goods to A, but retains possession, and while still in possession sells the goods over again to B, then B will get a good title and A will be left to his remedy in damages for breach of contract of sale.

(e) Buyer obtaining possession

Where a person having bought or agreed to buy goods obtains possession of the goods or the documents of title, the delivery of the goods or the transfer of the documents to any person receiving them in good faith under a contract of sale will pass a good title to that person: s. 25(1). By this provision, if a buyer gets possession of goods and sells them to a *bona fide* third party before he, the original buyer, obtains the title from the original seller, the *bona fide* third party gets a good title and the original seller is left to any claim he might have for damages against the original buyer. In *Blythswood Motors* v. *Lloyds & Scottish Finance* (1973) a motor vehicle was sold and delivered in return for a cheque which was later dishonoured. Before the seller had notice of the dishonour, the buyer in possession had sold the vehicle to a *bona fide* purchaser. It was held that the requirements of s. 25(1) were satisfied and that, accordingly, the buyer was able to pass a good title.

(f) Voidable title

When the seller has a voidable title to the goods but his title has not been avoided at the time of the sale, the buyer acquires a good title provided he bought in good faith: s. 23. See *Lewis* v. *Averay* (1972) (Chapter 11.1(c)).

16.5 IMPLIED TERMS

Sections 12, 13, 14 and 15 of the Act provide for the implication of certain terms which are much to the advantage of the buyer.

(a) Seller's title

Unless the parties agree otherwise, there is an implied condition on the part of the seller that in the case of a sale he has a right to sell the goods, and in the case of an agreement to sell, he will have a right to sell the goods at the time when the property is to pass: s. 12(1). There is also an implied warranty that the goods are free from any charge or encumbrance not disclosed to the buyer and that the buyer will enjoy quiet possession of the goods: s. 12(2). A seller will be in breach of the implied condition in s. 12(1) if he has no right to sell the goods lawfully. For example, in *Niblett* v. *Confectioners' Materials Ltd.* (1921), it was held by the Court of Appeal that the owner of goods which were detained by the Commissioners of Customs had sold the goods in breach of the implied condition that he had a right to sell.

Any exclusion clause purporting to exclude liability under s. 12 will be void: Unfair Contract Terms Act 1977, s. 6(1).

(b) Description

Where there is a contract of sale of goods by description, there is an implied condition that the goods will correspond with that description: s. 13. In *Beale* v. *Taylor* (1967), a car was offered for sale under the following description: 'Herald convertible, white, twin carbs.' It was in fact made up of two cars – the rear from a 1961 model and the front from an earlier model. It was held that the sale was by description and that the implied term in s. 13 was broken.

(c) Quality

Where the seller sells goods in the course of a business, there is an implied condition that the goods supplied under the contract are of merchantable quality, except that there is no such condition (1) as regards defects specifically drawn to the buyer's attention before the contract is made, or (2) if the buyer examines the goods before the contract is made, as regards defects which that examination ought to reveal: s. 14(2).

Goods are of merchantable quality within the meaning of s. 14(2) if they are as fit for the purpose or purposes for which goods of that kind are commonly bought as it is reasonable to expect having regard to any description applied to them, the price (if relevant) and all other relevant circumstances: s. 14(6). In *Cehave* v. *Bremer* (1975) it was held by the Court of Appeal that citrus pulp pellets which had deteriorated in transit but which were still usable for the purpose for which such pellets were normally used, namely, for animal feed, were of merchantable quality within the definition now set out in s. 14(6).

(d) Fitness for purpose

Where the seller sells goods in the course of a business and the buyer, expressly or by implication, makes known to the seller any particular purpose for which the goods are being bought, there is an implied condition that the goods supplied under the contract are reasonably fit for that purpose, whether or not that is a purpose for which such goods are commonly supplied, except where the circumstances show that the buyer does not rely, or that it is unreasonable for him to rely, on the skill or judgement of the seller: s. 14(3).

In *Griffiths* v. *Peter Conway Ltd.* (1939), the buyer had a Harris tweed coat specially made for her by the seller. The coat caused her to contract dermatitis. It was held by the Court of Appeal that since the coat would have caused no harm to normal skin and the seller could not have known of the buyer's sensitivity, there was no breach of the implied condition of fitness of purpose. In *Geddling* v. *Marsh* (1920) it was held that the seller of bottles of mineral water was liable for breach of the implied condition of fitness of purpose when an empty returnable bottle exploded, injuring the buyer.

(e) Sale by sample

A contract of sale is a contract of sale by sample where there is an express or implied term to that effect in the contract: s. 15(1).

In the case of a contract for sale by sample there is an implied condition:

(*a*) that the bulk will correspond with the sample in quality;
(*b*) that the buyer will have a reasonable opportunity of comparing the bulk with the sample;

(c) that the goods will be free from any defect, rendering them unmerchantable, which would not be apparent on reasonable examination of the sample: s. 15(2).

The Act further provides that if a sale is a sale by sample as well as by description it is not sufficient that the bulk of the goods corresponds with the sample if the goods do not also correspond with the description: s. 13(2).

(f) Contracts analogous to sale

The Supply of Goods and Services Act 1982 provides for the implication of terms about title, correspondence with description, quality, fitness for purpose and sample in contracts other than sale. These implied terms are similar to those in ss. 12 to 15 of the Sale of Goods Act 1979, but are adapted to bind (1) the transferor of goods in a contract (other than sale or hire-purchase) by which it is agreed to transfer the property in goods and (2) the bailor of goods in a contract of hire.

16.6 EXCLUSION OF SELLER'S LIABILITY

It is provided by s. 55(1) that where a right, duty or liability would arise under a contract of sale of goods by implication of law, it may (subject to the Unfair Contract Terms Act 1977) be negatived by agreement. This means that the exclusion of the seller's liability under ss. 12, 13, 14 and 15 by virtue of an exclusion clause will be subject ultimately to the Unfair Contract Terms Act 1977. This Act makes a distinction between liabilities under s. 12, on the one hand, and liabilities under ss. 13, 14 and 15, on the other, as follows:

(a) Liability under s. 12

Liability for breach of the obligations arising from s. 12 of the Sale of Goods Act (implied obligations as to title) cannot be excluded or restricted by reference to any contract term: Unfair Contract Terms Act, s. 6.

(b) Liability under ss. 13, 14 and 15

Implied obligations concerning description, quality, fitness and sample arising from ss. 13, 14 and 15 respectively cannot be excluded or restricted as against a person dealing as consumer: Unfair Contract Terms Act, s. 6(2). As against a person dealing otherwise than as consumer, the same liabilities can be excluded or restricted by reference to a contract term, but only in so far as the term satisfies the requirement of reasonableness: Unfair Contract Terms Act, s. 6(3).

(i) Dealing as consumer.
A party 'deals as consumer' in relation to another party if:

(*a*) he neither makes the contract in the course of a business nor holds himself out as doing so; and

(*b*) the other party does make the contract in the course of a business; and

(*c*) the goods passing under the contract are of a type ordinarily supplied for private use or consumption: Unfair Contract Terms Act: s. 12(1).

(ii) The requirement of reasonableness.
In relation to a contract term, the requirement of reasonableness is that the term shall have been a fair and reasonable one to be included having regard to the circumstances which were, or ought reasonably to have been, known to or in the contemplation of the parties when the contract was made: Unfair Contract Terms Act, s. 11(1).

In determining whether a contract term satisfies the requirement of reasonableness, regard shall be had in particular to the matters specified in Schedule 2 of the Unfair Contract Terms Act. The matters thus specified are:

(*a*) the relative strength of the bargaining position of the parties;

(*b*) whether the customer received an inducement to agree to the term;

(*c*) whether the customer knew or ought reasonably to have known of the existence and the extent of the term;

(*d*) where the term excludes any relevant liability if some condition is not complied with, whether it was reasonable to expect that compliance with that condition would be practicable;

(*e*) whether the goods were manufactured, processed or adapted to the special order of the customer.

For an example of the application of the reasonableness test by the Court of Appeal, see *Mitchell* v. *Finney Lock Seeds* (1983) (Chapter 10.5(f)).

(c) The Supply of Goods and Services Act 1982

As has been mentioned above, this Act provides for implied terms similar to those contained in ss. 12 to 15 of the Sale of Goods Act in contracts analogous to sale and in contracts for the hire of goods. The 1982 Act also provides for certain implied terms in contracts for the supply of services. The effectiveness of any exclusion clause purporting to exclude or limit liability under any such implied term is governed (as in sale of goods contracts) by the Unfair Contracts Terms Act 1977.

16.7 **BREACH OF CONTRACT OF SALE**

(a) Buyer's breach

The Sale of Goods Act 1979 provides remedies for the seller where the buyer is in default by failing to accept and pay for the goods or by failing to pay the price.

(i) Failure to take delivery.
When the seller is ready and willing to deliver the goods, and requests the buyer to take delivery, and the buyer does not within a reasonable time after such request take delivery of the goods, he is liable to the seller for any loss occasioned by his neglect or refusal to take delivery, and also for a reasonable charge for the care and custody of the goods: s. 37(1).

(ii) Failure to accept and pay for the goods.
Where the buyer wrongfully neglects or refuses to accept and pay for the goods, the seller may maintain an action against him for damages for non-acceptance: s. 50(1).

The measure of damages is the estimated loss directly and naturally resulting, in the ordinary course of events, from the buyer's breach of contract: s. 50(2).

Where there is an available market for the goods in question the measure of damages is *prima facie* to be ascertained by the difference between the contract price and the market or current price at the time or times when the goods ought to have been accepted or at the time of the refusal to accept: s. 50(3). Where the application of this *prima facie* rule does not result in fair compensation for the seller, it will not be applied. In *Thompson Ltd.* v. *Robinson Ltd.* (1955), the seller was able to recover as damages the profit which he would have made on the sale of a motor-car. In that case the seller was able to show that he could not sell all the cars available to him from the makers. In *Charter* v. *Sullivan* (1957) the position was different in that the seller could easily sell all the cars available to him of the make in question: the Court of Appeal applied the *prima facie* rule in subsection (3).

(iii) Failure to pay the price: remedy against the buyer.
Where, under a contract of sale, the property in the goods has passed to the buyer and he wrongfully neglects or refuses to pay for the goods according to the terms of the contract, the seller may maintain an action against him for the price of the goods: s. 49(1).

Where, under a contract of sale, the price is payable on a day certain irrespective of delivery and the buyer wrongfully neglects or refuses to pay such price, the seller may maintain an action for the price, although the property in the goods has not passed and the goods have not been appropriated to the contract: s. 49(2).

The price in a contract of sale may be fixed by the contract, or may be left to be fixed in a manner agreed by the contract, or may be determined by the course of dealing between the parties: s. 8(1). Where the price is not determined in this manner, the buyer must pay a reasonable price: s. 8(2).

(iv) Failure to pay the price: remedy against the goods.

Regardless of whether the property in the goods has passed to the buyer, the unpaid seller has, by implication of law: (1) a lien on the goods or a right to retain them for the price while he is in possession of them; (2) in case of the insolvency of the buyer, a right of stopping the goods in transit; and (3) a right of resale of the goods: s. 39(1).

A lien is a right exercisable by a creditor to obtain satisfaction of a debt by means of property of the debtor: it is a species of security.

(b) Seller's breach

The Sale of Goods Act 1979 provides remedies for the buyer where the seller is in default by failing to deliver the goods or by his breach of condition or breach of warranty.

(i) Failure to deliver the goods.

Where the seller wrongfully neglects or refuses to deliver the goods to the buyer, the buyer may maintain an action against the seller for damages for non-delivery: s. 51(1).

The measure of damages is the estimated loss directly and naturally resulting, in the ordinary course of events, from the seller's breach of contract: s. 51(2).

Where there is an available market for the goods in question the measure of damages is *prima facie* to be ascertained by the difference between the contract price and the market or current price at the time when the goods ought to have been accepted: s. 50(3).

(ii) Failure to deliver the goods: specific performance.

In any action for breach of contract to deliver specific or ascertained goods the court may, if it thinks fit, on the plaintiff's application direct that the contract shall be performed specifically: s. 52(1). This is an equitable power which will not be exercised where damages under s. 52(1) would be an adequate remedy. In *Sky Petroleum Ltd.* v. *V.I.P. Petroleum Ltd.* (1974) the court took the view that specific performance might be available where the buyer had no alternative supply of the goods in question.

(iii) Breach of condition.

Whether there is a breach of condition or breach of warranty depends in each case on the construction of the contract: s. 11(3). In the event of a breach of condition by the seller the buyer may have a right to reject the goods and to treat the contract as repudiated. This right may be lost if the buyer waives the condition, or elects to treat the breach of condition as a breach of warranty, or accepts the goods.

(iv) Breach of warranty.

Where there is a breach of warranty by the seller, or where the buyer elects (or is compelled) to treat any breach of condition as a breach of warranty, the buyer may maintain an action against the seller for damages for the breach of warranty: s. 53(1).

The measure of damages is the estimated loss directly and naturally arising, in the ordinary course of events, from the breach of warranty: s. 53(2). In the case of breach of warranty of quality such loss is *prima facie* the difference between the value of the goods at the time of delivery to the buyer and the value they would have had if they had fulfilled the warranty: s. 53(3).

SUMMARY

1 The law of sale of goods was codified by the Sale of Goods Act 1893, and was later consolidated by the Sale of Goods Act 1979.

2 A contract of sale of goods is a contract by which the seller transfers or agrees to transfer the property in goods to the buyer for a money consideration, called the price.

3 It is the duty of the seller to deliver the goods, and of the buyer to accept and pay for them, in accordance with the terms of the contract of sale.

4 The property in the goods passes when the parties intend that it shall pass.

5 The general rule is that no one can transfer a better title than that which he has (*nemo dat quod non habet*) but there are some important exceptions.

6 Sections 12 to 15 of the Sale of Goods Act provide for the implication of terms which are much to the advantage of the buyer. The implied terms are with regard to seller's title (s. 12), correspondence of the goods with description (s. 13), quality and fitness for purpose (s. 14) and correspondence of bulk with sample in quality (s. 15).

7 Liability under s. 12 cannot be excluded. Liability under ss. 13, 14 and 15 cannot be excluded as against a person dealing as a consumer: as against a person dealing otherwise than as consumer, the same liabilities can be excluded only in so far as the exclusion clause satisfies the requirement of reasonableness.

8 Where the buyer wrongfully refuses to accept and pay for the goods

the seller may claim damages. Where the buyer does not pay, the seller may claim the price of the goods; in some circumstances the seller may have a remedy against the goods themselves.

9 Where the seller wrongfully fails to deliver the goods the buyer may sue for damages or, in appropriate circumstances, he might be entitled to specific performance. Where the seller is in breach of condition the buyer may reject the goods and treat the contract as repudiated. Where the seller is in breach of warranty the buyer is left with his right to claim damages.

EXERCISES

1 Define a contract of sale of goods.

2 What are the duties of buyer and seller?

3 Distinguish between possession of the goods and the property in them?

4 When does the property in the goods pass from seller to buyer?

5 What are the exceptions to the general rule that no one can transfer a better title than that which he has?

6 What implied terms arise under s. 12 of the Sale of Goods Act?

7 Explain how the implied terms with regard to quality and fitness of the goods might arise under the Sale of Goods Act and the Supply of Goods and Services Act 1982.

8 In what circumstances does an implied term arise concerning the correspondence of the goods with the description? Mention two statutes in your answer.

9 What rules govern the validity of exclusion clauses which purport to exclude liability under the implied terms arising from ss. 12, 13, 14 and 15 of the Sale of Goods Act?

10 What are the remedies available to the seller in the event of the buyer's breach of contract?

11 What are the remedies of the buyer in the event of the seller's breach?

WORKSHOP

1 Joe bought a television set in the radio and electrical department of Harry's store. After the sale, the set was packed into a box, sealed and labelled with Joe's name and address. It was agreed that the set would be delivered next day. On the morning of the following day, through no fault of Harry or his staff, there was an explosion in the store and the

television set bought by Joe was damaged. Joe wishes to know whether he has any claim against Harry. Advise him.

2 Kenneth has contracted to sell his racehorse Goer to Jim for £14,600. Before delivery of the horse to Jim, Stewart, who has no knowledge of the sale to him, offers Kenneth £21,000 for Goer. Kenneth accepts this offer immediately and Stewart pays by cheque and takes Goer away with him. Explain, with reasons, whether Stewart gets a good title to the horse. In your answer, mention Jim's position.

3 Maudie sold and delivered her 'mini' motor-car to Sheila taking a cheque in payment. The cheque was later dishonoured. Before Maudie knew of the dishonour, Sheila had sold the mini to Frank, who bought it in entire good faith without notice of the dishonoured cheque. Explain the legal position of all parties and include a statement as to the property in the motor-car.

4 George bought a consignment of animal feed from Jane. By the agreement, payment was to be made on delivery. George accepted delivery and paid the price. However, due to a defect in the feed which was not noticeable on the brief inspection at the time of delivery, a number of George's pedigree animals have become ill and have died or are dying. Advise George as to any remedy which might be available to him under the Sale of Goods Act. What difference, if any, would it make to your advice if the contract contained a clause which provided that: 'The seller will not be responsible for any loss or damage suffered by the buyer as a result of using any product supplied by the seller under this contract'.

5 Ferdy bought half a ton of sand from Jenny, a builders' merchant. Ferdy intended to use the sand to make a sand-pit for his small children to play in. After the sand was delivered to his house, Ferdy discovered that it contained so much iron and other impurities that it was useless for making a sand-pit for children. Jenny has now sent her bill to Ferdy who does not wish to pay for the sand which is useless to him. Advise Jenny.

6 Adolphus, an art dealer has agreed to sell a rare painting by Holbein to Angela, delivery to take place at the close of an exhibition in which the picture is being shown. Before the exhibition is due to close, Angela discovers that Adolphus is negotiating to sell the painting to another client. Angela, who does not wish to lose this painting, seeks your advice. Advise her.

CONSUMER CREDIT

17.1 THE CONSUMER CREDIT ACT 1974

(a) The purpose of the Act

The Act establishes for the protection of consumers a new system, administered by the Director General of Fair Trading, of control of traders concerned with the provision of credit, or the supply of goods on hire or hire-purchase, and their transactions. This comprehensive new system is designed to replace previous legislation regulating moneylenders, pawnbrokers and hire-purchase traders and their transactions. Although the Act is not fully in force, this chapter describes the salient features of the system as it will be when completely established.

All section references are to sections of the Consumer Credit Act 1974 unless otherwise indicated.

(b) The Director General of Fair Trading

By s. 1, the duties of the Director General of Fair Trading (called 'the Director' in this chapter) are on the one hand administrative and adjudicatory and, on the other, advisory.

(i) Director's administrative duties.
It is the duty of the Director:

- (*a*) to administer the licensing system set up by the Act;
- (*b*) to exercise adjudicating functions in relation to the licensing system;
- (*c*) to superintend the working and enforcement of the Act and the regulations made under it; and
- (*d*) where necessary, himself to enforce the Act.

(ii) Director's advisory duties.
It is the duty of the Director to keep under review and from time to time advise the Secretary of State for Prices and Consumer Protection about:

(a) social and commercial developments in the United Kingdom and elsewhere relating to the provision of credit or bailment, and

(b) the working and enforcement of the Act and orders and regulations made under it.

17.2 REGULATED CONSUMER AGREEMENTS

Any agreement governed by the Act is called a 'regulated' agreement. These may be either consumer credit agreements or consumer hire agreements. There are several different kinds of regulated consumer credit agreements, each carefully defined by the Act. From these definitions it is clear that all forms of consumer credit are included, such as credit cards, bank overdrafts, voucher trading, cash loans and, indeed, any form of financial accommodation. As will be seen, distinctions are made between running-account credit and fixed-sum credit, between restricted-use credit and unrestricted-use credit, between debtor–creditor agreements and debtor–creditor–supplier agreements. The Act also recognises separately credit-token agreements and consumer hire agreements. There are special provisions for small agreements where payments do not exceed £30.

(a) Regulated consumer credit agreements

A regulated consumer credit agreement is a consumer credit agreement which is not an 'exempt' agreement under s. 16, i.e. it is one which is governed by the Act: s. 8(3).

To understand this important provision, further definitions must be considered.

(i) A personal credit agreement is an agreement between an individual (the debtor) and the creditor by which the creditor provides the debtor with credit of any amount. s. 8(1). For the purposes of the Act, 'individual' includes a partnership or other unincorporated body of persons not consisting entirely of bodies corporate: s. 189(1).

(ii) A consumer credit agreement is a personal credit agreement by which the creditor provides the debtor with credit not exceeding £5,000: s. 8(2).

(iii) An exempt agreement is a consumer credit agreement of a kind specified by s. 16 as being outside the control of the Act. These are mainly agreements where the creditor is a local authority, building society or a body specified in an order made by the Secretary of State. Such specified bodies will be charities, friendly societies, organisations of employers or employees and, in some cases, insurance companies.

(b) Running-account credit and fixed-sum credit

There are two types of credit according to whether there is a fixed-sum account or a running-account as follows.

(i) Running-account credit.
This is a facility under a personal credit agreement whereby the debtor is enabled to receive from time to time an amount or value such that any credit limit is not exceeded. Examples are bank overdrafts, credit cards and shop budget accounts: s. 10(1)

(ii) Fixed-sum credit.
This is any facility other than running-account credit whereby the debtor is enabled to receive credit, whether in one amount or in instalments. Examples are personal loans, bank loans, hire-purchase, credit sale and conditional sale agreements and voucher trading: s. 10(1).

(c) Restricted-use and unrestricted-use credit

Credit may be restricted or unrestricted in its use.

(i) Restricted-use credit.
A restricted-use credit agreement is a regulated consumer credit agreement:

- (*a*) to finance a transaction between the debtor and the creditor, or
- (*b*) to finance a transaction between the debtor and a person other than the creditor (the supplier), or
- (*c*) to refinance any existing indebtedness: s. 11(1).

Examples are hire-purchase, credit sale and conditional sale agreements (under which credit may be given either by the supplier or by a finance house), mail order credit, voucher trading, store budget accounts and loans for goods or services which are paid direct to the supplier of the goods or services.

'Conditional sale agreement' means an agreement for the sale of goods or land under which the purchase price or part of it is payable by instalments, and the property in the goods or land is to remain in the seller (notwithstanding that the buyer is to be in possession of the goods or land) until such conditions as to the payment of instalments or otherwise as may be specified in the agreement are fulfilled: s. 189(1).

'Credit-sale agreement' means an agreement for the sale of goods, under which the purchase price or part of it is payable by instalments, but which is not a conditional sale agreement: s. 189(1).

(ii) Unrestricted-use credit.
An unrestricted-use credit agreement is any regulated consumer credit

agreement which is not a restricted-use credit agreement: s. 11(2). Examples are bank overdraft facilities, cheque cards and loans under which the debtor has an unrestricted right of disposition.

(d) Debtor–creditor–supplier agreements

A debtor–creditor–supplier agreement is a regulated consumer credit agreement which is either:

(i) a restricted-use credit agreement to finance a transaction between the debtor and the creditor, e.g. a credit sale agreement where the seller finances the instalment credit for the buyer; or

(ii) a restricted-use credit agreement to finance a transaction between the debtor and the supplier, e.g. a loan from a finance company strictly for the purchase of a specified boat; or

(iii) an unrestricted-use credit agreement made by the creditor under pre-existing arrangements between himself and the supplier in the knowledge that the credit is to be used to finance a transaction between the debtor and the supplier - i.e., where the debtor is not strictly bound to use the credit for any particular purpose although he has such an intention.

(e) Debtor–creditor agreements

A debtor–creditor agreement is a regulated consumer credit agreement which is either:

(i) a restricted-use credit agreement to finance a transaction between the debtor and a person (the 'supplier') other than the creditor, but is not made by the creditor under pre-existing arrangements or in contemplation of future arrangements between himself and the the supplier (s. 13(a)); or

(ii) a restricted-use credit agreement to refinance any existing indebtedness of the debtor's whether to the creditor or another person (s. 13(b)); or

(iii) an unrestricted-use agreement which is not made by the creditor under pre-existing arrangements between himself and a person (the 'supplier') other than the debtor in the knowledge that the credit is to be used to finance a transaction between the debtor and the supplier (s. 13(c)).

(f) Credit-token agreements

A credit-token is a card, check, voucher, coupon, stamp, form, booklet or other document or thing given to an individual by a person carrying on a consumer credit business who undertakes either:

(i) that on production of it he will supply cash, goods or services on credit; or

(ii) that where, on the production of it to a third party, the third party supplies cash, goods or services, he will pay the third party for them in return for payment to him by the individual: s. 14(1).

Credit-token agreements are regulated agreements under the Act: s. 14(2). Examples of credit-tokens are bank cash cards for automatic cash machines, credit cards issued by stores to their customers, credit cards issued by credit card organisations and vouchers issued by voucher trading companies: s. 14.

(g) Consumer hire agreements

A consumer hire agreement is an agreement made by an individual (the hirer) for the bailment of goods to the hirer but which does not require the hirer to make payments exceeding £5,000. The agreement must be capable of subsisting for more than three months and must not be a hire-purchase agreement: s. 15(1). Consumer hire agreements are regulated agreements: s. 15(2).

Examples would be the hiring of equipment or a motor-car for a period of more than three months. Even commercial hirings would be within the definition if the hirer were a sole trader or a partnership firm, i.e. not a company.

(h) Small agreements

A small agreement is either:

(i) a regulated consumer credit agreement not exceeding £30, other than a hire-purchase or conditional sale agreement; or

(ii) a regulated consumer hire agreement which does not require the hirer to make payments exceeding £30.

In either case the agreement must be unsecured or secured by guarantee or indemnity only: s. 17(1).

17.3 ENTRY INTO CREDIT OR HIRE AGREEMENTS

(a) Preliminary matters

If regulations require specified information to be disclosed to the debtor or hirer before a regulated agreement is made the agreement will not be 'properly executed' if such regulations are not complied with: s. 55(1) and (2). (See 17.3(b) below).

'Antecedent negotiations' are any negotiations with the debtor or hirer conducted by the creditor, owner, credit-broker or supplier. The 'negotiator' is the person by whom such negotiations are conducted with the debtor or hirer: s. 56(1).

Where the negotiator is conducting negotiations on behalf of a credit-broker or supplier the negotiator will be deemed to be the agent of the creditor: s. 56(2).

(b) Making the agreement

(i) Signature.
A regulated agreement is not 'properly executed' unless the following conditions are satisfied:

- (*a*) a document in the prescribed form is signed by or on behalf of the creditor or owner; and
- (*b*) the document embodies all the express terms of the agreement; and
- (*c*) the document, when presented to the debtor or hirer for signature, is in such a state that all its terms are readily legible: s. 61(1).

(ii) Duty to supply copies of the agreement.
If an unexecuted agreement is presented personally to the debtor or hirer and he signs it but the creditor or owner does not, then the debtor or hirer is entitled to a copy of the unexecuted agreement on the spot and to a copy of the executed agreement within seven days of its being executed: ss. 62(1) and 61(3).

If an unexecuted agreement is presented personally to the debtor or creditor for signature and he signs, and the creditor or owner also signs on the spot, then a copy of the executed agreement must be given to the debtor or hirer immediately: s. 63(1).

If an unexecuted agreement is sent to the debtor or hirer for his signature, a copy must be sent at the same time and a further copy must be given to him within seven days of the agreement being made: s. 62(2) and s. 61(3).

(iii) Notice of cancellation rights.
An agreement is not 'properly executed' if the debtor or hirer is not given notice of any rights he may have to cancel the agreement: s. 64.

(iv) Improperly executed agreements.
Where an agreement is not 'properly executed' it can be enforceable against the debtor or hirer only by an order of the court: s. 65(1).

(c) Cancellation within the cooling-off period

(i) Cancellable agreements.

A regulated agreement may be cancelled by the debtor or hirer if the antecedent negotiations included oral representations made in the presence of the debtor or hirer by an individual acting as, or on behalf of, the negotiator. An agreement will not be cancellable, however, if it is signed by the debtor or hirer at premises at which any of the following carry on any business whether on a permanent or temporary basis – the creditor or owner, or the negotiator in any antecedent negotiations or any party (other than the debtor or hirer) to a linked transaction: s. 67.

(ii) Cooling-off period.

This period starts when the debtor or hirer signs the unexecuted agreement and ends at the end of the fifth day following the day on which he received the second statutory copy of the agreement or, where there is no second copy, the statutory notice of cancellation rights: s. 68.

(iii) Notice of cancellation.

If sent by post, notice of cancellation is deemed to be served at the time of posting even if lost in the post. The effect of such notice is to render the regulated agreement void as if it had never been entered into: s. 69.

(iv) Recovery of money and return of goods.

The Act contains (ss. 70 to 73) detailed provisions governing the restoration of money and goods following the cancellation of a regulated agreement. Essentially, they are as follows:

(a) money paid by the debtor or hirer can be recovered;
(b) the debtor or hirer can retain possession of any goods under the agreement as security for money to be repaid to him;
(c) money payable by the debtor or hirer ceases to be payable.

17.4 MATTERS ARISING DURING THE AGREEMENT

Sections 75 to 85 deal with various matters which might arise during the currency of credit or hire agreements. The most important of these matters are outlined below.

(a) Liability of the creditor for breaches by the supplier

If a debtor under certain kinds of debtor–creditor–supplier agreement has a claim for misrepresentation or breach of contract against the supplier, he has a like claim against the creditor: s. 75(1). The kinds of agreement subject to this provision are:

(i) a restricted-use credit agreement to finance a transaction between the the debtor and the supplier which is made by the creditor under pre-existing arrangements, or in contemplation of future arrangements, between himself and the supplier; and

(ii) an unrestricted-use credit arrangement which is made by the creditor under pre-existing arrangements between himself and the supplier in the knowledge that the credit is to be used to finance a transaction between the debtor and the supplier.

This provision renders the creditor (usually a finance house) liable *inter alia* for breaches of the implied terms about title, quality and fitness for purpose.

(b) Information under fixed-sum credit agreement

The creditor under a regulated fixed-sum agreement must, on the request of the debtor, supply him with a copy of the executed agreement together with a detailed statement of the account between them: s. 77(1).

(c) Liability for misuse of facilities

The debtor under a regulated consumer credit agreement does not become liable to the creditor for any loss arising from use of the credit facility by another person other than an agent of the debtor: s. 83(1). This provision does not apply to non-commercial agreements: s. 83(2). (A non-commercial agreement is one which is not made by the creditor or owner in the course of a business carried on by him: s. 189(1)). This provision does not prevent the debtor under a credit-token agreement from being made liable to the extent of £30 for loss to the creditor arising from the use of the credit-token by other persons during a period when the credit-token was not in the possession of the debtor: s. 84(1). The debtor is under no liability at all after he has given oral notice that the credit-token is lost or stolen: s. 84(3).

17.5 DEFAULT AND TERMINATION

(a) Default notices

Where a debtor is in breach of a regulated agreement the creditor or owner cannot obtain certain remedies unless he has served a default notice on the debtor or hirer: s. 87(1).

(i) The need for default notice.
Service of a notice is necessary before the creditor or owner can become entitled to:

(*a*) terminate the agreement; or

(*b*) demand earlier payment; or

(*c*) recover possession of goods or land; or

(*d*) treat any right conferred on the debtor or hirer as terminated, restricted or deferred; or

(*e*) enforce any security: s. 87(1).

(ii) Contents of a default notice.
The default notice must be in the prescribed form and specify:

(*a*) the nature of the alleged breach;

(*b*) if the breach is capable of remedy, what action is required to remedy it and the date before which that action is to be taken;

(*c*) if the breach is not capable of remedy, the sum (if any) required to be paid as compensation for the breach, and the date before which it is to be paid: s. 88(1).

Any date specified in a notice must not be less than seven days after the date of service of the notice: s. 88(2).

(iii) Compliance with a default notice.
If before the date specified for that purpose in the default notice the debtor or hirer takes the action specified the breach shall be treated as not having occurred: s. 89.

(b) Further restriction of remedies

(i) Retaking protected hire-purchase goods.
At any time when the debtor is in breach of a regulated conditional sale agreement or a regulated hire-purchase agreement, and the debtor has paid one-third or more of the price, and the property remains in the creditor, then the creditor is not entitled to recover possession of the goods except on an order of the court: s. 90(1).

If goods are recovered by the creditor in contravention of this provision the agreement will terminate, the debtor will be released from all liability and will be entitled to recover all money paid under the agreement: s. 91.

(ii) Entering premises to recover goods.
Except under an order of the court, the creditor or owner will not be entitled to enter any premises to take possession of goods subject to a regulated hire-purchase agreement, a regulated conditional sale agreement or a regulated consumer hire agreement: s. 92. Any entry in contravention of this provision will be actionable as a breach of statutory duty: s. 93.

(c) Early payment by the debtor

(i) The right to pay ahead of time.
The debtor under a regulated consumer credit agreement is entitled at any time, by notice to the creditor and the payment to the creditor of all amounts payable under the agreement, to discharge his indebtedness: s. 94(1).

Where the debtor takes advantage of this provision to pay early, he will be allowed a rebate of charges for credit: s. 95.

(ii) The duty to give information.
The creditor is under a duty, if so requested in writing by the debtor, to provide a statement of the amount required at any time to discharge the debtor under the early payment provisions. Such statement must be in the prescribed form and must show how the amount is calculated: s. 97(1).

(d) Termination of agreements

(i) Notice of termination in non-default cases.
The creditor or owner is not entitled to terminate a regulated agreement except by or after giving the debtor or hirer not less than seven days' notice of the termination: s. 98(1). The notice must be in the prescribed form or it will be ineffective: s. 98(3).

(ii) The right to terminate hire-purchase agreements.
The debtor under a regulated hire-purchase or conditional sale agreement has an indefeasible right to terminate the agreement at any time before the final payment is due: s. 99(1). In order to terminate the agreement, the debtor must give notice to whoever is authorised to receive instalments under the agreement: s. 99(1).

Where a regulated hire-purchase or regulated conditional sale agreement is terminated in a non-default case, the debtor is liable to pay to the creditor the amount by which one-half of the total price exceeds the aggregate of the sums paid and the sums due in respect of the total price immediately before the termination: s. 100. This so-called 50 per cent rule is subject to the agreement providing for a smaller payment or not providing for any payment: s. 100(1).

(iii) The right to terminate a hire agreement.
The hirer under a regulated consumer hire agreement has an indefeasible right to terminate the agreement by giving notice to whoever is authorised to receive sums payable under the agreement: s. 101(1). A notice under this provision must not expire earlier than eighteen months after the making of the agreement: s. 101(3). Apart from that, the minimum period of notice, unless the agreement provides for a shorter period, is as follows:

(*a*) if the agreement provides for payments at equal intervals, the minimum period of notice is the length of one interval or three months, whichever is less: s. 101(4).

(*b*) if the agreement provides for payments at differing intervals, the minimum period of notice is the length of the shortest interval or three months, whichever is less: s. 101(5).

(*c*) in any other case the minimum period of notice is three months: s. 101(6).

(iv) Exceptions to the right of termination of hire agreements.
Section 101(7) provides for three exceptions to the statutory right of termination of regulated hire agreements. They are as follows:

(*a*) any agreement which provides for the total payment of a sum in excess of £300 in any year; or

(*b*) any agreement where goods are bailed to the hirer for the purpose of his business and the goods are selected by the hirer and acquired by the owner for the purposes of the agreement at the request of the hirer; or

(*c*) any agreement where the hirer requires the goods for the purpose of bailing them to other persons in the course of his business.

(v) Termination statements.
If the debtor or hirer serves notice on the creditor or owner stating that the indebtedness has been discharged and requiring the creditor or owner to confirm the correctness of the statement, the creditor or owner must either comply or serve a counter-notice disputing the statement: s. 103.

17.6 SECURITY

(a) General matters

(i) Definition.
Section 189(1) provides a wide definition of 'security', embracing real security and personal security, as follows. Security means 'a mortgage, charge, pledge, bond, debenture, indemnity, guarantee, bill, note or other right provided by the debtor or hirer at his request (express or implied), to secure the carrying out of the obligations of the debtor or hirer under the agreement'.

(ii) Form and content of securities.
Any security provided in relation to a regulated agreement must be in writing: s. 105(1). The documents (security instruments) must, in form and content, comply with any relevant regulations: s. 105(2).

(b) The duty to give information

(i) The duty to give information to a surety: credit agreements.
The creditor under a regulated credit agreement (whether fixed-sum or running account) must give to any surety, on request, a copy of the executed agreement and a copy of the security instrument and a statement of the account between himself and the debtor: ss. 107(1) and 108(1). These provisions are not applicable to non-commercial agreements.

(ii) The duty to give information to a surety: hire agreements.
The owner under a regulated consumer hire agreement must give to a surety, on request, a copy of the executed agreement and a copy of the security instrument and a statement of the sums due and payable under the agreement: s. 109(1). This provision is not applicable to non-commercial agreements.

(iii) The duty to give information to the debtor or hirer.
The creditor or owner under a regulated agreement must give to the debtor or hirer, on request, a copy of any security instrument executed in relation to the agreement after the making of the agreement: s. 110(1).

(iv) The duty to give the surety a copy of the default notice.
When a default notice or a notice under s. 76(1) or s. 98(1) is served on a debtor or hirer, a copy of the notice must be served by the creditor or owner on any surety: s. 111(1).

If the creditor or owner fails to comply with this requirement, the security is enforceable only on an order of the court: s. 111(2).

(c) Negotiable instruments

(i) Restrictions on taking and negotiating instruments.
A creditor or owner must not take a negotiable instrument, other than a bank note or cheque, in discharge of any sum payable by the debtor or hirer or by the surety: s. 123(1). Nor may the creditor or owner negotiate a cheque taken by him from the debtor or hirer or from the surety except to a banker: s. 123(2). Nor may the creditor or owner take a negotiable instrument as security for the discharge of any sum payable by the debtor or hirer or by the surety: s. 123(3).

In the event of any contravention of the provisions of s. 123, the sum payable or the security, as the case may be, will be enforceable only on the order of the court: s. 124.

Finally, a person who takes a negotiable instrument in contravention of s. 123(1) or (3) is not a holder in due course, and is not entitled to enforce the instrument: s. 125.

17.7 JUDICIAL CONTROL

The Act contains provisions for the judicial enforcement of certain regulated agreements and securities, for extension of time orders, for protection of property orders and for the reopening of extortionate agreements.

(a) Enforcement orders in cases of infringement

Section 127 is concerned with the power of the court to make enforcement orders with regard to:

(i)   improperly executed agreements (s. 65(1)); or
(ii) improperly executed security instruments (s. 105(7)); or
(iii) failure to serve a copy of a notice to the surety (s. 11(2)); or
(iv) taking a negotiable instrument in contravention of s. 123(s.124).

The general rule is that the court must dismiss applications for such enforcement orders if it considers it just to do so: s. 127(1). If it appears just to do so, the court may in an enforcement order reduce or discharge any sum payable by the debtor or hirer, or any surety, so as to compensate him for prejudice suffered as a result of the contravention in question.

(b) Extension of time

If it appears just to do so the court may make a time order on the application of a debtor or hirer or in an action by a creditor or owner: s. 129(1). A time order must provide for one or both of the following:

(*a*) the payment by the debtor or hirer or any surety of any sum owed at such times and by such instalments as the court thinks reasonable;
(*b*) the remedying by the debtor or hirer of any breach of a regulated agreement (other than non-payment of money) within such period as the court may specify: s. 129(2).

(c) Protection orders

The court, on the application of the creditor or owner under a regulated agreement, may make such orders as it thinks just for protecting any property from damage or depreciation pending the determination of proceedings.

(d) Extortionate credit bargains

The general rule is that if the court finds a credit bargain extortionate it may reopen the credit agreement so as to do justice between the parties: s. 137(1).

(i) Definition.
In ss. 137 to 140, 'credit agreement' and 'credit bargain' have the following meanings respectively:

    (*a*) 'credit agreement' means any agreement between the debtor and the creditor by which the creditor provides the debtor with credit of any amount, and

    (*b*) 'credit bargain': (1) where no transaction other than the credit agreement is to be taken into account in computing the total charge for credit, means the credit agreement; or (2) where one or more other transactions are to be so taken into account, means the credit agreement and those other transactions, taken together: s. 137(2).

(ii) When bargains are extortionate.
A credit bargain is extortionate if it:

    (*a*) requires the debtor or a relative of his to make payments which are grossly exorbitant; or

    (*b*) otherwise grossly contravenes ordinary principles of fair dealing: s. 138(1).

(iii) Reopening of extortionate agreements.
On the application of, or at the instance of, the debtor or a surety, a credit agreement may be reopened if the court thinks just on the ground that the credit bargain is extortionate: s. 139(1). In reopening the agreement, the court may make an order relieving the debtor or a surety from the payment of any sum in excess of that fairly due and reasonable: s. 139(2).

SUMMARY

1   The Consumer Credit Act 1974 was passed to establish a comprehensive system of consumer protection for all types of credit.

2   The Director General of Fair Trading has the duty to administer the system and to advise the Secretary of State as to the working of the Act.

3   An agreement which is governed by the Act is called a 'regulated agreement'.

4   The Act defines the following: 'personal credit agreement', 'consumer credit agreement', 'running-account credit', 'fixed-sum credit', 'restricted-use credit', 'unrestricted-use credit', 'debtor–creditor–supplier agreement', 'debtor–creditor agreement', 'credit-token agreement', 'consumer hire agreements' and 'small agreements'.

5   The debtor or hirer is entitled to copies of the unexecuted or executed agreement according to the circumstances.

6   All regulated agreements must be in the prescribed form and signed by the parties.

7   Certain agreements may be cancelled by notice during the cooling-off period.

8   The creditor in a debtor–creditor–supplier agreement is liable for the default of the supplier.

9   Where a debtor is in breach of a regulated agreement the creditor or owner cannot obtain the usual remedies unless he has served a default notice on the debtor or hirer.

10   The debtor under a regulated consumer credit agreement has a right to pay ahead of time.

11   The debtor under a regulated hire-purchase or conditional sale agreement has an indefeasible right to terminate the agreement at any time before payment is due. The hirer under a regulated consumer hire agreement generally has a similar right, but there are some important exceptions.

12   Any security provided in relation to a regulated agreement must be in writing and must comply in form and content with any relevant regulations.

13   Sureties, debtors and hirers are entitled, on request, to be provided with copies of the executed agreement and security instrument.

14   The court will deal with applications for enforcement orders as it considers just.

EXERCISES

1   State the purpose of the Consumer Credit Act 1974.

2   List the duties of the Director General of Fair Trading under the Act.

3   Define a regulated consumer credit agreement.

4   Distinguish in detail between restricted-use credit agreements and unrestricted-use credit agreements.

5   What is a credit-token agreement?

6   What is a consumer hire agreement?

7   Explain the procedure for making a properly executed regulated agreement.

8   What is the procedure for cancellation within the cooling-off period?

9   How may the creditor become liable for the default of the supplier?

10   Explain the function of a default notice.

11   What right has the debtor to pay ahead of time?

12   Has the debtor under a regulated hire-purchase agreement a right of termination?

13 Explain the hirer's right to terminate a regulated consumer hire agreement. What exceptional cases are there?

14 What may constitute 'security' under the Act?

15 What rights has a surety to obtain documents and information from the creditor or owner? Has the debtor or hirer a similar right?

16 When may the court make an enforcement order? What other judicial controls are provided for in the Act?

THE ASSIGNMENT OF THINGS IN ACTION

Things in action are to be compared with things in possession. For example, a contract right to recover money is a thing in action, whereas a book or a chair is a thing in possession.

A 'thing in action' or, to call it by its ancient name, a 'chose in action', is personal property of a kind which can ultimately be enforced by legal action and not by taking actual physical possession.

Examples of things in action are contract rights of all kinds, company shares, rights under a trust, insurance policies, patents, copyrights, postal orders, legacies and many more.

A thing in action which is of a kind enforceable by the courts of common law before 1875 is called a legal thing in action, e.g. a creditor's right to the payment of a debt.

A thing in action which is of a kind enforceable by the courts of equity before 1875 is called an equitable thing in action, e.g. a right under a trust.

19.1 ASSIGNMENT

(a) The assignment of legal things in action

There are usually three parties involved in an assignment, namely, the assignor, the assignee and the debtor (or person otherwise liable originally to the assignor). Where, for example, X owes £100 to Y, and Y assigns the right to recover this debt to Z, the parties are X the debtor, Y the assignor and Z the assignee.

The common law did not permit such an assignment as would give the assignee the right to sue in his own name to recover the debt from the debtor, although it might allow the assignee to claim against the assignor in the event of non-payment if the claim could be founded on breach of contract. Where, however, the assignor was prepared to allow the assignee to use his name, then the assignee could sue the debtor in the name of the assignor. This cumbersome procedure was not necessary where the Crown was the assignee, nor where the instrument assigned was negotiable, either by custom or by statute.

The courts of equity regarded the assignment as binding on the conscience of the assignor, recognising therefore that the assignee had a kind of property in the assigned thing in action, and not merely a procedural right to sue. In *Fitzroy* v. *Cave* (1905), it was explained as follows:

> 'At common law a debt was looked upon as a strictly personal obligation, and an assignment of it was regarded as a mere assignment of a right to bring an action at law against the debtor. But the courts of equity took a different view. They admitted the title of an assignee of a debt, regarding it as a piece of property, an asset capable of being dealt with like any other asset, and treating the necessity of an action at law to get it in as a mere incident.'

In equity, the assignor could be compelled to allow the assignee to use his name in an action against the debtor.

There are no strict formal requirements for a valid equitable assignment of a legal thing in action. Form and language are immaterial so long as the meaning and intention are clear.

(b) The assignment of equitable things in action

It is necessary to distinguish between absolute and non-absolute assignments of equitable things in action. An absolute assignment is one by which the entire interest in the thing in action is intended to be assigned unconditionally to the assignee. It is not necessary, however, for the assignor to deprive himself for ever of the property transferred. For example, an assignment of an entire thing in action for the purpose of security is none the less an absolute assignment.

Non-absolute assignments may be conditional assignments, assignments by way of charge or assignments of part only of a thing in action.

A conditional assignment is one which is subject to the happening of an event which is not certain. For example, where the interest assigned is expressed to remain with the assignee until a specified payment be made to him.

An assignment by way of charge occurs where a fund is specified from which the assignee is to be paid, the fund itself not being assigned in part or in whole.

The effects of equitable assignments may be summarised as follows:

(i) Legal things in action.

As mentioned above, equity compels the assignor to allow the assignee to use his name in proceedings against the debtor.

(ii) Equitable things in action.

In the case of an absolute assignment of an equitable thing in action, the assignee could bring his action in a court of equity in his own name. In such cases it was not necessary to join the assignor as a party to the action, for the entire thing had been transferred, leaving no rights in the assignor to be considered by the court. In such cases, equity would not require the presence of the assignor in court. Such assignments have been, since 1875, recognised by the Supreme Court in its equitable jurisdiction.

In the case of a non-absolute assignment of an equitable thing in action, equity required the assignee to join the assignor as a party in the action against the debtor. This process would enable the court to take the assignor's remaining interest into account. For this purpose his presence in court would be required.

(c) Statutory assignment

A method of statutory assignment which would enable the assignee of a legal thing in action to sue in his own name was first introduced by the Judicature Act 1873 and is now re-enacted in section 136 of the Law of Property Act 1925 as follows:

Any absolute assignment by writing under the hand of the assignor (not purporting to be by way of charge only) of any debt or other legal thing in action, of which express notice in writing has been given to the debtor, trustee, or other person from whom the assignor would have been entitled to claim such debt or thing in action, is effectual in law (subject to equities having priority over the right of the assignee) to pass and transfer from the date of such notice:

   (*a*) the legal right to such debt or thing in action;

   (*b*) all legal and other remedies for the same; and

   (*c*) the power to give a good discharge for the same without the concurrence of the assignor.

An assignment will be valid and effective under this provision only if it is absolute and in writing and, further, notice of it must have been given to the debtor. The law regarding equitable assignments is not affected by section 136. The reference to 'legal thing in action' in the section referred to has been held to mean 'lawful thing in action', with the result that both legal and equitable things in action are assignable under the statute.

18.2 RESTRICTIONS ON THE EFFECTIVENESS OF ASSIGNMENT

An assignment may be subject to notice having been given to the debtor and it will always be subject to the equities. These matters will be seen as the commercial disadvantages of assignment as compared with the transfer of a negotiable instrument.

(a) Notice to the debtor

Notice of the assignment to the debtor has different functions according to whether the assignment is statutory or equitable.

(i) Statutory assignment.
In order to satisfy the requirements of section 136 of the Law of Property Act 1925, express notice in writing of the assignment must have been given to the debtor, trustee or other person from whom the assignor would have been entitled to claim the debt or thing in action. Section 136 also provides that the assignment takes effect from the date of the notice. It is clear that no statutory assignment can take place without notice. In the absence of notice, the attempted statutory assignment would probably be effective as an equitable assignment.

(ii) Equitable assignment.
Although notice to the debtor is not a strict requirement to validate an equitable assignment, the absence of notice may affect the assignee's title to the thing in action. For instance, if the debtor without notice pays the assignor, the assignee will have no claim against the debtor and, furthermore, in the case of two or more assignments of the same thing in action, the assignees will be entitled according to the priorities in time of their respective notices.

(b) Subject to the equities

In both statutory and equitable assignments, the assignee takes 'subject to the equities' having priority over the right of the assignee. This means that, as against the assignee, the debtor may plead any defence or counterclaim that he could have pleaded against the assignor at the time of the notice. If, for example, A assigns to B a debt of £80 which is owed by C and, under another transaction between A and C, the sum of £10 accrued to C from A before notice of the assignment, B's claim as assignee will be subject to C's right to set off the sum of £10 against the amount assigned, i.e. the assignment will be effective as to £70 only.

Similarly, if the assignor's title is defective in any way at all, the assignee will take no better title than that which the assignor had. This is an application of the principle that no one can pass a better title than that which he has: *nemo dat quod non habet.*

(c) Negotiability

The risk taken by the assignee effectively rendered assignment as unsuitable for some commercial and financial transactions. Originally by the custom of merchants, and later by statute, certain instruments were given the characteristics of negotiability. Share warrants to bearer, Treasury Bills, promissory notes and, most important of all, bills of exchange are all negotiable instruments, having the characteristics of negotiability.

The characteristics of negotiability are as follows:

(i) The instrument is such that it can be put into a state in which title will pass by mere delivery or, in the case of bills of exchange, by indorsement and delivery.

(ii) Title will pass free from the equities and other defects.

(iii) The holder of the instrument can sue all prior parties in his own name.

SUMMARY

1   A thing in action is personal property of a kind which can ultimately be enforced by legal action and not by taking actual physical possession.

2   Things in action may be legal or equitable.

3   At common law it was not possible to assign a thing in action.

4   The courts of equity recognised that the assignee had a kind of property in the assigned thing in action. In equity, the assignor could be compelled to allow the assignee to use his name in proceedings against the debtor. Equity acts on the conscience of the assignor.

5   An absolute assignment is one by which the entire interest in the thing in action is assigned unconditonally.

6   In the case of an absolute assignment of an equitable thing in action, the assignee could bring an action in a court of equity in his own name. Such actions are now within the jurisdiction of the Supreme Court.

7   An assignment which satisfies the strict requirements of s. 136 of the Law of Property Act 1925 passes from the date of notice to the debtor (*a*) the legal right to the thing in action, (*b*) all remedies for it and (*c*) the power to give a good discharge for it.

8   Notice to the debtor is essential in the case of a statutory assignment and advisable in the case of an equitable assignment.

9   An assignee takes subject to the equities, i.e. as against the assignee, the debtor may plead any defence or counterclaim that he could have

pleaded against the assignor at the time of the notice to him. In other words, the assignee takes subject to any defects in the assignor's title.

10 The characteristics of negotiability are (*a*) the instrument can be put in a state in which title will pass by mere delivery or, in the case of a bill of exchange, by indorsement and delivery, (*b*) title will pass free from the equities and other defects and (*c*) the holder of the instrument can sue all prior parties in his own name.

EXERCISES

1 Define 'thing in action'.

2 Explain the difference between a legal thing in action and an equitable thing in action.

3 Does the common law allow the assignment of a thing in action?

4 What do you understand by 'an equitable assignment of a legal thing in action'?

5 How did equity permit the assignment of equitable things in action? Where is the equitable jurisdiction today?

6 Distinguish between absolute and non-absolute assignments.

7 State fully the requirements of an assignment under s. 136 of the Law of Property Act 1925.

8 What is the requirement of notice to the debtor? How is it significant with regard to the effectiveness of an assignment?

9 The assignee takes subject to the equities. Explain.

10 State the characteristics of negotiability.

11 What do you think are the advantages of negotiation over assignment from the commercial point of view?

WORKSHOP

1 Which, if any, of the following are things in action: a share certificate, a contract right, a dog, an insurance policy, a house, a bill of lading and a right under a trust?

2 Joe owes £300 to Lisa. Lisa tells Lucy that she can have the £300 from Joe if she, Lucy, will deliver her car to her. If Lucy delivers the car, can she sue Joe for the £300?

3 George is of full age and is the beneficiary under a trust. He has written to Susan to say that he wishes to transfer all of his rights under the trust to her. Susan now wishes to know what principles govern the drafting of an instrument of assignment to be signed by George. She also wishes to

know whether any other document is necessary to complete the assignment.

4 Percy has a share warrant to bearer and wishes to transfer all rights in it to Harold in the simplest possible way. Advise him.

5 Fanny contracted to buy a new piano from Agatha for £650. After receiving the money (£650), Agatha in writing assigned the full amount to Michael. One week after the assignment, Fanny wrote to Agatha saying that the piano was defective and would cost £100 to put right. Michael wishes to claim the full amount (£650) from Agatha. Advise him.

6 Keith has assigned a debt owed to him by Henry by a full statutory assignment to Bertrand. Before Henry had notice of the assignment, he paid the amount in full to Keith. Keith is now insolvent and Bertrand wishes to know whether he has a claim against Henry. Advise him.

BILLS OF EXCHANGE

Unless otherwise indicated, all section references in this chapter are to the Bills of Exchange Act 1882.

19.1 NEGOTIABILITY

(a) Negotiable instruments

Where a thing in action is assigned, the assignee takes subject to the equities and any other defects in the title of the assignor. The assignee must also make sure that prompt notice of the assignment is given to the debtor in order to preserve his rights as assignee. The assignee's great disadvantage is that he can never be absolutely certain that he will get a perfect title transferred to him. Where, on the other hand, there is a transfer of a negotiable instrument the position of the transferee is quite different from that of the assignee. Negotiable instruments have been invested by custom or by statute with the special characteristics of negotiability. These characteristics are:

(i) the instrument can be put into a state in which title will pass by mere delivery or, in the case of a bill of exchange, by indorsement and delivery.

(ii) title passes on negotiation free from the equities and other defects.

(iii) the holder of the instrument can sue all prior parties in his own name. (It must be remembered that a negotiable instrument may be used to finance a series of transactions and may be thus negotiated several times in its life.)

The commercial advantages of negotiation over assignment are obvious.

Examples of negotiable instruments are promissory notes, dividend warrants, debentures payable to bearer, share warrants, Treasury Bills and bills of exchange, including cheques.

Examples of instruments which are not negotiable are bills of lading, postal orders, share certificates and insurance policies.

The question whether or not any particular kind of instrument is negotiable depended originally on mercantile usage.

(b) Use of bills of exchange

Negotiability means that an honest transferee for value can depend upon being paid under the instrument. This facilitates the use of bills of exchange as instruments of credit for various commercial purposes, but particularly:

(i)   to raise short-term finance for trade and industry; or
(ii) to enable a seller or exporter to obtain cash soon after the dispatch of the goods and, at the same time,
(iii) to enable the buyer or importer to defer payment, at least until he is in possession of the goods.

For all the above purposes, the parties to a bill of exchange usually rely on the services of an accepting house which is prepared to make itself ultimately liable on the bill. An accepting house is a merchant banking house specialising in the acceptance of bills of exchange. Acceptance is carried out under previous arrangements called 'credits' set up in favour of the banker's customers.

An ordinary cheque is a bill of exchange, but its usual purpose is simply to enable the customer to draw on a banker for the provision of cash to the customer himself or a creditor whereas, in the case of a commercial bill, there will be a series of transactions, in each of which the bill will be given in return for value.

(c) The Bills of Exchange Act 1882

The Act is a codification of the law of bills of exchange, cheques and promissory notes. Important amendments to the law governing cheques were made by the Cheques Act 1957.

19.2 DEFINITION AND FORM OF A BILL

(a) Definition

A bill of exchange is an unconditional order in writing, addressed by one person to another, signed by the person giving it, requiring the person to whom it is addressed to pay on demand or at a fixed or determinable future time a sum certain in money to or to the order of a specified person, or to bearer: s. 3(1).

An instrument which does not comply with these conditions, or which orders any act to be done in addition to the payment of money, is not a bill of exchange: s. 3(2).

An order to pay out of a particular fund is not unconditional within the meaning of this section; but an unqualified order to pay, coupled with (*a*) an indication of a particular fund out of which the drawee is to reimburse himself or a particular account to be debited with the amount, or (*b*) a statement of the transaction which gives rise to the bill, is unconditional: s. 3(3).

A bill is not invalid by reason that it is not dated, or that it does not specify the value given, or that any value has been given for it, or that it does not specify the place where it is drawn or the place where it is payable: s. 3(4).

(b) Analysis of s. 3(1).

The statutory definition contains the following elements. A bill is

(i) an unconditional order in writing
(ii) addressed by one person (*the drawer*)
(iii) to another (*the drawee*), who becomes *the acceptor* on signing the face of the bill,
(iv) signed by the person giving it (*the drawer*)
(v) requiring the person to whom it is addressed (*the drawee/acceptor*)
(vi) to pay
(vii) on demand, or at a fixed or determinable future time
(viii) a sum certain in money
(ix) to, or to the order of, a specified person or to bearer (*the payee*).

(c) The parties to a bill

The parties to a bill of exchange are the following:

(i) The drawer is the party who signs the bill as an order given to another person (the drawee) requiring him to pay the amount of the bill. By drawing the bill, the drawer undertakes that it will be accepted and paid by the drawee. He also undertakes that, in the event that the bill is dishonoured, he will compensate the holder or any indorser who has been compelled to pay on the bill.

(ii) The drawee is the party to whom the bill is addressed ordering him to pay, i.e. the bill is drawn upon him. He is not liable on the bill unless he has signed the bill as accepting it. He is then called the acceptor. The acceptor signs across the face of the bill to undertake that he will pay whoever is the holder of the bill at the date of maturity.

(iii) An indorsee is a party to whom the cheque is negotiated by the payee. Each subsequent indorsee becomes, in effect, a payee.

(iv) An indorser is a party to whom the bill is payable as payee or indorsee, but who negotiates his rights by way of indorsement to an indorsee. He does so by indorsement on the back of the bill. Each time a bill is negotiated the indorser makes himself liable on the bill to subsequent indorsees.

(d) The face of a bill

Figure 19.1 is an illustration of a bill drawn by Buyers Limited of Derby on John Marchant & Co. in favour of Selling Company Limited for the sum of £17,000 payable thirty days after sight. It is, of course intended that John Marchant & Co. (as merchant bankers) will duly accept the bill and it is likely that Sellers Limited will indorse the bill to an indorsee who will then, in effect, be the payee and so on. This bill will mature, i.e. become payable, thirty days after sight by the drawee.

Fig 19.1

```
£17,000                          Derby
                                 7   December   1985

       30 days after sight pay to Selling Company Limited
       or order the sum of seventeen thousand pounds for
       value received.
                                 (Signed)
                                 Buyers Limited

   To John Marchant & Co.
   London.
```

(e) Inland and foreign bills

An inland bill is a bill which is or on the face of it purports to be (a) both drawn and payable within the British Islands, or (b) drawn within the British Islands upon some person resident therein. Any other bill is a foreign bill: s. 4(1).

(f) Payable on demand

A bill is payable on demand (a) which is expressed to be payable on demand, or at sight, or on presentation; or (b) in which no time for payment was expressed: s. 10(1).

Where a bill is accepted or indorsed when it is overdue, it shall, as regards the acceptor who so accepts, or any indorser who so indorses it, be deemed a bill payable on demand: s. 10(2).

(g) Payable at future time

A bill is payable at a determinable future time within the meaning of the Act which is expressed to be payable (1) at a fixed period after date or sight or (2) on or at a fixed period after the occurrence of a specified event which is certain to happen, though the time of happening may be uncertain: s. 11.

(h) Acceptance

(i) Definition and requisites of acceptance.
The acceptance of a bill is the signification by the drawee of his assent to the order of the drawer: s. 17(1).

An acceptance is invalid unless it complies with the following conditions, namely:

(*a*) It must be written on the bill and signed by the drawee. The mere signature of the drawee without addition is sufficient.
(*b*) It must not express that the drawee will perform his promise by other means than the payment of money: s. 17(2).

(ii) Time for acceptance.
A bill may be accepted before it has been signed by the drawer, or while otherwise incomplete: s. 18(1); or when it is overdue, or after it has been dishonoured by a previous refusal to accept, or by non-payment: s. 18(2). When a bill payable after sight is dishonoured by non-acceptance, and the drawee subsequently accepts it, the holder, in the absence of any different agreement, is entitled to have the bill accepted as of the date of first presentment to the drawee for acceptance: s. 18(3).

(iii) General and qualified acceptance.
A general acceptance assents without qualification to the order of the drawer. A qualified acceptance in express terms varies the effect of the bill as drawn: s. 19(2).

In particular, an acceptance is qualified which is:

(*a*) conditional, that is to say, which makes payment by the acceptor dependent on the fulfilment of a condition therein stated;
(*b*) partial, that is to say, an acceptance to pay part only of the amount for which the bill is drawn;
(*c*) local, that is to say, an acceptance to pay only at a particular specified place; an acceptance to pay at a particular place is a general acceptance,

unless it expressly states that the bill is to be paid there only and not elsewhere;

(*d*) qualified as to time;

(*e*) the acceptance of some one or more of the drawees, but not of all: s. 19(2).

(j) Delivery

Every liability on a bill, whether it be the drawer's, the acceptor's, or an indorser's, is incomplete and revocable, until delivery of the instrument in order to give effect to it: s. 21(1). However, where an acceptance is written on a bill, and the drawee gives notice to or according to the directions of the person entitled to the bill that he has accepted it, the acceptance then becomes complete and irrevocable: s. 21(1).

19.3 CAPACITY AND AUTHORITY OF THE PARTIES

(a) Capacity of the parties

Capacity to incur liability as a party to a bill is co-extensive with capacity to contract: s. 22(1). Where a bill is drawn or indorsed by an infant, minor, or corporation having no capacity or power to incur liability on a bill, the drawing or indorsement entitles the holder to receive payment of the bill, and to enforce it against any other party to it: s. 22(2).

(b) Signature essential to liability

No person is liable as drawer, indorser, or acceptor of a bill who has not signed it as such: provided that:

(i) where a person signs a bill in a trade or assumed name, he is liable on it as if he had signed it in his own name; and

(ii) the signature of the name of a firm is equivalent to the signature by the person so signing of the names of all persons liable as partners in that firm: s. 23.

(c) Forged or unauthorised signature

Subject to the Act, a forged or unauthorised signature is wholly inoperative, and no right to retain the bill or to give a discharge for it or to enforce payment against any party to it can be acquired through or under that signature: s. 24. Where the bill has been negotiated several times, the effect of a forged indorsement is to break the chain of title. Where the drawer's signature is forged, the instrument is not a bill of exchange.

274

(d) Signing a bill as agent

Where a person signs a bill and adds words to his signature indicating that he signs for or on behalf of a principal, or in a representative character, he is not personally liable on it; but the mere addition to his signature of words describing him as an agent, or as filling a representative character, does not exempt him from personal liability: s. 26(1).

19.4 THE CONSIDERATION FOR A BILL

(a) Value and holder for value

Valuable consideration for a bill may be constituted by:

(*a*) any consideration to support a simple contract;
(*b*) an antecedent debt or liability: s. 27(1).

Provision (*b*) is an exception to the rule of past consideration.

Where value has at any time been given for a bill the holder is deemed to be a holder for value as regards the acceptor and all parties to the bill who became parties prior to such time: s. 27(2).

(b) Accommodation bill or party

An accommodation party is a person who has signed a bill as drawer, acceptor or indorser, without receiving value for it, and for the purpose of lending his name to some other person: s. 28(1).

An accommodation party is liable on the bill to a holder for value and it is immaterial whether, when that holder took the bill, he knew the party to be an accommodation party or not: s. 28(2).

(c) Holder in due course

A holder in due course is a holder who has taken a bill, complete and regular on the face of it, under the following conditions, namely:

(*a*) that he became the holder of it before it was overdue, and without notice that it had been previously dishonoured, if such was the fact; and
(*b*) that he took the bill in good faith and for value, and that at the time the bill was negotiated to him he had no notice of any defect in the title of the person who negotiated it: s. 29(1).

This very important definition can be analysed as follows:

(i) Holder.
A holder in due course must be a holder of the bill and it follows that if

there has previously been a forgery or an unauthorised signature the chain of title is broken and no person can thereafter be a holder of any kind.

(ii) Complete and regular.
A person taking an inchoate bill, i.e. one which is lacking some material detail, cannot be a holder in due course, even though he may have authority to complete the bill. Also, where a bill is marked in an irregular manner such as 'not negotiable' any person taking it cannot be a holder in due course.

(iii) Before it was overdue.
Where a bill is expressed to be payable at a fixed or determinable future time it will be overdue on the day following that time.

(d) Presumption of value and good faith

Every party whose signature appears on a bill is *prima facie* deemed to have become a party to it for value: s. 30(1).

Every holder of a bill is *prima facie* deemed to be a holder in due course: s. 30(2).

19.5 THE NEGOTIATION OF BILLS

(a) Negotiation

A bill is negotiated when it is transferred from one person to another in such a manner as to constitute the transferee the holder of the bill: s. 31(1).

A bill payable to bearer is negotiated by delivery: s. 31(2).

A bill payable to order is negotiated by the indorsement of the holder completed by delivery: s. 31(3).

Where the holder of a bill payable to his order transfers it for value without indorsing it, the transfer gives the transferee such title as the transferor had in the bill, and the transferee in addition acquires the right to have the indorsement of the transferor: s. 31(4).

(b) Requisites of a valid indorsement

By section 32 an indorsement, in order to operate as a negotiation, must comply with the following conditions:

(i) It must be written on the bill and signed by the indorser. His signature is sufficient.
(ii) It must be an indorsement of the entire bill.
(iii) Where a bill is payable to the order of two or more payees or indorsees

who are not partners, all must indorse unless one has authority to indorse for the others.

(iv) Where, in a bill payable to order, the payee or indorsee is wrongly designated, or his name is misspelt, he may indorse the bill as it describes him, adding, if he thinks fit, his proper signature.

(v) Where there are two or more indorsements on a bill, each indorsement is deemed to have been made in the order in which it appears on the bill, until the contrary is proved.

(vi) An indorsement may be made in blank or special. It may also be restrictive.

(c) Indorsement in blank and special indorsement

An indorsement in blank specifies no indorsee and a bill so indorsed becomes payable to bearer: s. 34(1).

A special indorsement specifies the person to whom or to whose order, the bill is to be payable: s. 34(2). The provisions of the Act relating to a payee apply to an indorsee under a special indorsement: s. 34(3).

When a bill has been indorsed in blank, any holder may convert the blank indorsement into a special indorsement: s. 34(4).

(d) Restrictive indorsement

An indorsement is restrictive which prohibits the further negotiation of the bill or which expresses that it is a mere authority to deal with the bill as thereby directed and not a transfer of the ownership of it, as, for example, if a bill be indorsed 'Pay D only', or 'Pay D for the account of X', or 'Pay D or order for collection': s. 35(1).

A restrictive indorsement gives the indorsee the right to receive payment of the bill and to sue any party to it that his indorser could have sued, but gives him no power to transfer his rights as indorsee: s. 35(2).

The chief effect of these provisions is that a restrictive indorsement restricts or destroys the transferability of the bill according to the tenor of the restriction. It follows that a restrictively indorsed bill is not a negotiable instrument in the hands of the indorsee. He can take no better title than that of his transferor, which may be non-existent, defective or subject to the equities.

The indorsee can transfer such rights as he has under the bill to the extent that the indorsement expressly permits: s. 35(3).

(e) Negotiation of an overdue or dishonoured bill

Where a bill is negotiable in its origin, it continues to be negotiable until it has been *(a)* restrictively indorsed or *(b)* discharged by payment or otherwise: s. 36(1).

When an overdue bill is negotiated, it can be negotiated only subject to any defect of title affecting it at its maturity and, from then on, no person who takes it can acquire or give a better title than that which the person from whom he took it had: s. 36(2). Strictly, this provision means that, subject to s. 36(1) (*a*) and (*b*), an overdue bill can only be transferred for value – it cannot be 'negotiated' in the true sense of the word.

(f) Rights of the holder

The rights and powers of the holder of a bill are as follows:

(i) He may sue on the bill in his own name: s. 38(1).
(ii) Where he is a holder in due course he holds the bill free from any defect of title of prior parties, as well as from mere personal defences available to prior parties among themselves, and may enforce payment against all parties liable on the bill: s. 38(2).
(iii) Where his title is defective (*a*) if he negotiates the bill to a holder in due course, that holder obtains a good and complete title to the bill, and (*b*) if he obtains payment of the bill the person who pays him in due course gets a valid discharge for the bill: s. 38(3).

This provision must be read together with section 29 which defined holder in due course (19.4(c) above). The most important point is that a holder in due course obtains a title free from all equities.

19.6 GENERAL DUTIES OF THE HOLDER

In order to ensure that he obtains the rights available to him under the Act, there are certain general duties required from the holder of a bill.

(a) When presentment for acceptance is necessary

(i) Where a bill is payable after sight, presentment for acceptance is necessary in order to fix the maturity of the instrument: s. 39(1).
(ii) Where a bill expressly stipulates that it must be presented for acceptance, or where a bill is drawn payable elsewhere than at the residence or place of business of the drawee, it must be presented for acceptance before it can be presented for payment: s. 39.

(b) Time for presenting a bill payable after sight

When a bill payable after sight is negotiated, the holder must either present it for acceptance or negotiate it within a reasonable time: s. 40(1). If he does not, the drawer and all indorsers prior to that holder are discharged: s. 40(2). In determining what is a reasonable time, the nature of the bill, trade usage and the facts of each particular case must be taken into account: s. 40(3). As a result of this provision, the holder of an unaccepted bill must take heed that, unless he either negotiates it or presents it for acceptance within a reasonable time, he may lose his right of recourse against the drawer and all indorsers.

(c) Non-acceptance

When a bill is duly presented for acceptance and is not accepted within the customary time, the person presenting it must treat it as dishonoured by non-acceptance. If he does not, the holder will lose his right of recourse against the drawer and indorsers: s. 42. Where non-acceptance occurs, the holder must take heed of this provision. The drawer and prior parties are entitled to notice of the non-acceptance, failing which they may be discharged from liability to the holder.

(d) Dishonour by non-acceptance and its consequences

A bill is dishonoured by non-acceptance:

(a) when it is duly presented for acceptance, and acceptance is refused or cannot be obtained; or
(b) when presentment for acceptance is excused and the bill is not accepted: s. 43(1).

When a bill is dishonoured by non-acceptance, an immediate right of recourse against the drawer and indorsers accrues to the holder, and no presentment for payment is necessary: s. 43(2).

From this provision it can be seen that there are three ways in which a bill is dishonoured by non-acceptance: first, where acceptance is refused; secondly, where acceptance cannot be obtained and, thirdly, where acceptance is excused and there is non-acceptance.

(e) Rules as to presentment for payment

If a bill is not duly presented for payment the drawer and indorsers will be discharged. A bill is duly presented for payment if the following rules are complied with:

(i) Where the bill is not payable on demand, presentment must be made on the day it falls due.
(ii) Where the bill is payable on demand presentment must be made within a reasonable time after its issue in order to render the drawer liable, and a reasonable time after indorsement in order to render the indorser liable.
(iii) Presentment must be made by the holder or his agent at a reasonable

hour on a business day, at the proper place, to the drawee or his agent.

(iv) The proper place for presentment may be:

- *(a)* the place (if any) specified in the bill;
- *(b)* the address of the drawee or acceptor if given in the bill;
- *(c)* the drawee's place of business if known, otherwise his ordinary residence;
- *(d)* in any other case, wherever the drawee or acceptor can be found, or at his last place of business or residence.

(f) Dishonour by non-payment

A bill is dishonoured by non-payment *(a)* when it is duly presented for payment and payment is refused or cannot be obtained or *(b)* when presentment is excused and the bill is overdue and unpaid: s. 47(1). When a bill is dishonoured by non-payment, an immediate right of recourse accrues to the holder: s. 47(2). This right of recourse should be compared with that which accrues in the event of dishonour by non-acceptance under section 43 (19.6(d) above).

(g) Notice of dishonour and the effect of non-notice

When a bill has been dishonoured by non-acceptance or by non-payment, notice of dishonour must be given to the drawer and each indorser, and any drawer or indorser to whom notice is not given is discharged: s. 48.

(h) Rules as to notice of dishonour

By section 49 notice of dishonour must be given in accordance with the following rules:

- *(i)* The notice must be given by or on behalf of the holder or indorser who, at the time, must himself be liable on the bill.
- *(ii)* Notice may be given by an agent either in his own name or in the name of any party entitled to give notice, whether that party be his principal or not.
- *(iii)* Where notice is given by or on behalf of the holder, it enures for the benefit of all subsequent holders and all prior indorsers who have a right of recourse against the party to whom it is given.
- *(iv)* Where notice is given by or on behalf of an indorser so entitled, it enures for the benefit of the holder and all indorsers subsequent to the party to whom notice is given.
- *(v)* The notice may be given in writing or by personal communication,

and may be in any terms to identify the bill and intimate that it has been dishonoured.

(vi) The return of a dishonoured bill to the drawer or an indorser is deemed sufficient notice of dishonour.

(vii) A written notice need not be signed.

(viii) Notice may be given to a party or to his agent.

(ix) Where the drawer or indorser is dead, notice must be given to a personal representative.

(x) Where the drawer or indorser is bankrupt, notice may be given to the party or to the trustee.

(xi) Where there are two or more drawers or indorsers who are not partners, notice must be given to each of them.

(xii) Notice may be given as soon as the bill is dishonoured and must be given within a reasonable time thereafter.

(j) **Illustration**

On the dishonour of a bill, the holder should give notice to every party. This will ensure that each of them will remain liable to him. The holder may, if he wishes, give notice only to his own immediate transferor, who should then pass the notice down the line of prior indorsers until the drawer is reached by notice from the first indorsee.

For the purpose of illustration:

let   D be the drawer,

        P be the payee to whom the bill is issued,

        I1 be the first indorser after the payee,

        I2 be the second indorser,

        I3 be the third indorser,

        I4 be the fourth indorser,

        I5 be the fifth indorser,

        H be the holder at the time of dishonour, and

        A be the acceptor.

To be certain of preserving his right of recourse against all prior parties, H must give notice of dishonour to them all. If, however, H gives notice to I5, who then gives notice to I4, who then gives notice to I3, who then gives notice to I2, who then gives notice to I1, who then gives notice to P, who then gives notice to D, then H's rights of recourse will have been preserved as if he had himself given notice to all parties. It should be clear that, on dishonour, the drawer at the end of the chain of liability is the party ultimately liable on the bill. Whether he has any right of recourse against the drawee/acceptor will depend on the nature of the arrangement or contract between them.

19.7 **LIABILITIES OF PARTIES**

(a) **Funds in the hands of the drawee**

A bill, of itself, does not operate as an assignment of funds in the hands of the drawee and available for the payment of it. The drawee of a bill who does not accept it is not liable on the instrument: s. 53(1). This means that if the drawee holds funds provided by the drawer, he is under no obligation *on the bill* to comply with the order of the drawer. He is not liable on the bill unless and until he accepts it. The person named as drawee who refuses to accept the bill may, nevertheless, be liable in some cases to the person who draws the bill on him, but such liability will be outside the bill, e.g. in contract, according to the circumstances.

(b) **Liability of the acceptor**

The acceptor of a bill, by accepting it, undertakes that he will pay it according to the tenor of his acceptance: s. 54(1).

Further, by accepting the bill, the acceptor is precluded from denying to a holder in due course:

- (*a*) the existence of the drawer, the genuineness of his signature, and his capacity and authority to draw the bill;
- (*b*) in the case of a bill payable to drawer's order, the then capacity of the drawer to indorse, but not the genuineness and validity of his indorsement;
- (*c*) in the case of a bill payable to the order of a third person, the existence of the payee and his then capacity to indorse, but not the genuineness or validity of his indorsement: s. 54(2).

This provision gives some very important rights to the holder in due course. In the event of a claim by the holder in due course against the acceptor in case of dishonour, the acceptor will be estopped from denying (1) the existence of the drawer, (2) the genuineness of the drawer's signature, (3) the capacity and authority of the drawer to indorse the bill and (4) the existence of the payee and his capacity to indorse the bill.

(c) **Liability of drawer or indorser**

The drawer of a bill undertakes that, on due presentment, it will be accepted and paid according to its tenor, and that if it be dishonoured he will compensate the holder or any indorser who is compelled to pay it, provided the requisite proceedings on dishonour be duly taken: s. 55(1). He is precluded from denying to a holder in due course the existence of the payee and his then capacity to indorse: s. 55(1).

The indorser of a bill undertakes that, on due presentment, it will be accepted and paid according to its tenor and that, if it be dishonoured, he will compensate the holder or a subsequent indorser who is compelled to pay it, provided the requisite proceedings on dishonour be duly taken: s. 55(2)(*a*).

The indorser is precluded from denying to a holder in due course the genuineness and regularity of the drawer's signature and all previous indorsements: s. 55(2)(*b*).

He is also precluded from denying to his immediate or a subsequent indorsee that the bill was, at the time of his indorsement, a valid and subsisting bill, and that he had then a good title to it: s. 55(2)(*c*).

Sections 54 and 55 should be considered together. From them it is clear that the drawer is the party ultimately liable on the bill unless the drawee has accepted it, in which case he (the drawee) is ultimately liable. The sections also give important rights to the holder in due course, especially through the estoppel provisions.

(d) Transferor by delivery and transferee

Where the holder of a bill payable to bearer negotiates it by delivery without indorsing it, he called a 'transferor by delivery': s. 58(1).

A transferor by delivery is not liable on the bill: s. 58(2).

A transferor by delivery warrants to his immediate transferee, being a holder for value, that the bill is what it purports to be, that he has a right to transfer it, and that at the time of the transfer he was not aware of any fact which rendered it valueless: s. 58(3).

It is important to notice that this provision applies only to bearer bills. It should be compared with s. 31(4) which deals with the transfer of a bill payable to order without an indorsement (19.5(a) above).

19.8 THE DISCHARGE OF A BILL

(a) Payment in due course

A bill is discharged by payment in due course by or on behalf of the drawee or acceptor. 'Payment in due course' means payment made at or after the maturity of the bill to the holder in good faith and without notice that his title to the bill is defective (if such be the case): s. 59(1).

Payment in due course is akin to the discharge of a contract by performance. It is, of course, the usual way in which a bill is discharged.

(b) Acceptor the holder at maturity

When the acceptor of a bill is the holder of it at or after its maturity, in his own right, the bill is discharged: s. 61. This would, of course, be a most unusual manner of discharge.

(c) Express waiver

When the holder of a bill at or after its maturity absolutely and unconditionally renounces his rights against the acceptor, the bill is discharged. The renunciation must be in writing unless the bill is delivered up to the acceptor: s. 62(1).

(d) Cancellation

Where a bill is intentionally cancelled by the holder and the cancellation is apparent on the bill, it is discharged: s. 63(1).

In like manner, any party liable on a bill may be discharged by the intentional cancellation of his signature by the holder. It follows that, in such a case, any indorser who would have had a right of recourse against the party whose signature is cancelled is also discharged: s. 63(2).

(e) The alteration of a bill

Where a bill or acceptance is materially altered without the assent of all parties liable, the bill is avoided except as against a party who has himself made the alteration and subsequent indorsers: s. 64(1).

Where the alteration is not apparent and the bill is in the hands of a holder in due course, his rights are not affected, i.e. he may avail himself as if the bill had not been altered: s. 64(1).

19.9 ACCEPTANCE AND PAYMENT FOR HONOUR

(a) Acceptance for honour supra protest

Where a bill has been protested for dishonour by non-acceptance and is not overdue, any person other than a party may, with the consent of the holder, intervene and accept the bill *supra protest,* for the honour of any party liable, or for the honour of the person for whose account the bill is drawn: s. 65(1).

A bill may be accepted for honour for part only of the sum for which it is drawn: s. 65(2).

An acceptance for honour must (*a*) be written on the bill and (*b*) be signed by the acceptor for honour: s. 65(3).

Acceptance for honour is designed to avoid the inconvenience and embarrassment caused by the refusal of the drawee to accept and pay the amount of the bill. The acceptor for honour will usually have made arrangements to be compensated by the drawer or the indorser for whose honour he is accepting the bill.

(b) Liability of the acceptor for honour

The acceptor for honour undertakes that he will, on due presentment, pay the bill according to the tenor of his acceptance, if it is not paid by the drawee, provided it has been duly presented for payment and protested for non-payment, and that he receives notice of these facts: s. 66(1).

The acceptor for honour is liable to the holder and to all parties to the bill subsequent to the party for whose honour he has accepted: s. 66(2).

(c) Presentment to the acceptor for honour

Where a dishonoured bill has been accepted for honour *supra protest*, or contains a reference in case of need, it must be protested for non-payment before it is presented for payment to the acceptor for honour, or referee in case of need: s. 67(1).

(d) Payment for honour supra protest

Where a bill has been protested for non-payment, any person may intervene and pay it *supra protest* for the honour of any party liable on it, or for the honour of the person for whose account the bill is drawn: s. 68(1).

Where a bill has been paid for honour, all parties subsequent to the party for whose honour it is paid are discharged, but the payer for honour is subrogated for, and succeeds to both the rights and duties of, the holder as regards the party for whose honour he pays, and all parties liable to that party: s. 68(5).

It is not required that acceptance for honour should precede payment for honour although this is often the case.

SUMMARY

1   Negotiable instruments have been invested by custom or by statute with the special characteristics of negotiability.

2   The characteristics of negotiability are (1) the instrument can be put into a state in which title will pass by mere delivery or, in the case

of a bill of exchange, by indorsement and delivery, (2) title passes on negotiation free from the equities and other defects, and (3) the holder of the instrument can sue all prior parties in his own name.

3   'Bill of exchange' is defined in s. 3(1).

4   The parties to a bill are the drawer, the drawee, the payee and the indorsers.

5   The acceptance of a bill is the signification by the drawee of his assent to the order of the drawer.

6   Capacity to incur liability as a party to a bill is co-extensive with capacity to contract.

7   No person is liable on a bill unless he has signed it.

8   Valuable consideration for a bill may be constituted by an antecedent debt or liability.

9   A holder in due course is a holder who has taken a bill, complete and regular on the face of it, under the following conditions, namely, (1) that he became the holder of it before it was overdue, and without notice that it had been previously dishonoured, if such was the fact, and (2) that he took the bill in good faith and for value, and that at the time the bill was negotiated to him he had no notice of any defect in the title of the person who negotiated it.

10   A bill is negotiated when it is transferred from one person to another in such manner as to constitute the transferee the holder of the bill. A bill payable to bearer is negotiated by delivery. A bill payable to order is negotiated by indorsement of the holder completed by delivery.

11   A holder in due course holds the bill free from any defect of title of prior parties, as well as from mere personal defences available to prior parties among themselves, and may enforce payment against all parties liable on the bill.

12   A bill may be dishonoured by non-payment or by non-acceptance.

13   A bill is discharged by payment in due course by or on behalf of the drawee or acceptor.

14   The statutory definition of a bill of exchange is

> an unconditional order in writing, addressed by one person to another, signed by the person giving it, requiring the person to whom it is addressed to pay on demand or at a fixed or determinable future time a sum certain in money to or to the order of a specified person, or to bearer.

An instrument which does not comply with these conditions or which orders any act to be done in addition to the payment of money is not a bill of exchange.

EXERCISES

1 What are the advantages of a negotiable instrument over an instrument the rights under which can merely be assigned?

2 Explain the commercial function of a bill of exchange.

3 Give the full statutory definition of a bill of exchange.

4 What is the effect on the bill of a forged signature?

5 There is a special rule in regard to the consideration for a bill. State it.

6 Define carefully 'holder in due course' and compare his rights with those of any other kind of holder.

7 How is a bill negotiated?

8 When is presentment for acceptance necessary?

9 What are the consequences of dishonour by non-acceptance?

10 There are rules governing presentment of a bill for payment. State them.

11 What notice must be given in case of dishonour by either non-acceptance or non-payment? State the rules governing such notice.

12 The acceptor is estopped from denying certain matters to a holder in due course. What are they?

13 Explain the liability of the drawer or an indorser of a bill.

14 What is the liability of a transferor by delivery?

15 What is payment in due course? How many other ways are there for the discharge of a bill?

16 What is 'acceptance for honour *supra protest*'? In what circumstances might it occur?

17 Compare the liabilities of the acceptor for honour with those of an accommodation party.

18 What is the effect of payment for honour *supra protest?* Who may be a payer for honour? Does acceptance for honour always precede payment for honour?

WORKSHOP

1 The bill below (Figure 19.2) is drawn in favour of Jenny Wren. Advise her when it can be presented for payment.

2 Consider again the bill in Figure 19.2. What would be the effect if Bartholomew had written the words 'NOT NEGOTIABLE' across the face of it?

3 Consider the bill below (Figure 19.3). Does it satisfy the requirements of the Bills of Exchange Act as regards the time at which it becomes payable?

Fig 19.2

```
┌────────────────────────────────────────────────────────────┐
│  £3,000                                       London         │
│                                               2 October 1985 │
│                                                              │
│       Pay  to  Jenny  Wren  or  order  the  sum  of  Three   │
│       thousand pounds for value received.                    │
│                                               Batholomew Eagle│
│                                                              │
│  To Rudolf & Co.                                             │
│  London EC2                                                  │
│                                                              │
└────────────────────────────────────────────────────────────┘
```

Fig 19.3

```
┌────────────────────────────────────────────────────────────┐
│  £760                                         Birmingham     │
│                                               17 December 1985│
│                                                              │
│       Pay to Edwin Brown or order six weeks after the        │
│       death of his father the sum of seven hundred and       │
│       sixty pounds.                                          │
│                                               Henry Green    │
│                                                              │
│  To Adams & Co.                                              │
│  Newcastle                                                   │
│                                                              │
└────────────────────────────────────────────────────────────┘
```

4 Consider again the bill in Figure 19.3. If, on presentment for acceptance it is accepted in the following terms, what is the effect on the bill? '*Accepted payable in my office in Newcastle.*'

5 Make up a specimen bill, by yourself today, upon John Robinson of Guildford, payable thirty days after sight in favour of Richard Dolittle. When would you expect this bill to be presented for acceptance, assuming that you gave it today to the payee?

6 A bill is drawn on Osbert by Alice in favour of Peter and payable three months after date. Peter negotiates the bill to Paul by special indorsement. Before he signs the bill, Paul loses it and it is found by Sykes, who forges a special indorsement by Paul in favour of Dorothy. Dorothy negotiates the bill to Walter. Assume that value was given at each stage of the bill's transfer. What is the effect of the forgery on each of the parties to the bill?

7   A bill is drawn on Patsy by Tom in favour of Arthur and payable three months after sight. The amount is £43,000. Arthur negotiated the bill by special indorsement to Timothy who presented it for acceptance to Patsy. Patsy refused to accept the bill. Consider the rights of all parties to the bill.

8   Warner drew a bill for £1,000 on Gillian in favour of Donald, payable thirty days after date. Donald negotiated the bill by special indorsement to Sidney who negotiated it similarly to Sherlock. Sherlock duly presented the bill for acceptance and Gillian accepted. Sherlock then negotiated the bill to Samuel who presented the bill for payment. In the event of dishonour by non-payment to Sherlock, advise him as to his rights, if any, with regard to all parties.

CHEQUES AND PROMISSORY NOTES

All section references in this chapter are to the Bills of Exchange Act 1882, unless otherwise indicated.

'The bank undertakes to receive money and to collect bills for its customer's account. The proceeds so received are not to be held in trust for the customer, but the bank borrows the proceeds and undertakes to repay them. The promise to repay is to repay at the branch of the bank where the account is kept and during banking hours. It includes a promise to repay any part of the amount due, against the written order of the customer addressed to the bank at the branch, and as such written orders may be outstanding in the ordinary course of business for two or three days, it is a term of the contract that the bank will not cease to do business with the customer except upon reasonable notice. The customer, on his part, undertakes to exercise reasonable care in executing his written orders so as not to mislead the bank or to facilitate forgery. I think it is necessarily a term of such contract that the bank is not liable to pay their customer the full amount of his balance until he demands payment from the bank at the branch at which the current account is kept.' *Joachimson* v. *Swiss Bank Corporation* (1921), per Atkin L.J.

20.1 CHEQUES ON A BANKER

(a) Definition

A cheque is a bill of exchange drawn on a banker and payable on demand: s. 73(1).

A cheque is, thus, a special kind of bill of exchange and is subject to all the provisions of the Act regarding the drawing, indorsement and payment, etc., of demand bills subject to the special provision dealt with in this chapter. As has been seen in the previous chapter, a bill can be used to finance a series of otherwise disconnected transactions, each transferor in his turn taking consideration in return for the negotiation of the bill. In theory, a cheque could be used in the same way. There is nothing to prevent a cheque from being negotiated a number of times. However, the usual practice is to draw the cheque on a banker in favour of the payee, who will then present the cheque for payment. In this way, the cheque has a simple, but important, function, namely, a convenient method of making payments without actually handling cash.

(b) Presentment of a cheque for payment

Where a cheque is not presented for payment within a reasonable time of its issue, the drawer is not totally discharged as in the case of any other demand bill (s. 45); he is, by s. 74(1), discharged only to the extent to which he has suffered loss from the delay in presentment. In the usual course, the drawer suffers no loss or damage for unreasonable delay in presentment for payment, in which case the drawer's legal liability to pay the amount of the cheque continues for the statutory period of six years from the date of the cheque.

(c) Revocation of a banker's authority

The duty and authority of a banker to pay a cheque drawn on him by his customer are terminated by (1) countermand of payment or (2) notice of the customer's death: s. 75.

Countermand of payment simply means stopping the cheque by giving due notice to the banker to that effect. Full details of the cheque to be stopped must be given in writing to the banker. Where the customer has used a cheque guarantee card to support the cheque that cheque cannot be stopped if the sum is within the sum guaranteed by the terms of the card.

Where a customer has died, the banker must continue to honour his cheques until reliable notice of the death is received.

Apart from the above-mentioned provisions, the banker's duty and authority to pay cheques will be terminated as follows:

(i) where insolvency proceedings have commenced against the customer, i.e. bankruptcy in the case of an individual or partnership firm or winding-up in the case of a body corporate; or

(ii) where the court has ordered the banker to stop payments out of a particular account, e.g. to satisfy a liability for contempt of court; or

(iii) where the banker receives reliable notice of the customer's insanity.

20.2 CROSSED CHEQUES

(a) General and special crossings defined

Where a cheque bears across its face an addition of:

(*a*) the words 'and company' or any abbreviation of them between two parallel transverse lines, either with or without the words 'not negotiable'; or

(*b*) two parallel transverse lines simply, either with or without the words 'Not negotiable';

that addition constitutes a crossing, and the cheque is crossed generally: (Figure 20.1) s. 76(1).

Fig 20.1 *Examples of general crossings*

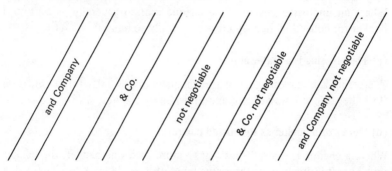

Where a cheque bears across the face of it an addition of the name of a banker, either with or without the words 'not negotiable', that addition constitutes a crossing and the cheque is crossed specially (Figure 20.2) and to that banker: s. 76(2). The crossing should include the name of *one* banker only.

Fig 20.2 *Examples of special crossings*
Note: The two transverse parallel lines are not essential to a special crossing.

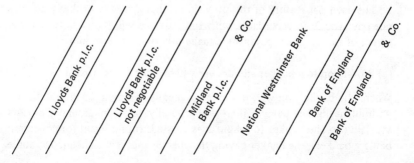

Although the crossing marked 'account payee' is not mentioned in the Act, this type of crossing received judicial recognition in *Bevan* v. *The National Bank* (1906). As a result of this and subsequent decisions, any banker who collected for some account other than that of the named payee would risk a claim for negligence against him by that payee.

(b) Crossing by the drawer or after issue

A cheque may be crossed generally or specially by the drawer: s. 77(1). Where a cheque is uncrossed, the holder may cross it generally or specially: s. 77(2). Where a cheque is crossed generally the holder may cross it specially: s. 77(3). Where a cheque is crossed generally or specially, the holder may add the words 'not negotiable': s. 77(4).

Where a cheque is crossed specially, the banker to whom it is crossed may again cross it specially to another banker for collection: s. 77(5). Where an uncrossed cheque, or a cheque crossed generally, is sent to a banker for collection, he may cross it specially to himself: s. 77(6).

(c) The crossing is a material part

A crossing is a material part of the cheque and it is unlawful to obliterate it or alter it in any way except as authorised by the Act: s. 78.

(d) Duties of a banker as to crossed cheques

Where a cheque is crossed specially to more than one banker, the banker on whom it is drawn must refuse payment of it: s. 79(1). A special crossing should name one banker only. If two bankers are named (except where one is the collecting agent for the other) the paying banker must refuse payment.

Where the drawee banker of a cheque crossed with two bankers' names nevertheless pays it, he is liable to the true owner of the cheque: s. 79(2).

The drawee banker incurs a similar liability where he
(1) pays a cheque crossed generally otherwise than to a banker; or
(2) if crossed specially, otherwise than to the banker to whom it is crossed: s. 79(2).

The essential feature of this provision is that a drawee banker who does not pay strictly in accordance with the crossing, will be liable to the true owner of the cheque if payment is made otherwise than to him.

(e) Protection to a banker and drawer where a cheque is crossed

Where the banker, on whom a crossed cheque is drawn, in good faith and without negligence pays it, if crossed generally, to a banker, and if crossed specially, to the banker to whom it is crossed, (or his agent for collection being a banker), the banker paying the cheque and, if the cheque has come into the hands of the payee, the drawer, will both be entitled to the same rights and be placed in the same position as if payment had been made to the true owner of the cheque: s. 80.

This is an important protection to both banker and drawer, who can never be certain that the payment for the crossed cheque is being collected for the true owner. Both drawee banker and the drawer have a defence against a claim by the true owner if the payment was made in accordance with the crossing, in good faith and without negligence.

(f) Banker paying a demand draft whereon an indorsement is forged

When a bill payable to order or on demand is drawn on a banker, and the banker on whom it is drawn pays the bill in good faith and in the ordinary course of business, it is not incumbent on the banker to show that the indorsement of the payee or any subsequent indorsement was made by or under the authority of the person whose indorsement it purports to be, and the banker is deemed to have paid the bill in due course, although that indorsement was forged or made without authority: s. 60. This provision makes allowance for the fact that, unless there are specific grounds for suspicion, the drawee banker, who must honour his customer's cheque, is in no position to make a check upon the credentials of the person presenting the cheque. If there has been a forged indorsement, the banker will be deemed to have paid in due course provided that he paid in good faith and in the ordinary course of business. This provision should be carefully compared with that of s. 80 dealt with above (20.2(e)).

(g) The effect of a crossing on a holder

Where a person takes a crossed cheque which bears on it the words 'not negotiable', he will not have and will not be capable of giving a better title to the cheque than that which the person from whom he took it had: s. 81. It will be remembered that an instrument expressed to be 'not negotiable' is outside the definition of a bill of exchange in s. 3(1).

20.3 THE CHEQUES ACT 1957

This Act makes provision for the modern function of a cheque, i.e. as a means of payment to a payee from a bank customer's account. In almost all instances, the indorsement of the payee is intended to discharge the instrument rather than to effect a negotiation as in the case of a bill of exchange having the usual commercial function. The Act gives protection to a banker paying an unindorsed cheque or an irregularly indorsed cheque.

It also gives protection to a banker who collects the amount for a customer who has no title to the instrument.

(a) Protection of bankers paying unindorsed or irregularly indorsed cheques

Where a banker in good faith and in the ordinary course of business pays a cheque drawn on him which is not indorsed or is irregularly indorsed, he does not, in doing so, incur any liability by reason only of the absence of, or irregularity in, the indorsement, and he is deemed to have paid it in due course: Cheques Act, s. 1(1). This protection is afforded to the paying banker only where he pays in the ordinary course of business and in good faith. Sub-section (2) goes on to extend similar protection in the case of dividend warrants and banker's drafts.

(b) Rights of bankers collecting cheques not indorsed by holders

A banker who gives value for, or has a lien on, a cheque payable to order which the holder delivers for collection without indorsing it, has such (if any) rights as he would have had if, upon delivery, the holder indorsed it in blank: Cheques Act, s. 2. This section applies to cheques only.

(c) Unindorsed cheques as evidence of payment

An unindorsed cheque which appears to have been paid by the banker on whom it is drawn is evidence of the receipt by the payee of the sum payable by the cheque: Cheques Act, s. 3. This provision brings unindorsed cheques into line with indorsed cheques as regards evidence of payment. In either case, the cheque is a sufficient receipt for the amount.

(d) Protection of bankers collecting payment of cheques, etc.

Where a banker, in good faith and without negligence

- (a) receives payment for a customer of a cheque; or
- (b) having credited a customer's account with the amount of the cheque, receives payment of it for himself;

and the customer has no title, or a defective title to the cheque, the banker does not incur any liability to the true owner by reason only of having received payment for it: Cheques Act, s. 4(1). Sub-section (2) provides that this protection extends not only to cheques but also to certain other documents.

In all, the provision applies to
- (i) cheques;
- (ii) any document issued by a customer of a banker which though not

a bill of exchange, is intended to enable a person to obtain payment from that banker of the sum mentioned in the document;

(iii) any document issued by a public officer to enable a person to obtain payment from the Paymaster General of the sum mentioned in it but which is not a bill of exchange; and

(iv) any draft payable on demand drawn by a banker upon himself, whether payable at the head office or some other office of the bank.

It should be noticed that this protection is only for collecting bankers and is applicable to all cheques, open or crossed, as well as to other specified instruments.

20.4 PROMISSORY NOTES

(a) Definition

A promissory note is an unconditional promise in writing made by one person to another signed by the maker, engaging to pay, on demand or at a fixed or determinable future time, a sum certain in money, to, or to the order of, a specified person or to bearer: s. 83(1). This definition should be compared carefully with the definition of a bill of exchange given in s. 3(1).

An instrument in the form of a note payable to maker's order is not a note within the meaning of this provision unless and until it is indorsed by the maker: s. 83(2). A note by the maker promising to pay himself is obviously useless unless it is indorsed. Such a note with the maker's special indorsement becomes payable to the indorsee or, with a blank indorsement, it becomes payable to the bearer.

(b) Delivery necessary

A promissory note is inchoate and incomplete until it is delivered to the payee or bearer: s. 84.

(c) Joint and several notes

A promissory note may be made by two or more makers, and they may be liable on it jointly or jointly and severally according to its tenor: s. 85(1). Where a note runs 'I promise to pay' and is signed by two or more persons it is deemed to be their joint and several note: s. 85(2). Whether the liability is joint or joint and several, each person signing is liable in full if sued on the note. The only difference is that, in the case of joint liability, in the event of the death of the party signing as such, his estate will not be liable. In such a case, liability on the note will remain in the other party or parties who signed.

(d) Note payable on demand

Where a note payable on demand has been indorsed, it must be presented for payment within a reasonable time of the indorsement. If the note is not presented within a reasonable time, the indorser will be discharged: s. 86(1).

(e) Presentment of a note for payment

Where a promissory note is in the body of it made payable at a particular place, it must be presented for payment at that place in order to render the maker liable. In any other case, presentment for payment is not necessary in order to render the maker liable: s. 87(1).

Presentment for payment is necessary in order to render the indorser of a note liable: s. 87(2). Where a note is in the body of it made payable at a particular place, presentment at that place is necessary in order to render an indorser liable: s. 87(3); but where a place of payment is indicated by way of memorandum only, presentment at that place is sufficient to render the indorser liable, though a presentment to the maker elsewhere, if sufficient in other respects, will also suffice: s. 87(3).

This is a perfectly reasonable provision with regard to the liability of an indorser in that he cannot be compelled to pay the amount of the note until it has been presented to the maker, i.e. the party primarily liable. This is very much the same liability as the indorser of a bill of exchange.

(f) Liability of the maker

The maker of a promissory note by making it: (1) engages that he will pay it according to its tenor and (2) is precluded from denying to a holder in due course the existence of the payee and his then capacity to indorse: s. 88. This is a reasonable provision designed to estop the maker from denying to a holder in due course that the payee exists and had capacity. The advantage given to a holder in due course is obvious.

(g) Application of the Act to notes

The provisions of the Bills of Exchange Act 1882 relating to bills of exchange apply, with some exceptions and with necessary modifications, to promissory notes: s. 89(1). In applying those provisions, the maker of a note will be deemed to correspond with the acceptor of a bill, and the first indorser of a note will be deemed to correspond with the drawer of an accepted bill payable to drawer's order: s. 89(2).

SUMMARY

1   A cheque is a bill of exchange drawn on a banker and payable on demand: s. 73.

2   The duty and authority of a banker to pay a cheque may be terminated by (1) countermand of payment, (2) notice of customer's death, (3) commencement of insolvency proceedings, (4) court order or (5) notice of customer's insanity.

3   A crossing which includes the name of one banker is a special crossing to that banker. A crossing without a banker's name is a general crossing.

4   A banker who collects for any person other than the named payee on a cheque which is crossed 'account payee' will risk a claim for negligence at the suit of that payee.

5   The drawee banker incurs a liability to the true owner of a cheque if he pays a cheque crossed generally otherwise than to a banker or if he pays a cheque crossed specially otherwise than to the banker named in the crossing: s. 79.

6   Where the banker on whom a crossed cheque is drawn, in good faith and without negligence pays it, if crossed generally, to a banker and, if crossed specially, to the banker to whom it is crossed, the banker paying the cheque will be placed in the same position as if payment had been made to the true owner: s. 80.

7   Where a banker in good faith and in the ordinary course of business pays a cheque drawn on him which is not indorsed or is irregularly indorsed, he does not, in doing so, incur any liability by reason only of the absence of, or irregularity in, the indorsement, and he is deemed to have paid it in due course: Cheques Act, s. 1.

8   Where a banker, in good faith and without negligence receives payment for a customer of a cheque or, having credited a customer's account with the amount of the cheque, receives payment of it for himself, and the customer has no title, or a defective title to the cheque, the banker does not incur any liability to the true owner by reason only of having received payment for it: Cheques Act, s. 4.

9   A promissory note is an unconditional promise in writing made by one person to another signed by the maker, engaging to pay, on demand or at a fixed or determinable future time, a sum certain in money, to, or to the order of, a specified person or to bearer: s. 83.

10   Where a note payable on demand has been indorsed, it must be presented for payment within a reasonable time of the indorsement or the indorser will be discharged: s. 86.

11   The maker of a note is precluded from denying to a holder in due course the existence of the payee: s. 88.

EXERCISES

1   Define a cheque.

2   Explain the difference between the role of the banker, on the one hand as his customer's drawee and, on the other, as collector for his customer's account.

3   What is the position of the drawer of a cheque which is not presented for payment within a reasonable time of its issue?

4   In what ways may the authority and duty of a banker to pay cheques be revoked?

5   Explain carefully the difference between general crossings and special crossings. Give some examples of each and mention the legal significance of each.

6   Comment on the crossing with the words 'account payee'.

7   What are the duties of the drawee banker where a cheque is crossed specially to two other bankers?

8   What protection does a drawee banker lose if he pays a crossed cheque negligently or without good faith?

9   What is the effect of a crossing on the holder?

10   What protection does the Cheques Act give to a drawee banker who pays an unindorsed cheque?

11   Summarise the provisions contained in section 4(1) and (2) of the Cheques Act.

12   What is a promissory note?

13   Explain the rules governing joint notes and joint and several notes.

14   When is presentment of a note for payment necessary?

WORKSHOP

1 Consider the statement from the judgement of Atkin L.J. in *Joachimson* v. *Swiss Bank Corporation* (1921) set out at the head of this chapter. Analyse this statement and, from your analysis, draw up a list of the banker's obligations to his customer and a list of the customer's obligations to the banker.

2 Take the definitions set out in sections 3(1) and 74(1), respectively, and amalgamate them so as to form a detailed definition of a cheque.

3 Sally draws a cheque in favour of Percy which he mislays and does not present for ten months after its issue to him. During this period, Sally's bank becomes insolvent and goes into liquidation, paying its ordinary creditors only ten pence in the pound. Payment cannot be obtained by Percy, who now has decided to sue Sally for the full amount owing on the contract for which the cheque was given. Advise Sally.

4 Olga drew a cheque on her bank, the Outwest Banking Company Ltd., in favour of Douglas. She crossed the cheque and wrote in the crossing 'account payee'. James stole the cheque from Douglas and forged an indorsement to himself and gave the cheque to his own bank for collection. The bank collected the amount from the Outwest Banking Company Ltd. and credited James' account, which is overdrawn. Douglas has now discovered what has happened. He wishes to know whether he has a right of action against James' bank. Advise him.

5 Ivan drew a cheque in favour of Penelope, crossing it specially to her banker. Penelope dropped the cheque in the street and it was found by Buster who indorsed it to himself by forging Penelope's signature. Buster's bank, on receiving the cheque, collected and paid the amount into his account. Buster is now in prison and he has no funds. Penelope wishes to know whether she can claim against Buster's bank for the repayment of the amount of the cheque.

6 Andy drew a cheque payable to Goodstores Limited for goods received. He crossed the cheque with two transverse parallel lines only. Amy, a clerk in the office at Goodstores Limited, stole the cheque and wrote the name of her own bank between the lines, forged her boss's signature and thus obtained payment into her own current account. Comment on the liability, if any, of Amy's banker.

7 Chips, a dishonest youth, found a cheque drawn by Esther in favour of Julia, in a railway carriage. The cheque was crossed generally with the words 'not negotiable'. Chips gave the cheque to Martin in exchange for a bicycle. Esther has, in the meantime, put a stop on the cheque. What rights, if any, has Martin?

8 Walter sends to his bank, Westland Bank, a cheque drawn by Delilah and payable to Winston. The cheque is crossed with the words 'Texan Bank p.l.c.' between the lines. This cheque is received by Westland Bank together with Walter's paying-in book. Advise Westland Bank.

APPENDIX

THE UNFAIR CONTRACT TERMS ACT 1977

PART I

AMENDMENT OF LAW FOR ENGLAND AND WALES AND NORTHERN IRELAND

Introductory

1.—(1) For the purposes of this Part of this Act, 'negligence' means the breach—

- (*a*) of any obligation, arising from the express or implied terms of a contract, to take reasonable care or exercise reasonable skill in the performance of the contract;
- (*b*) of any common law duty to take reasonable care or exercise reasonable skill (but not any stricter duty);
- (*c*) of the common duty of care imposed by the Occupiers' Liability Act 1957 or the Occupiers' Liability Act (Northern Ireland) 1957.

(2) This Part of this Act is subject to Part III; and in relation to contracts, the operation of sections 2 to 4 and 7 is subject to the exceptions made by Schedule 1.

(3) In the case of both contract and tort, sections 2 to 7 apply (except where the contrary is stated in section 6(4)) only to business liability, that is liability for breach of obligations or duties arising—

- (*a*) from things done or to be done by a person in the course of a business (whether his own business or another's);

  or
- (*b*) from the occupation of premises used for business purposes of the occupier;

and references to liability are to be read accordingly.

(4) In relation to any breach of duty or obligation, it is immaterial for any purpose of this Part of this Act whether the breach was inadvertent or intentional, or whether liability for it arises directly or vicariously.

Avoidance of liability for negligence, breach of contract, etc.

2.–(1) A person cannot by reference to any contract term or to a notice given to persons generally or to particular persons exclude or restrict his liability for death or personal injury resulting from negligence.

(2) In the case of other loss or damage, a person cannot so exclude or restrict his liability for negligence except in so far as the term or notice satisfies the requirement of reasonableness.

(3) Where a contract term or notice purports to exclude or restrict liability for negligence a person's agreement to or awareness of it is not of itself to be taken as indicating his voluntary acceptance of any risk.

3.–(1) This section applies as between contracting parties where one of them deals as consumer or on the other's written standard terms of business.

(2) As against that party, the other cannot by reference to any contract term–

(*a*) when himself in breach of contract, exclude or restrict any liability of his in respect of the breach; or

(*b*) claim to be entitled–

(i) to render a contractual performance substantially different from that which was reasonably expected of him, or

(ii) in respect of the whole or any part of his contractual obligation, to render no performance at all,

except in so far as (in any of the cases mentioned above in this subsection) the contract term satisfies the requirement of reasonableness.

4.–(1) A person dealing as consumer cannot by reference to any contract term be made to indemnify another person (whether a party to the contract or not) in respect of liability that may be incurred by the other for negligence or breach of contract, except in so far as the contract term satisfies the requirement of reasonableness.

(2) This section applies whether the liability in question–

(*a*) is directly that of the person to be indemnified or is incurred by him vicariously;

(*b*) is to the person dealing as consumer or to someone else.

Liability arising from sale or supply of goods

5.—(1) In the case of goods of a type ordinarily supplied for private use or consumption, where loss or damage—

(*a*) arises from the goods proving defective while in consumer use; and

(*b*) results from the negligence of a person concerned in the manufacture of distribution of the goods,

liability for the loss or damage cannot be excluded or restricted by reference to any contract term or notice contained in or operating by reference to a guarantee of the goods.

(2) For these purposes—

(*a*) goods are to be regarded as 'in consumer use' when a person is using them, or has them in his possession for use, otherwise than exclusively for the purposes of a business; and

(*b*) anything in writing is a guarantee if it contains or purports to contain some promise or assurance (however worded or presented) that defects will be made good by complete or partial replacement, or by repair, monetary compensation or otherwise.

(3) This section does not apply as between the parties to a contract under or in pursuance of which possession or ownership of the goods is passed.

6.—(1) Liability for breach of the obligations arising from—

(*a*) section 12 of the Sale of Goods Act 1893 (seller's implied undertakings as to title, etc.);

(*b*) section 8 of the Supply of Goods (Implied Terms) Act 1973 (the corresponding thing in relation to hire-purchase).

cannot be excluded or restricted by reference to any contract term.

(2) As against a person dealing as consumer, liability for breach of the obligations arising from—

(*a*) section 13, 14 or 15 of the 1893 Act (seller's implied undertakings as to conformity of goods with description or sample, or as to their quality or fitness for a particular purpose);

(*b*) section 9, 10 or 11 of the 1973 Act (the corresponding things in relation to hire-purchase),

cannot be excluded or restricted by reference to any contract term.

(3) As against a person dealing otherwise than as consumer, the liability

specified in subsection (2) above can be excluded or restricted by reference to a contract term, but only in so far as the term satisfies the requirement of reasonableness.

(4) The liabilities referred to in this section are not only the business liabilities defined by section 1(3), but include those arising under any contract of sale of goods or hire-purchase agreement.

7.—(1) Where the possession or ownership of goods passes under or in pursuance of a contract not governed by the law of sale of goods or hire-purchase, subsections (2) to (4) below apply as regards the effect (if any) to be given to contract terms excluding or restricting liability for breach of obligation arising by implication of law from the nature of the contract.

(2) As against a person dealing as consumer, liability in respect of the goods' correspondence with description or sample, or their quality or fitness for any particular purpose, cannot be excluded or restricted by reference to any such term.

(3) As against a person dealing otherwise than as consumer, that liability can be excluded or restricted by reference to such a term, but only in so far as the term satisfies the requirement of reasonableness.

(4) Liability in respect of

    (*a*) the right to transfer ownership of the goods, or give possession; or

    (*b*) the assurance of quiet possession to a person taking goods in pursuance of the contract,

cannot be excluded or restricted by reference to any such term except in so far as the term satisfies the requirement of reasonableness.

(5) This section does not apply in the case of goods passing on a redemption of trading stamps within the Trading Stamps Act 1964 or the Trading Stamps Act (Northern Ireland) 1965.

Other provisions about contracts

8.—(1) In the Misrepresentation Act 1967, the following is substituted for section 3—

    3. If a contract contains a term which would exclude or restrict—

        (*a*) any liability to which a party to a contract may be subject by reason of any misrepresentation made by him before the contract was made; or

(*b*) any remedy available to another party to the contract by reason of such a misrepresentation,

that term shall be of no effect except in so far as it satisfies
the requirement of reasonableness as stated in section 11(1)
of the Unfair Contract Terms Act 1977; and it is for those
claiming that the term satisfies that requirement to show
that it does.

(2) The same section is substituted for section 3 of the Misrepresentation
Act (Northern Ireland) 1967.

9.–(1) Where for reliance upon it a contract term has to satisfy the
requirement of reasonableness, it may be found to do so and be given
effect accordingly notwithstanding that the contract has been terminated
either by breach or by a party electing to treat it as repudiated.

(2) Where on a breach the contract is nevertheless affirmed by a party
entitled to treat it as repudiated, this does not of itself exclude the requirement of reasonableness in relation to any contract term.

10. A person is not bound by any contract term prejudicing or taking
away rights of his which arise under, or in connection with the performance
of, another contract, so far as those rights extend to the enforcement of
another's liability which this Part of this Act prevents that other from
excluding or restricting.

Explanatory provisions

11.–(1) In relation to a contract term, the requirement of reasonableness
for the purposes of this Part of this Act, section 3 of the Misrepresentation
Act 1967 and section 3 of the Misrepresentation Act (Northern Ireland)
1967 is that the term shall have been a fair and reasonable one to be included
having regard to the circumstances which were, or ought reasonably to
have been, known to or in the contemplation of the parties when the
contract was made.

(2) In determining for the purposes of section 6 or 7 above whether
a contract term satisfies the requirement of reasonableness, regard shall
be had in particular to the matters specified in Schedule 2 to this Act;
but this subsection does not prevent the court or arbitrator from holding,
in accordance with any rule of law, that a term which purports to exclude
or restrict any relevant liability is not a term of the contract.

(3) In relation to a notice (not being a notice having contractual

effect), the requirement of reasonableness under this Act is that it should be fair and reasonable to allow reliance on it, having regard to all the circumstances obtaining when the liability arose or (but for the notice) would have arisen.

(4) Where by reference to a contract term or notice a person seeks to restrict liability to a specified sum of money, and the question arises (under this or any other Act) whether the term or notice satisfies the requirement of reasonableness, regard shall be had in particular (but without prejudice to subsection (2) above in the case of contract terms) to—

(a) the resources which he could expect to be available to him for the purpose of meeting the liability should it arise; and

(b) how far it was open to him to cover himself by insurance.

(5) It is for those claiming that a contract term or notice satisfies the requirement of reasonableness to show that it does.

12.—(1) A party to a contract 'deals as consumer' in relation to another party if—

(a) he neither makes the contract in the course of a business nor holds himself out as doing so; and

(b) the other party does make the contract in the course of a business; and

(c) in the case of a contract governed by the law of sale of goods or hire-purchase, or by section 7 of this Act, the goods passing under or in pursuance of the contract are of a type ordinarily supplied for private use or consumption.

(2) But on a sale by auction or by competitive tender the buyer is not in any circumstances to be regarded as dealing as consumer.

(3) Subject to this, it is for those claiming that a party does not deal as consumer to show that he does not.

13.—(1) To the extent that this Part of this Act prevents the exclusion or restriction of any liability it also prevents—

(a) making the liability or its enforcement subject to restrictive or onerous conditions;

(b) excluding or restricting any right or remedy in respect of the liability, or subjecting a person to any prejudice in consequence of his pursuing any such right or remedy;

(c) excluding or restricting rules of evidence or procedure;

and (to that extent) sections 2 and 5 to 7 also prevent excluding or restricting liability by reference to terms and notices which exclude or restrict the relevant obligation or duty.

(2) But an agreement in writing to submit present or future differences to arbitration is not to be treated under this Part of this Act as excluding or restricting any liability.

14. In this Part of this Act—

'business' includes a profession and the activities of any government department or local or public authority;

'goods' has the same meaning as in the Sale of Goods Act 1893;

'hire-purchase agreement' has the same meaning as in the Consumer Credit Act 1974;

'negligence' has the meaning given by section 1(1);

'notice' includes an announcement, whether or not in writing, and any other communication or pretended communication; and

'personal injury' includes any disease and any impairment of physical of mental condition.

SCHEDULE 2

'GUIDELINES' FOR APPLICATION OF REASONABLENESS TEST

The matters to which regard is to be had in particular for the purposes of sections 6(3), 7(3) and (4), 20 and 21 are any of the following which appear to be relevant—

(a) the strength of the bargaining positions of the parties relative to each other, taking into account (among other things) alternative means by which the customer's requirements could have been met;

(b) whether the customer received an inducement to agree to the term, or in accepting it had an opportunity of entering into a similar contract with other persons, but without having to accept a similar term;

(c) whether the customer knew or ought reasonably to have known of the existence and extent of the term (having regard, among other things, to any custom of the trade and any previous course of dealing between the parties);

(d) where the term excludes or restricts any relevant liability if some condition is not complied with, whether it was reasonable

at the time of the contract to expect that compliance with
that condition would be practicable;

(e) whether the goods were manufactured, processed or adapted to
the special order of the customer.

INDEX

A

abatement of nuisance
  defence to tort 76
absolute liability 201–2
absolute ownership 52
absolute privilege
  defence against defamation 80
acceptance
  bills of exchange 272–3
  buyer's failure to accept goods
    240
  communication 139, 140
  contracts 137, 138–40
acceptance for honour
  bills of exchange 283–4
acceptor
  holder at maturity 283
  liability on bills of exchange 281
accommodation party
  bills of exchange 274
accord and satisfaction
  discharge of contracts 200
account payee
  crossed cheques 292
accountability
  partners 226
accounting
  false 68
accounting reference date 126
accounts
  companies 126
accounts stated
  with minors 184
Acts of Parliament 10–12
actual bodily harm 65–6
actus reus 59–60, 62, 64, 65, 66
administration of justice
  contracts prejudicial to 179
Admiralty Court 31
affirmation
  disentitlement to rescission
    168
agency 48,
  general 212
  partnership and 223

pretended 217
special 212
agency agreement 214–16
agency of necessity 213–14
agent
  implied duties 215
  signing bills of exchange 274
  third parties and 216–17
agreement
  agency by 212–13
  authenticity of 162–72
  contracts 135, 136, 137–42
  discharge by 199–201
All England Reports 22
alteration
  bills of exchange 283
ancient demesne 8
annual general meetings
  companies 125
apparent authority 213
apparent partners 228
appointment
  judges 31–2
appropriation 67
arbitration clauses 181
arrest
  lawful 76
Articles of Agreement
  contracts 148
articles of association
  companies 118–19
assault and battery 65, 72
assault occasioning actual bodily
    harm 65–6
assent
  acceptance of contract 138–9
  unqualified, to offer 138–9
assets
  partnerships 228
assignment
  absolute 262–3
  equitable 262–3
  non-absolute 262–3
  statutory 263–4
association
  unincorporated 47–8

312

314

goods
failure to accept and pay for 240
interference with 73-4
supplied to minors 184
transfer of property in 232-4
goodwill
business 181
Grand Assize 4
Gray's Inn 43
grievous bodily harm 63, 66
gross returns
sharing 222
group accounts 129
guarantee
contracts of 176-7

H

heads of claim 194
Henry II 4
High Court of Justice 20, 28
30-1, 32-4
hire agreements
duty to give information to
surety 256
entry into 249-51
termination 254-5
hire purchase agreements
termination 254
hire purchase goods
retaking 253
holder
at maturity 283
bills of exchange 277-80
title to crossed cheque 293
unindorsed cheques 294
holder in due course
bills of exchange 274-5
holding company 129
holding out
partner 223-4
House of Commons 11-12
House of Lords 11-12, 19, 26-9
husbandry service 7

I

illegal contracts 178-80
illegality
dissolution of partnership 227
implied authority 212-13

implied duties
agents 215
principals 215-16
implied terms
contracts 148-50
contracts for services 239
contracts other than sale 238
sale of goods 236-8
incomplete negotiation
contracts 151
Incorporated Council of Law
Reporting 21
indemnity
of agents 216
indorsement
bills of exchange 275-6
forged 273, 293
in blank 276
indorser
bills of exchange 271
liability on bills of exchange 282
Industrial Tribunals 37
injunction
negative terms of contract 196
injury
causation and remoteness 90-3
risk of 89
inland bill 271
Inner Temple 43
Inns of Court 41, 43
insane person
contract by 186
insanity
general defence 61
partner 227
insider dealing 127
Institute of Legal Executives 42-3
Institutes of the Laws of England
23
intention
of parties to contract 147-8,
232-3
intention to create legal relations
136, 137, 145-7
interests
company directors 124-5
in land 104, 105, 107-10
interference with goods 73-4
interpretation
statutes 14-16

intoxication
general defence 61

J

judges
appointment 31-2
County Court 34
Court of Appeal 29-30
Crown Court 31
High Court 30
Judicial Committee of the Privy
Council 38
judicial control
credit agreements 257-8
juries 40-1
justice
contracts prejudicial to 179
justices of the peace 35
justification
defence against defamation
79-80

K

King's Peace 5
King's writ 4
knight service 102

L

land
Crown ownership 101-2
interest in 4
sale or disposition 177-8
trespass to 74
land ownership
beneficial 103
land tenure 101-2
lapse
of offer 142
law
historical background 3-8
impact of European Court
39-40
mistake at 163-4
subsidiary source 22-4
Law Commission 12, 13, 15
law merchant 8
law reform
by statute 12

law reports 20-2
Law Reports 21
Law Society 41, 42
lawful discipline or arrest
defence to tort 76
leapfrog procedure 28
leaseholds 51, 107
legal estates 104
legal executives 42-3
legal interests
in land 104, 107-10
legal mortgages 107-8
charges 104
legal profession 41-3
legal relations
intention to create 136, 137, 145-7
legal things in action
assignment of 261-2
legislation 6-7, 10-17
autonomic 14
delegated 13
liability
acceptor for honour 284
defined 50
limitation or exclusion 151-3
maker of promissory notes 296
on bills of exchange 273
parties to bills of exchange 281-2
partners 223
seller's 238-9
libel 78-80
licence
coupled with interest 109
entry to land 108-9
lien
on principal's property 216
life imprisonment 63
limitation of actions 196-7
limited company 47
limited liability 117
Lincoln's Inn 43
liquidated damages 194-5
liquidation
see winding up 127-9
literal rule
construction of statutes 15
Littleton, Sir Thomas 23
Lloyd's List Reports 22
loans
to minors 184